Differences That Matter

Social Policy and the Working Poor in the United States and Canada

DAN ZUBERI

ILR Press *an imprint of*
Cornell University Press
Ithaca and London

First published 2006 by Cornell University Press
First printing Cornell Paperbacks, 2006
Printed in the United States of America

Library of Congress Cataloging-in-Publication Data

Zuberi, Dan.
    Differences that matter : social policy and the working poor in
the United States and Canada / Dan Zuberi.
        p. cm.
    Includes bibliographical references and index.
    ISBN-13: 978-0-8014-4407-4 (cloth : alk. paper)
    ISBN-10: 0-8014-4407-1 (cloth : alk. paper)
    ISBN-13: 978-0-8014-7312-8 (pbk. : alk. paper)
    ISBN-10: 0-8014-7312-8 (pbk. : alk. paper)
    1. Poverty—Government policy—United States.   2. Poverty
—Government policy—Canada.   3. Working poor—United
States.   4. Working poor—Canada.   5. Social policy—United
States.   6. Social policy—Canada.   7. Public welfare—United
States.   8. Public welfare—Canada.   I. Title.
HC110.P6Z83   2006
362.5'5610973—dc22

                                                    2005035783

Cornell University Press strives to use environmentally responsible suppliers and materials to the fullest extent possible in the publishing of its books. Such materials include vegetable-based, low-VOC inks and acid-free papers that are recycled, totally chlorine-free, or partly composed of nonwood fibers. For further information, visit our website at www.cornellpress.cornell.edu.

Cloth printing   10 9 8 7 6 5 4 3 2 1
Paperback printing   10 9 8 7 6 5 4 3 2

To the memory of my *mormor*,

Marta Höckert, 1908–2002,

who taught me that loving and caring

are the most important things in life.

CONTENTS

ACKNOWLEDGMENTS

Although for some research can be a solitary process, I feel fortunate that my research allows me to meet and talk to so many interesting people. One of the ironies of qualitative research methods is that those who I would most like to thank for their help with this book—the hotel-industry workers and others I interviewed—must remain anonymous in order to protect their identities. At times, their struggles broke my heart. Their strength amazed me. Their quiet fortitude, sense of humor, and openness to sharing their stories, hardships, achievements, fears, and hopes was heartwarming. They may toil invisibly behind the scenes in windowless back rooms, in jobs that are repetitive and at times demeaning, but their conditions of work do not lessen their humanity. They taught me a lot.

I owe a debt of gratitude to many people for their help with this book. First and foremost, I extend a huge thank you to Katherine S. Newman at Princeton University. She was incredibly supportive of this research project from the beginning. Kathy Newman helped me develop the research design and supported me through the fieldwork, analysis, writing, and rewriting of this work, reading several drafts of each chapter and providing invaluable feedback every time. I am fortunate to have had the chance to work with and get to know such an outstanding scholar. I could not have completed this book without her help and inspiration. She provided the academic model and resources for me to pursue such an exciting project, even when I lived on the other side of the continent.

I also thank William Julius Wilson at Harvard University, whose scholarship on urban poverty has long been an inspiration for me. I feel very fortunate to have had the opportunity to get to know him personally and work with him at the formative stages of my academic career. Mary C. Waters, also at Harvard, provided immeasurable help with my research, offering valuable feedback and revisions that have improved the quality of the book. I also learned from her excellent research on immigrants and debates in the immigration literature as well as from her insights about qualitative research. I extend a special thank you to Jeffrey Reitz at the University of Toronto, whom I was lucky enough to meet while planning the Global Hotel study. He introduced me to Canadian scholarship on race, ethnicity, and immigration and has been a steadfast supporter of my research since then. Together, these four scholars have had the greatest influence on this book.

Many others helped me with useful advice and support. I particularly thank Christopher Jencks at Harvard's Kennedy School of Government (KSG), who recommended I study the hotel industry. I also thank at Harvard: Mary Jo Bane, Mariko Chang, David Ellwood, Marshall Ganz, Jason Kaufman, Jane Mansbridge, Brian Mandell, Pamela Metz, Gary Orfield, Orlando Patterson, James Quane, Edward Walker, Rick Weissboard, Julie Boatwright Wilson, and Sidney Verba. Although, sadly, I never had the opportunity to get to know her personally, a presentation at the Inequality Summer Institute 2000 at the KSG by Susan C. Eaton of her groundbreaking research on staff at nursing homes inspired me to interview low-wage service-sector employees.

At the University of British Columbia in Vancouver, Neil Guppy's sponsorship during the fieldwork stage of my research made it possible for me to complete my interviews and participant observation in Vancouver. Kate Bush provided excellent transcription services, and Karen Fang provided some wonderful Chinese language translating. At the University of Washington, Jennifer Edwards provided tremendous help when I was setting up to interview hotel employees in Seattle. I also thank Debra Minkoff, Barbara Reskin, and Stewart Tolney at the University of Washington. I was lucky to meet Timothy Smeeding of Syracuse University, and David Reisman of Harvard University, at the Luxembourg Income Study (LIS) during summer 2000. They and the LIS staff, especially David Jesuit, did a stellar job of teaching me to use LIS data to compare the United States and Canada.

Through the Inequality and Social Policy program at Harvard, I was fortunate to meet many wonderful scholars from across the United States who study poverty and inequality. I particularly enjoyed meeting Kathryn Edin and Frank Furstenberg of the University of Pennsylvania, who provided early positive feedback about my research design.

When I was studying for my master's degree at Oxford, Michael Noble and my advisor, George Smith, strongly encouraged me to continue to pursue my doctorate and sociological research as a career. Patricia Fernandez-Kelly, at Princeton University, is the original source of my academic inspiration, and her passionate commitment to helping improve the lives of the urban poor continues to motivate me.

I am fortunate to have Clyde Hertzman, director of the Human Early Learning Partnership (HELP) and professor in the Department of Health Care and Epidemiology at the University of British Columbia (UBC), as an enthusiastic mentor and supporter of my research. I thank him for the incredible opportunity of a postdoctoral fellowship, co-funded by the Canadian Institute for Advanced Research, which allowed me to focus on revising this book while starting an exciting new research project on Vancouver's eastside elementary schools. The HELP staff and affiliates at UBC have also been wonderful to work with. I especially thank Hillel Goelman and Paul Kershaw as well as Jacqueline Smit Alex, Catherine Coxall, Barry Forer, Eileen Grant, Alison Holley, Lori Irwin, Keely Kinar, Veronica Lapointe, Wendy Li, Aubrey Lim, Calvin Lo, Nancy Meagher, Mari Pighini, Brenda Poon, Iraj Pouresami, Kate Trafford, Michelle Wiens, and David Wu. I reserve special thanks for Peter Schaub, the staff geographer at HELP, who made and remade the maps for this book and also reviewed several draft chapters, lending valuable insights about urban planning and geography. His enthusiasm for the project, mapping, and the eastside Vancouver neighborhood where he grew up was contagious and inspirational. Tragically, Peter passed away in the summer of 2005 from a heart attack at age twenty-six, devastating all of those fortunate to have known him.

I appreciate the support and encouragement of other UBC faculty: Joan Anderson, Bruce Baum, Alexia Bloch, Gillian Creese, Julian Dierkes, Liz Dunn, Brian Elliott, Nancy Gallini, Amy Hanser, Greg Feldman, Martha Foschi, Slyvia Fuller, Laura Janara, Thomas Kemple, Darrin Lehman, Judith Lynam, Robert MacDonald, Charles Menzies, David Pokotylo, Becki Ross, David Tindall, Gerry Veenstra, Sabrina Wong, and Elvin Wyly. I also thank Daniel Cohn, Karl Froschauer, Arlene Tigar McLaren, Jane Pulkingham, Gary Teeple, and Ann Travers at Simon Fraser University and Hospital Employees' Union researcher Marcy Cohen for their encouragement.

I thank my peers at Harvard for their encouragement: Irene Bloemraad, Ajay Chaudry, Leslie Cintron, Carrie Conaway, David Harding, Matissa Hollister, Tomás R. Jiménez, Andrew Karch, Peter Moskos, Wendy Roth, Patrick Sharkey, Mario Small, Arjumand Siddiqi, Natasha Warikoo, Celeste Watkins, and Justin Wolfers.

I have enjoyed the opportunity to travel to many interesting conferences over the past several years to share my research ideas and findings; this has helped me immeasurably in thinking through dilemmas and generating new insights. I particularly thank Michèle Lamont and Peter A. Hall, at Harvard, for inviting me to present my research findings to the Canadian Institute for Advanced Research meeting, Successful Societies: The Dynamics of Collective Development. I also thank Jacques Bertrand, Gerard Bouchard, Peter Evans, Leanne Son Hing, Jane Jensen, Daniel Keating, Ron Levi, Nancy Ross, William Sewell, Dietlind Stolle, and Ann Swidler for their feedback. In addition, I received valuable feedback from presentations to the Sociology Department at Harvard University, the Department of Anthropology and Sociology at the University of British Columbia, and the Department of Sociology and Anthropology at Simon Fraser University. The Sociology Department at Harvard also provided funding for me to present my research at the Aage Memorial Conference in Stockholm, Sweden. I benefited from presenting at the Association for Canadian Studies in the United States (ACSUS) colloquium at Simon Fraser's Harbour Centre campus and at the annual meetings of the International Sociological Association in Brisbane, Australia; the American Sociological Association; and the Society for the Study of Social Problems (SSSP) in San Francisco. I thank the Sociology and Social Welfare section of the SSSP and the Labor and Employment Relations Association (LERA) for their awards recognizing this work.

This research project could not have happened without the generous financial support from several sources. I am extremely grateful to the Canada-U.S. Fulbright Foundation for awarding me a Fulbright scholarship to carry out this research. I also thank the Harvard Frank Knox Memorial fellowship and a U.S. National Science Foundation Integrative Graduate Education and Research Traineeship Grant (NSF No. 9870661) to Harvard for critical support. The Multi-Disciplinary Program on Inequality and Social Policy provided valuable academic and research support.

I especially thank Fran Benson of Cornell University Press, who has been a truly wonderful editor and supporter of this research. Her enthusiasm for this book and helpful advice has been wonderful for me and dramatically improved the final product. It has been great to work with Karen Laun, the manuscript editor, and Susan Barnett, the copy supervisor at Cornell University Press. Julie F. Nemer did an amazing job copyediting the manuscript. I also thank Peter Adler at the University of Denver and one anonymous reviewer, whose feedback guided me through the revisions of the manuscript.

Parts of chapters 2 and 4 appeared originally in the *International Journal of Comparative Sociology*, 45(1–2) (2004): 87–110. Those passages are reproduced here with permission from Sage Publications Ltd. from Daniyal Zuberi, *Transfers Matter Most: How Changes in Transfer Systems of Canada and the United States Explain the Divergence in Household Poverty Levels from 1974–1994*, © Sage Publications, 2004.

Many great friends over the years have put the spark and laughter in my life while I have been researching and writing this book. Craig Winters was there right from the beginning, accompanying me on my first trip to Vancouver. Elena Mansour has been a wonderful friend through it all. David Pinto-Duschinsky wins the award for the most frequent visitor to the Pacific Northwest; while at the KSG, he helped me think through the idea of doing a Seattle-Vancouver comparative study, and I truly appreciate his friendship and helpful advice. David Alire Garcia wins second place for frequent visits to the Pacific Northwest, and I feel lucky to have a good friend who is also such a great writer and is passionate about progressive causes.

Jeremy Weinstein and Rachel Gibson have been one of my favorite couples for a long time. I want to thank Jeremy for his wonderful support and friendship from the first day of graduate school at the KSG, when we sat next to each other in the doctoral math enrichment class. His amazing and critically important research on Africa is also an inspiration for me. I thank Joiwind and

Amit Ronen, who brought lots of laughter and fun times into my life; Molly and Ty Terkel, the best of San Francisco, who have been good friends to me and my family; and Anand Das and Shilpa Patel, who have kept me inspired with their friendship and commitment to helping others.

I also feel very fortunate to have become close friends with Antje Ellermann and Alan Jacobs in Vancouver. Our hikes, trips to the pub, eagle walks, and camping and island adventures have been great escapes I have cherished, and I look forward to many fun times in the future. I also appreciate many wonderful evenings with Shannon Daub and Ryan Blogg; at dinners and folk music festivals, it has been great getting to know them. Kyle Horner and Kyla Tienhaara took me snowshoeing—a Canadian tradition—for the first time; they are now missed but fortunate to be studying in Amsterdam. I thank Robin Duschesneau for letting me crash on his couch many times over the course of my fieldwork. I also thank the Bulman-Fleming family; Josh Flax; Aslam and Amber Khan; Mark Koehler; Jon Pitts; Richard, Barbara and Ricky Tatum; Trish and Noel Winston; and Daniel Wood, who pushes his students to write to change the world.

I thank my parents, Mo and Lilly Zuberi, for their strong encouragement and support of my academic interests from an early age. They provided the resources and opportunities that helped me get my dream job as a researcher and professor. Although many parents have to help some of their children financially through an extended adolescence that includes four years of college, few endure periodic requests for emergency loans for another eight postgraduate years. My dad and mom helped me out time and again and made sure I always had everything I needed to keep going as I pursued my dream and completed my doctorate and this book.

My wonderful sisters are simply the best. Anita Zuberi, who is becoming an urban poverty scholar in her own right as a doctoral student at Northwestern University, has been a wonderful confidant and friend. Sofia Zuberi, whose globe-trotting has had her living in Nice, Antibes, San Francisco, Grenoble, Rome, and London, has shared with me her friendship, her international adventures, and her comparative insights.

My grandfather—or *morfar* in Swedish—Karl-Erik Hockert, is ninety-five-years-old and has lived a global life worth emulation; I thank him for the inspiration to be creative and his love of travel. And I also thank my aunts and uncles, Gunilla and Peter Tamm, Akhbar and Farida Zuberi, and Göran and Kian Höckert, as well as my cousins for their support.

In Vancouver, I am fortunate to have become part of a new, second family. Campbell Robinson and Helen Robinson have become great friends, sharing countless meals and enjoyable outings. Cam used his finely honed editing skills, perfected from publishing so many letters to the editor in *The Globe and Mail*, to provide some excellent editorial advice on an early draft of this book. Leslie Robinson, Ken Hildebrand, five-year-old Kate, and just-born Graham have been a pleasure to befriend; their kindness and companionship are much appreciated. Michelle Robinson, Charles Lepoutre and new addition Georges have always been kind hosts and taught me a lot about Quebec. Toni and David Owen and Jean Vivian have always been very generous and welcoming every time I have had the pleasure of seeing them. And of course, I thank Dante, for being good company while I write.

My biggest thanks goes to my partner, Joanna Robinson, who has been incredibly supportive of me throughout the process of researching and writing this book. I feel so lucky that we met as volunteers for a UN conference on civic participation in Vancouver. She read and provided invaluable feedback on many drafts of each chapter. Joanna also taught me a lot about social policy in Canada, about the growing international struggle against poverty and war, and about the importance of protecting the environment. But, more important, she provided the light in my life, and I treasure our long walks through city streets and the forest, warm moments alone and with friends, sitting out on our balcony until late in the night, delicious dinners, and swimming together in oceans and pools. I love sharing the journey of life together with her.

Differences That Matter

Vancouver Skyline

Seattle Skyline

CHAPTER 1

Introduction

It is 5:30 a.m. on an early spring morning in the Pacific Northwest. Pigeons mut-
ter, squawk, and whistle outside bedroom windows on Capitol Hill. One hundred
twenty miles to the north, the sun hits the peaks of the North Shore mountains as
the first buses carry drowsy passengers on their way to work. In Seattle, Washing-
ton, and Vancouver, British Columbia, delivery trucks roll down largely empty
streets as the workers on the morning shift prepare for the new day.
  Both cities are carved out of the Pacific Ocean rainforests—flourishing in fre-
quent misty rains—in valleys surrounded by towering snow-capped mountains.
From the frontier beginnings of these cities, the forest—in shades of green from
emerald to olive—has defined their development and life. Living amid the forest
and mountains, the residents of both cities enjoy a wonderful quality of life com-
pared to many other North American urbanites. Seattle and Vancouver, thriving
postindustrial mid-size global cities where east meets west, are often on the cutting
edge of urban development.

Sujita Hassam and Karen Hsu are ethnic minority immigrants who work for
the Globe Hotel[1]—a major multinational hotel chain—in Seattle and Vancouver, respectively. Their stories illuminate some of the major themes of this
book. They work at the bottom of the labor markets of each country, in jobs
that offer few rewards, for a firm that straddles an international border that
sharply demarcates two contrasting social policy regimes. The United States,
with its comparatively weak welfare state and laissez-faire tradition, and
Canada, with its history of strong safety nets and interventionist social policy,
offer divergent contexts through which the working poor must navigate.

Sujita's Story
Sujita Hassam is a forty-one-year-old ethnic Indian woman who moved to
the United States from Fiji in fall 2000. As she described it to me, life in Fiji was
fraught with difficulties and hardships. After finishing high school, Sujita

Hassam went to work in a garment factory where she labored under difficult conditions in order to make ends meet: "I didn't go on to university because my father was very poor," she told me. "I was getting like $1.45 per hour and every week we get the wages, a check, [for] $50 per week. It was very hard for us."[2] (In this book, all dollar amounts are presented unconverted in the currency of the hotel worker's current residence, unless otherwise noted).

After working at the garment factory, Sujita Hassam began a new job as a cashier for a clothing store, earning only slightly more money than in the factory: "I was getting $1.60. When I was cashier in the shop, I was getting there like one week $70." It was not enough for her to make ends meet.

> No it was not enough [to pay the rent and expenses]. But we have to think about the money. We just get the wages, we think about the money, and then we think if we want to buy food, clothes. Then we have to go to shop. . . . if we think anything nice, we want to buy, we cannot buy. We just think about that and come home. We just think a lot for the food.

Although she now laughs at the memory, Sujita Hassam spent five years working under these conditions to help support her family. During that time, her mother passed away and her father became ill. Because Sujita Hassam was single, she became the family matriarch, caring for her sick father and helping to raise her brother and sister-in-law's children, with whom she lived. "It was very hard for me," she said. Many of the immigrants working in the hotel industry in Seattle and Vancouver faced similar difficult economic circumstances in their home countries, before immigrating to North America.

One day Sujita Hassam met Rajiv Garithamy, a Fijian-American man of ethnic Indian background who was vacationing in Fiji. They soon fell in love, and he asked her to marry him and move to the United States—to California, no less—to be with him. It was a dream come true; a dream long deferred and finally given up on after thirty-eight years of matchmaking for others. Her first few months in California were wonderful. "It was really pretty great. It was very pretty. I like it."

During the first few months of their marriage, Sujita Hassam noticed that a Mexican woman frequently visited. When she asked her husband "What is this? He say, my friend my friend." Then, "one day I went to find a job, I stay my husband's sister's house. I said [to him] I'll not come back [tonight], I'll come tomorrow. But when I came [to] my apartment, I saw my husband was with her in my bedroom." Rajiv Garithamy's sister broke the news to her "that day, I catch him"; she discovered to her dismay that he already had a wife. "He was already married, and he did not tell me he got two kids. . . . He told me nothing. He had two kids, one was 5, one was 10." When she asked his sister why she had supported their marriage when she knew her brother was already married,

Rajiv's sister told her, "they [his family] do not like her, then we marry with an Indian girl we like." They told her, "And we thought, you gonna marry, then he gonna leave her. She [Rajiv Garithamy's sister] thought he will leave her, but he never did." Rajiv Garithamy's family wanted him to marry an ethnic Indian, and so he had kept his first marriage a secret. Sujita Hassam's discovery brought the whole world crashing down on her shoulders.

Angie Makora, a friend from Fiji who lives in Seattle, encouraged Sujita Hassam to move up the coast and marry her brother—Amit Hassam—whom Sujita had met in Fiji ten years earlier. Five months before we met, she did just that. After marrying Amit, Sujita Hassam found part-time work at a very difficult machine-operator job in a Tacoma-area factory where her new husband also worked. "Oh it was very hard job," she recalled. "Everything do with the machine. Cut every kind of rubber and everything. Press things and everything they use in the roofs." She earned $8 per hour for her labor. Her husband continues to work at the factory and also works a second part-time job in a school cafeteria as a custodian. His sixteen-year-old daughter, Maureen Hassam, who joined him in Seattle from Fiji two years earlier, is currently a student at Rainier Valley High in southeast Seattle, where many other hotel workers who I interviewed in Seattle live. Many immigrants in both Seattle and Vancouver had worked in low-wage factory jobs, for example, in garment factories, or in the kitchens of ethnic-food restaurants, before gaining employment in the hotel industry.

While Sujita Hassam was still on-call at the factory, she decided she wanted more hours of work. First, she found a new job as a room attendant for the Low-Cost Motel in Tacoma. She worked there for only three weeks, earning $6.90 per hour. She disliked this job because she was not able to secure enough hours and did not receive a uniform. She also hated cleaning what she described as really "stinky" rooms, particularly where people had pets living with them. She told me, "They bring dogs and kitties and they put inside the room, and when you go inside it smells very bad. Oh yeah." So she decided to look for another job. "I applied to a lot of places, mostly I applied for the hospital. But they [the hospital] told me they are going to phone me in like 6 months. I said, 'that's a long time, I cannot wait.'" After dropping off a resume in response to an ad in the paper, she was called in to interview for a room attendant position at the Globe Hotel Seattle. She went through two major interviews and was pleased and surprised to get the job, starting at $7.75 per hour. During her interview, Katharina Renska—the chief housekeeper—asked her about her past work experience and her family situation, including the age of her husband's daughter. Why? Perhaps managers screen out potential employees who may face problems accessing reliable child care. In both Seattle and Vancouver, it was surprising to find that few of the hotel workers were lone (single) parents.

Sujita Hassam said she enjoyed working at the Globe Hotel Seattle; she dreams of working as a registered nurse (RN) or of finding employment in a hospital again, "where the money is." In California, she had worked in a hospital for a national food-service company. "I just work there for four months and they were paying me like $8.50 something, and they said after 3 months they going to put your [wage] rate up." She recently met with a personnel officer at a Seattle hospital, who said she could get a food-service job in three months; this job also included the possibility of taking RN training courses. Sujita Hassam plans to wait and see.

Sujita Hassam was frustrated about the low wages paid at her hotel. She said she thought that her job at the Globe Hotel would be better if the hotel were unionized because employees would get regular pay increases: "Why I think if union it would be better? If they work hard and after 1 year or 2 and they are only giving you like $7 [per hour], you can probably use union for something like this." At the same time, she realized how difficult it can be to unionize a workplace. The garment factory she had worked for in Fiji closed down as it was being unionized: "3,000 people working there, and they closed it because the union come, so no more job." Only a small and declining percentage of hotel jobs in Seattle are unionized.

Life for the working poor is stressful in Seattle. The Hassam family rents a one-bedroom apartment. Maureen Hassam sleeps in the living room. Sujita Hassam described the apartment as "somewhat crowded," with leaks and roaches. The landlord continues to promise, but not deliver on the promise, to spray the apartment for insect infestation. He charges them a $70 fine if they are even one day late on the $600 monthly rent. In the five months prior to the interview, the Hassams were late paying the rent four times—incurring $350 in fines—and had their phone cut off twice because they could not pay their bill. Their utility bills add up to $250 or more per month for electricity, garbage service, and water. There is no room in their budget for any unexpected expenses or extravagant expenditures. Sujita Hassam described paying the household bills as "very difficult." These material hardships land on the Hassams, despite the fact that the two adults hold multiple jobs. They regularly borrow from Maureen Hassam, who works thirty hours per week at Burger Barn, a fast-food franchise. Amit Hassam also borrows money from Arthur Lowell, a white co-worker at the school cafeteria, although the family tries its best to pay him back quite quickly. At the time of the interview, Sujita Hassam said they had about $2,000 in the bank. She was not sure, but she thought her husband might have a little retirement savings. Living on the edge financially is not unusual among workers in Seattle, with many hotel employees reporting difficulties making ends meet.

Amit Hassam commutes to Tacoma by car; Sujita Hassam takes the bus to work. On a typical day, she gets up at 5:00 a.m. so that she can shower and prepare for her husband and step-daughter to leave for work and school. Then, she catches the 6:30 a.m. bus downtown to make sure she is not late for her 8:30 a.m. shift. Sujita Hassam estimates that last year, she earned only $7,000 before taxes and her husband earned $23,000 working two jobs. Despite their low income, she tries to send money and gifts back to her relatives in Fiji whenever possible. Every few months, they donate a small amount of money to their church and a local hospital.

Sujita Hassam lacks health insurance coverage. Although the Globe Hotel provides health insurance benefits, she is trapped in the new employee waiting period. Her husband pays $50 per month for health insurance, a limited plan lacking dental coverage. Her step-daughter is covered by a Washington state health program, so she has been to the doctor and dentist in the past year. But Sujita Hassam has no health insurance coverage, which worried her: "Yeah, I am worried. Because I am thinking if I haven't got any [health] insurance and maybe someday I'm gonna sick. And if I go to the doctor, I am going to have pay a lot without the insurance."

The family is very vulnerable to financial catastrophe in the event of a health emergency. Problems with health insurance coverage and accessing health care are much more frequent for workers in Seattle than in Vancouver. After three months, Sujita Hassam will qualify for health insurance coverage benefits for herself but not for the rest of her family. If she switches employers in order to improve her wages—as she and many working poor hope to do—she will probably have to start again in terms of waiting periods for essential benefits such as health insurance coverage.

As with most Seattle workers without health and/or dental insurance, Sujita Hassam has not received regular preventative medical checkups. Her last doctor's visit was her pre-emigration checkup in Fiji over two years ago. She wants to go to the doctor, but without health insurance she feels she is unable to afford medical and dental care. Her job benefits are meager; she is eligible for one week of paid vacation and six paid sick days this year. The job benefits are less generous in Seattle than in Vancouver, in part because of differences in labor policy that set different minimum standards for workers in each city.

Hotel workers in Seattle live in and around poorer neighborhoods compared to Vancouver. They experience more problems with crime and greater feelings of personal insecurity. Sujita Hassam's family lives southeast of downtown Seattle, close to Rainier Avenue, in a neighborhood close to shops. Sujita Hassam has noticed some "sketchy in and out" activity next door as well as cars cruising up and down the block (enough to scare her and cause her to bolt the door). Yet she has not seen a police officer or cruiser in her area since moving in. In the past few months, the Hassams have been the victims of petty thefts, which have left Sujita Hassam feeling personally insecure; for example, someone stole Maureen Hassam's expensive pants from the dryer in the common laundry room.

Although her husband brings her to the homes of many other Indian immigrant families, the Hassams do not belong to any official groups or clubs. Sujita Hassam is more socially isolated in Seattle than she was during her brief residence in California: "Different there [in California], I was with my auntie, there was a lot of Indian people. Here I don't have any friends, just my husband and my daughter." She reports she is happy in her new marriage and is grateful because, she reflects, she was never really happy before. She has a positive general feeling about the Rainier Valley high school her step-daughter attends. She thinks her teacher is nice, and she has met with her occasionally.

Sujita Hassam dreams of buying a two-bedroom home. Her husband thinks they should move to a Tacoma suburb—closer to his job at the factory but a much farther commute for her. Despite their hardships and insecure financial position, Sujita Hassam is still optimistic about her future. She perceived her family as being squarely in the middle class of U.S. society, but her story illustrates the significant obstacles and hardships facing recent-immigrant, working-poor families in U.S. cities. Even with the support of family resources and working as many jobs as possible, many live on the edge of poverty in neighborhoods with a low quality of life, isolated from mainstream society. They also often lack access to health insurance and preventative medical care. Without a new rung on the ladder of the urban service-sector economy to provide stable living-wage jobs for recently arrived, low-skilled immigrants, the second and third generations of these families are at risk for downward assimilation into the growing ranks of the urban poor.

Karen's Story

Karen Hsu is a forty-nine-year-old mother with two teenage children who lives with her husband and mother-in-law. She was born in Guangdong, China, and moved to Vancouver, British Columbia, Canada, in 1980. When I asked why she had moved to Vancouver, she said, "My mother and my sister, my brother already here." In China, she had completed only two years of high school. She quickly took advantage of educational opportunities after arriving in Vancouver; she took night courses in English as a Second Language (ESL) at Redlows High School from 1980 to 1985.

Karen Hsu's first job in Vancouver was as a seamstress in a factory. After toiling for several years—earning $3 per hour—in this difficult low-paying job, she met her husband, Lee Hsu. Lee Hsu currently works full-time as an electrician and takes on occasional handyman jobs. They were married in 1983. Soon after, she was laid off at the garment factory and began collecting unemployment insurance benefits. A Canadian government program—through Human Resources and Development Canada (HRDC)—paid Karen Hsu's tuition and expenses to attend a six-month hospitality training course while she was unemployed. Many immigrant hotel workers I interviewed in Vancouver reported benefiting from these federal training programs. Through the course work and, especially, internship placements, these training programs have lifted many from insecure poverty-wage jobs to more secure, living-wage jobs.

A close friend of Karen Hsu, Lucy Chen, had recently begun working at the Globe Hotel Vancouver. She recommended that Karen Hsu apply to the Laundry Department, where a position had recently opened. She got the job and began working at the Globe Hotel Laundry Department at double her previous seamstress wage—earning $6 per hour—and held that job for nine years. During this time, the hotel began outsourcing most of its laundry to subcontractors, and the staff scrambled to find job openings in other departments. It was stressful, she said, "Everyone want to go for the other job."

Today only two staff members continue to work in the Laundry Department of the Globe Hotel Vancouver. "And now everything go outside . . . so it's more difficult for the two people there." Fortunately, Karen Hsu's hospitality certificate and selection privileges under the union contract helped her switch jobs within the hotel and secure a position as a room attendant while maintaining her seven-year seniority. After years of regularly scheduled wage increases, Karen Hsu currently earns $14.84 per hour and has generous extended health and other benefits, including five weeks of paid vacation per year. Union-organizing rules in Canada and British Columbia—in contrast to the United States and Washington state—create a context in which a much higher percentage of hotel-industry workers are unionized in Vancouver than in Seattle.

When we met, Karen Hsu had worked in this establishment for twenty years and planned to continue until she retires: "maybe work over there five or ten years, retired." Her union-based seniority privileges allow Karen Hsu to work two or three days a week during the winter slow season and full-time the rest of the year. She described the job, "Yeah, it's a hard work but it's okay. If you want the money, it's okay." Karen Hsu's story shows how stable unionized positions in the service sector can provide workers with a mainstream middle-class quality of life and resources.

Karen Hsu estimated that she and her husband earn a combined pretax annual income of $45,000. Although taxes are higher in general in Canada than the United States, the income tax burden on the working poor is less in Canada, especially for parents, because of generous tax credits. Karen Hsu estimated they paid about $2,000 in taxes the previous year and received a $200 refund. Karen Hsu's story contrasts with Sujita Hassam's in ways that reveal how working-poor families in Seattle must rely much more heavily on personal resources to make ends meet than do those in Vancouver.

In 1987, Karen Hsu and her husband purchased a large five-bedroom home with a basement apartment about one block away from where they had been renting. In Vancouver, many single-family homes include a basement suite or small apartment, which homeowners rent out in order to help with their mortgage payments. The Hsus used to rent this apartment out for $600 per month; today, Karen Hsu's mother-in-law lives in the apartment. Their neighborhood is located southeast of the downtown core, close to Kingsway, and is similar to other neighborhoods where many other hotel workers I interviewed live. The Hsus live in a classic split level, probably built in the late 1960s. The rambling house provided what she describes as "just the right amount of space" for her, her husband, their two teenage children, and her mother-in-law. They have two cars, a 1997 Geo Tracker and an older 1989 Chevy Lumina, although she generally commutes to work by bus—a forty-five-minute trip each way. Karen Hsu appreciates the quality of life in her eastside Vancouver neighborhood and considers it a good place to raise her children. The impact of public infrastructure investment is obvious here. Karen Hsu's neighborhood boasts community centers and other family-friendly institutions. Both Karen Hsu and her fifteen-year-old son, Daniel Hsu, thought of their neighborhood as safe, and the family has no plans to move in the next several years.

During our interview, Daniel Hsu sat at the kitchen table with us and helped translate some of the questions and answers for his mother. A tall, lanky young man, he was happy to share his opinions. When I asked if there was an issue with crime in their neighborhood, he said, "Nothing happened here, for the past four years." Karen Hsu is very proud of her son, who just gained acceptance to a gifted and talented enrichment program at his high school. He told me the school has "very high math standards." Daniel Hsu also takes courses during the summer months through a summer school program and finds time to do some volunteer work as well. They also have a twelve-year-old daughter, Lucy. Like many immigrants, the Hsu family relied on their extended family for child care when their kids were young. While Karen Hsu and her husband worked, her mother and mother-in-law, as well as other relatives, watched after the children. "My mother-in-law, my mother and cousin. My father-in-law. Everyone help. Everybody help me." When I asked if she had paid them, she replied, "No afford to pay. I don't want to pay." Daniel chimed in, "Calling favors."

Karen Hsu's mother-in-law is unfortunately now quite ill and requires regular dialysis; yet the family has never had to worry about health expenses because of Canada's universal health insurance. The Canadian universal health insurance system mitigates financial stress that otherwise might be provoked by health crises. The family's regular doctor's office is located ten minutes from Karen Hsu's home by car. She had recently visited because of "shoulder pain," but does not have any major health problems. In the past year, she estimated that she visited the doctor four to five times. Her son went to the doctor once and her daughter twice. Although Canada's publicly financed medical plans do not cover dental work, all of them had recently been to the dentist for a teeth cleaning. The Hsus report making small annual donations to the British Columbia Children's Hospital.

Though her job is fairly low-skilled, Karen Hsu perceived her family as being squarely in the middle of the middle class in Canadian society, reflecting a subjective sense of class location. In 1999, the Hsu family went on a family vacation touring China for one month. Her son Daniel jokingly remembered, "China, mosquito bite town." With a paid-off home, rental property, and no credit card debt, the Hsu's largest regular monthly expenses include $200 for property taxes, $700–800 for food, $220 for hydro (utility bills), $200 for life insurance, and $300 per month for piano lessons. They have about $3,000 in savings and some retirement savings as well, but the majority of their equity is tied up in their own home. Karen Hsu's story is not unusual among room attendants and other hourly employees who I interviewed in Vancouver.

Overview

How do social and labor policy differences affect the quality of life and hardships experienced by the working poor in the United States and Canada? Chapter 2 describes previous research on urban poverty and the working poor, as well as findings from comparative research on the United States and Canada. It also contrasts trend data on poverty and inequality between the two countries since the mid-1970s to show how differences in social transfers explain these macro-level divergences.

Chapter 3 tells the story of my research, outlining the methodology of the Global Hotel study. I describe my research design and the sampling and procedures that I used. Descriptions of the four hotel sites and of the divisions of each hotel—Housekeeping, Maintenance Engineering, and Guest Services—set the scene.

Chapter 4 focuses on the differences in labor policy between the United States and Canada and the impact of these differences on hotel-industry employees in Seattle and Vancouver. First, labor policy differences, in particular those relating to union-organizing rules and procedures, are described. These differences have resulted in a dramatic divergence between the two countries in the past forty years: from the 1950s to the 1970s, approximately 30 percent of the nonagricultural labor force in the United States and Canada belonged to a union; after forty years of divergence, 35 percent of Canada's labor force presently belongs to a union compared to less than 14 percent in the United States.[3] What are the implications of this difference for hotel workers in Seattle and Vancouver? Directly, unionized hotel jobs provided better benefits, job security, and work conditions. Indirectly, higher levels of union coverage in Canada have translated into stronger labor policy and other social policies that help all low-income workers.

Chapter 5 examines the impact of the differences in the health-care systems of the United States and Canada on the hotel employees and their families. The large and growing percentage of uninsured people in the United States is well established. It stands at 14 percent of the population—over 44 million people —larger than entire population of Canada.[4] Yet there has been little systematic research on how health-care policy differences matter for the working poor.

Maintaining continuous health insurance coverage is a problem for many hotel workers in Seattle, despite the provision of health insurance benefits by the hotel. The main culprit is the waiting period for health insurance benefits, which ranges from three to six months and often longer for family coverage. Despite the fact that the hotels provide health benefits, over 25 percent of the employees in Seattle did not have health insurance at the time of their interview. Each time they change jobs, low-wage workers face the prospect of a new probationary period, even if the employer provides health insurance benefits. Even with insurance, many found the employee health benefits inadequate to prevent financial catastrophe and fewer sought and received preventative care in Seattle. In contrast, the universal health-care system in Canada decouples financial considerations from most health-care experiences. The findings suggest that the problems of the current health-care policy regime in the United States go well beyond individuals simply lacking health insurance.

Chapter 6 focuses on how differences in social welfare policies between the United States and Canada affect the quality of life and material hardships of hotel workers and their families. What differences are most important? In Vancouver, unemployment insurance provides the most important protection for hotel employees against material hardship. In Seattle, unemployment programs fail the working poor. The low replacement rate of benefits prevents unemployment insurance from acting as an effective social safety net; unemployment benefits for Seattle hotel workers are well below the income that can be earned in a minimum-wage job.

Few hotel workers in either city reported relying on public-assistance benefits, with the exception of minimal support benefits temporarily received by recently arrived refugees. In Vancouver, other government programs prevent hardships by providing financial assistance directly or helping workers build up financial resources in order to protect themselves during economic downturns. These programs include paid maternity leave, government-subsidized savings programs, workers' compensation, mandatory vacation benefits, and subsidized day care. A comparison of income supplements for low-income parents with children, such as the U.S. Earned Income Tax Credit and the Canadian Child Tax Credit, reveals that the current Canadian system provides nearly double the supplement to families in Vancouver than the U.S. system provides in Seattle. In Seattle, without government help, employees rely mostly on extended family or personal resources and on working multiple jobs to make ends meet in difficult economic times. More also live with extended families to make ends meet.

Chapter 7 examines how public infrastructure investment differences—in transit, neighborhood, and community institutions—affect the experiences of the hotel workers outside the workplace. The more egalitarian pattern of public investment in Canada, compared to the United States, means that income differences between families or individuals do not dictate the quality of life to the same degree in Vancouver as in Seattle. More workers in Vancouver were positive about their neighborhoods, almost uniformly describing them as "nice." They had access to more institution-rich communities, such as government-funded community centers. Seattle employees did not report using community centers and other neighborhood institutions as much and described more problems with crimes, such as theft and muggings.

Chapter 8 describes the cumulative and interactive impact of these differences on how workers see themselves and their families in society and on their perceptions of what the future has in store for them. Fewer hotel workers in Vancouver perceived themselves to be far below the middle rung of the socioeconomic hierarchy than in Seattle. Workers in Vancouver with children were also somewhat more positive about their children's futures. In Seattle, more workers expressed concern about their own place in society as well as hope in their predictions of their children's futures.

Chapter 9 outlines policy recommendations based on the findings of this study. What kinds of policies and institutions would improve the lives of Sujita Hassam and Karen Hsu and the millions of other working poor in the United States and Canada? Specific policy reforms are discussed for the local, state/provincial, and federal levels. This chapter goes beyond arguing for specific policy changes—it is a call for action. It proposes democratic community organizing at the grassroots level to build coalitions to work across divides and fight for changes to improve the quality of life for all Americans and Canadians.

Chapter 10 concludes the book with a summary of the main findings and discussion of their theoretical implications. In a global era, when branches of multinational franchises are opening in cities around the world, it is vitally important to understand the impact of government policy on the lives of low-income service-sector workers and their families. Social policies directly affect the quality of life and levels of material hardship experienced by working-poor families. The findings of the Global Hotel study reinforce the importance of a multidimensional analysis of equality involving more than income. The findings also contribute to the study of urban poverty.

An analysis of life in the postindustrial city also requires looking at larger forces outside of the city itself. Macro-level economic, social, and cultural forces intersect with state institutions and policies to shape the barriers and resources of people who are living, working, and striving to make ends meet. The systematic differences in the micro-level lived experiences of hotel workers, working in the same jobs for the same multinational companies in two different policy regimes, make clear that there is nothing inevitable about the globalization of the economy and rising levels of inequality and poverty. In countries experiencing growing poverty, what has been lacking is the collective will and imagination to live up to the democratic dream that can only realized on a foundation of equality of opportunity and outcomes.

CHAPTER 2

Poverty and Policy in the
United States and Canada

Urban Poverty and the Focus on Public Assistance

Much of the sociological research on urban poverty has focused myopically on public-assistance recipients, particularly in the United States. The reason is, in part, as Mark Robert Rank describes (and explodes) in *One Nation Underprivileged*,[1] the pervasive myth that the poverty problem is a values problem. Dating back even before the poor laws of Victorian England and the decrepit poor houses described by Charles Dickens, the "blaming the victim" approach to poverty has a long and disgraceful Anglo history.[2] According to this perspective, if only the poor would change their behavior and start following the rules—especially getting a job and getting married before having children—then poverty would be eliminated. Through the confounding lenses of race and segregation, arguments that the "poor are responsible for their plight" morphed into "culture of poverty" debates about urban poor ethnic minorities and ultimately transformed into welfare-reform debates.[3] My Global Hotel study adds more empirical evidence, from a cross-national comparative perspective, to support Mark Robert Rank's reframing of poverty in the United States from a problem of individual failings of those living in poverty to one of the failure of government policies and institutions to keep up with changes in the economy and society.[4] Poverty can be reduced dramatically in the United States if the political will exists.

The U.S. official poverty line is set at an extremely low level—and compared to median income, it has been falling in relative value since its creation in the mid-1960s. Mark Robert Rank provides a useful thought experiment for readers not in poverty (although real enough for students living in temporary poverty):

Now imagine that, instead of the income you currently have coming in for this month, next month you will be receiving only 29% of your income. The other 71% of your income is suddenly gone. That 71% is the distance between your current standard of living and the standard of living of those at the edge of poverty. Yet as noted, this represents poverty at its most opulent level. Forty-one percent of poor individuals have income less than one-half of the poverty line. For a family of four this would be $9,052, or 14% of the national median income.[5]

Imagine raising a family of four on a $9,052 annual income!

Ironically, studies examining the impact of welfare reform legislation have helped identify the large and growing ranks of the working poor as both an understudied and serious social problem. In *Making Ends Meet,* Kathryn Edin and Laura Lein focus on how lone mothers in four U.S. cities generated income and paid their bills.[6] Through snowball sampling and repeated in-depth interviewing, Edin and Lein gain a more accurate picture of the actual income and expenditures of lone parents, getting almost all respondents to account for how they had earned within $50 of the money they reported spending. Edin and Lein's findings are surprising—they find higher levels of material hardship among the working poor, even higher than among public-assistance recipients. Although working-poor parents might—on paper—have a higher income than public-assistance recipients, they also had much higher expenses due to the requirements of combining work and family obligations. These burdens included higher childcare, wardrobe, health insurance/health-care, and transit obligations than public-assistance recipients. At the same time, Edin and Lein find a serious underreporting of work (formal and informal) by public-assistance recipients. Virtually all public-assistance recipients had some other outside source of income to make ends meet. For example, few lone-parent respondents initially reported that they earned income through informal work or received child support from the fathers of their children.[7]

Researchers studying the impact of welfare reform in the United States have begun to examine the low-wage labor market more critically as they observe the challenges that former public-assistance recipients—largely lone mothers with children—have making ends meet on poverty wages. Sharon Hays' *Flat Broke with Children*[8] shatters much of the rhetoric and myths surrounding the 1996 Personal Responsibility and Work Opportunity Reconciliation Act (PWORA) reforms. These reforms impose two-year term limits on the receipt of public assistance and a five-year benefit lifetime cap. Based on three years of in-depth fieldwork interviewing caseworkers and over one hundred welfare recipients at welfare offices in two typical American cities, "Sunbelt" and "Arbordale," her research exposes what the much-hyped PWORA reforms have meant for caseworkers and welfare recipients actually dealing with the implementation of this nationwide policy experiment.

Viewed from the perspective of Carol and Kendra—two low-income lone mothers interviewed by Hays—the PWORA welfare reforms were far from the resounding success touted in the media and by researchers at conservative-leaning think tanks. Hays describes the actual consequences from the perspective of the welfare-office employees and recipients. Her work exposes fundamental contradictions in the legislation, which she characterizes as promoting "independence" through "Pavlovian behavioral modification." Welfare reform added a few positive supports to help women get and keep jobs. Yet these benefits—which largely helped only the best-off recipients—came at the cost of a host of punitive measures and even more bureaucratic control and quagmire. In a style suited to an Orwell novel, welfare reform attempts to create independence and self-sufficiency, largely for lone mothers raising children, through jobs in the low-wage labor market or through filling a mother's "proper" role in a two-parent, male-breadwinner, *Leave It to Beaver* mythological family.[9] The road to unstable employment at poverty wages in the low-wage labor market is made all the more rocky by the onerous rules and regulations of the welfare system. Mistakes are punished by sanctions. The system forces these mothers to take the first available job, but then allows no recourse for them to leave the position, no matter how bad or untenable, without being punished by losing the critical money they use to feed, clothe, and house their children.

That millions of dollars and volumes of research resulted in these largely punitive public-assistance reforms is tragic. Hays' work also suggests that much more research needs to be done on the working poor. She demonstrates that the implementation into practice of lofty policy ideas about the value of work as part of welfare reform is actually proving to be a cruel social experiment foisted on a vulnerable and powerless group in U.S. society. And Hays' findings suggest that the worst is yet to come, when hundreds of thousands of lone mothers with children hit their five-year lifetime-benefit limits. Books by journalists, including Jason DeParle's *American Dream: Three Women, Ten Kids and a Nation's Drive to End Welfare* and David Zucchino's *Myth of the Welfare Queen,* confirm the complex interactions of factors—policies, work, and families—that confront the day-to-day lives of low-income U.S. families.[10]

The Working Poor

Questions about the working poor have only begun to be addressed by current research. Barbara Ehrenreich, a journalist and honorary sociologist, put the low-wage labor market to the test herself in *Nickel and Dimed.*[11] Her struggles trying to make it as a Merry Maid, hotel room attendant, restaurant server, and big-box-store employee reveal how tough it can be for many low-income workers in the United States to find stable secure housing, pay bills, and put food on the table—and that is without young children in tow.

The sociology of the working poor is not new, but it is underdeveloped. The lack of research partly reflects the larger invisibility of the working poor in the collective imagination. Perhaps the daily repetitive toil and seemingly mundane struggles of finding stable secure housing and putting healthy food on the table are not quite "sexy" or sensational enough in the new "risk society" with its many social problems, real and imaginary.[12]

Scholarly attention has focused extensively on one segment of the working poor—live-in nannies, cleaners, and home cleaners. At the nexus of gender and immigration—with the homes of the wealthy as the formal workplace—qualitative studies of the cleaning and nanny businesses are a developing field in both North America and abroad.[13] Other research has focused largely on working-class culture,[14] focusing on how those working in these job positions see themselves, their work experience, and their families, hopes, and opportunities.

Service-Sector Work

Research has been slowly advancing on lower-tier work in certain segments of the service sector. Stuart Tannock, in *Youth at Work*,[15] studied the lives of grocery store and fast-food workers in unionized job settings in similar U.S. and Canadian cities. His research describes the job routines of the workers, as well as their hopes and aspirations, and challenges the myth that these jobs are populated exclusively by young workers in transition to higher degrees and professional jobs. His work does not, however, examine the impact of U.S.-Canadian policy differences on the workers.

In *No Shame in My Game*,[16] Katherine Newman focuses on a different subset of the working poor—the employees of Harlem's fast-food industry living in urban poor neighborhoods of New York City. Her findings cast doubt on the notion that traditional family and work values no longer exist in urban poor neighborhoods. The research also reveals many of the challenges facing African-American and Latino New Yorkers trying to survive in stigmatized poverty-wage service-sector jobs. Newman's research builds on the important findings of previous scholarship on urban poor neighborhoods.

In *When Work Disappears*, William Julius Wilson finds that residents of Chicago's very-high-poverty neighborhoods are limited in their search for employment by a combination of low-resource social networks, employer discrimination, low cultural capital, poor-quality public schools, and low levels of neighborhood social organization resulting from broader macro-social forces, such as the declining demand for low-skilled workers (in interaction with the historical legacy of race discrimination).[17] Residents of urban poor neighborhoods experience high levels of crime and violence, limited employment prospects, and weak governmental and institutional support.

Hotel Research

Recent research specifically about the hotel industry includes Patricia Adler and Peter Adler's *Paradise Laborers*,[18] which focuses on workers in several resort hotels in Hawaii. They examine how the hotel industry draws from the secondary labor market, exploiting certain segments of society and dividing the labor market by creating contingent skilled and semi-skilled work positions. They find that "Hotels are notoriously ghettoized in their allocation of labor. Some of the Ali'i resorts' departments were marked by gender assignment, others by age, and still others by ethnicity."[19] I found similar job-position segregation in Seattle and Vancouver hotels; for example, exclusively "girls"—as they are ubiquitously called—work as room attendants and exclusively men work as housemen and maintenance engineers. Indeed, I am amazed at the similarities between the Hawaiian resort hotels studied by the Adler and Adler and the hotels in Seattle and Vancouver, even the use of Filipino migrant workers in similar job positions. This book supports the generalizability of many of their findings.

Paradise Laborers also does an excellent job examining the oppressive characteristics of many kinds of employment as part of the growing 24/7 postindustrial postmodern service economy. As described from empirical research by Harriet Presser in *Working in a 24/7 Economy,* the expansion of nonstandard work hours has most deleteriously affected workers on the bottom rungs of the service sector.[20] In the hotel industry, as Adler and Adler find, "Losing standardized weekends prevented employees from being home on traditional family or religious days, when their spouses or children might be home from school or work and social occasions were planned."[21] Although the new 24/7 service-dominated economy has improved convenience for North Americans, societal institutions have not caught up to the convenience economy—leaving low-skilled workers, often from disadvantaged groups, to bear the brunt of the changes. My book is less about the job routines and stratification of work within the hotel per se and more about how broader macro- and micro-level social and labor policies and institutions affect the hotel workers' quality of life and material hardships.

The "Heroic" Working Poor

David Shipler, a journalist and author, takes a broader view on the issues of working poverty in *The Working Poor,* which touches on many different subgroups of the working poor in the United States, including the urban poor, former public-assistance recipients, recent immigrants, rural poor, and migrant farmworkers.[22] With broad strokes, he relates the stories of several working-poor families with a focus on the long-term deleterious impact of poverty and material hardships on children. He approaches the question by explicitly challenging exclusively cultural (right-wing) and structural (left-wing) explanations for the hardships experienced by working-poor families.

Shipler's stories are heart wrenching, particularly the cases of child neglect and abuse. Through interviews with health and social service workers, he relates some of the most horrific stories of those working on the front line with low-income parents and their children. Although his focus on many of the worst-off working poor tends to sensationalize some of the causes of working poverty and discounts the central role of structural causes, such as low wages and weak government protections, in favor of cultural arguments, his work highlights the most tragic and devastating consequences of poverty for families, communities, and the country. It reinforces the vital need for more research into understanding the working poor and what policy levers may help low-income working parents in the United States.

Shipler's work foregrounds this book through his partial focus on the "heroic" working poor. As an example, Shipler shares the story of the Tran family, refugees from Vietnam living in California. Their "success" is that "within four months of arriving as refugees from Vietnam in 1998, three of the five family members were working at jobs whose low wages pooled, brought in $42,848 a year. Within five months of arrival, they had saved enough to pay cash for two used cars. Less than a year later, the two oldest children were at community college."[23] Shipler emphasizes the personal factors that were critical for the Tran family's "success" in the United States: "the right combination of drive, opportunity, thrift, education, health, connections, and mutual support . . ."[24] More specifically, "When a cohesive family has multiple wage-earners who believe in their own competence, have the skills, know how to find jobs, manage their money with care, and never retreat in the face of hardship. If this sounds heroic, it is. There is no room for mistake or misfortune—not for drugs, not for alcohol, not for domestic violence, not for illness or injury, not for anything less than high diligence."[25] Many of the workers in my Global Hotel study have stories similar to the Tran family.

Low-skilled workers and their families take center stage in this study alongside a focus on how the low-wage labor market and a broad array of social policies interact. Many sociologists tend to underplay or ignore the critical role played by government policy and the labor-market institutions of advanced industrial countries in shaping social stratification and social mobility. Furthermore, social policy studies often overlook related issues, such as public investment in transportation, recreation, schooling, public safety, and environmental regulation, which—above and beyond labor-market regulation— help to determine (or soften) the consequences of being poor. More generally, recent research on advanced industrial countries has increasingly demonstrated the importance of public policy and institutions on a nation's levels of inequality, social stratification, and poverty.[26] Through the focus on policy impacts from the perspective of working-poor families in a cross-national comparative context, this book considers these issues from a new perspective. As a cross-national study of similar employees working in the same jobs for the same corporations in Seattle and Vancouver, I am able to isolate and analyze the impact of social policy differences on the employees' lives.

U.S.-Canadian Comparative Research

Although Gøsta Esping-Andersen categorizes the United States and Canada into the same neoliberal welfare state model in his book *Three Worlds of Welfare Capitalism*,[27] the two countries have diverged in certain policy domains over the past forty years. Canada has developed a universal health insurance system, in contrast to the current U.S. health-care system of mixed public and private coverage. Canada's labor laws also erect far fewer barriers for workers to unionize their workplace. My research focuses on the impact of these kinds of policy and institutional divergences on hotel workers in Seattle and Vancouver who work in the same jobs for the same hotel chains.

At the heart of my research is the following puzzle. The United States and Canada had very similar economies and levels of stratification after the end of World War II. Despite undergoing an almost identical shift from a largely manufacturing-based economy to a service-sector-dominated economy over the past fifty years, Canada has not experienced the rise in relative household poverty or inequality that the United States has. Why not?

We turn to the findings of other U.S.-Canadian comparative scholars. Seymour Martin Lipset, the well-known political sociologist, argues in his book *Continental Divide*, "Knowledge of Canada or the United States is the best way to gain insight into the other North American country. Nations can be understood only in the comparative perspective. And the more similar the units being compared, the more possible it should be to isolate the factors responsible for the differences between them. Looking intensely at Canada and the United States sheds light on both of them."[28] The United States and Canada certainly share many similarities, including comparable living standards, demographics, and similar occupational structures. Both the United States and Canada have experienced similar economic and social transformations in the post–World War II era, including the shift to a service-sector-dominated economy and the rapid entry of women into the formal labor market. As David Card and Richard B. Freeman, both economists, point out:

> Canada and the United States are as close economically and socially as any pair of countries in the world. The two nations share similar cultural traditions and enjoy comparable living standards. Both countries have highly educated and

skilled workforces, with similar industrial and occupational structures. Many of the same firms and unions operate on both sides of the border. . . .

Throughout the past century Canada and the U.S. have shared similar economic experiences. Both were major recipients of the European immigration and capital flows; more recently, both have experienced large in-flows of non-European immigrants. Both escaped the destruction of World Wars I and II. Both had "baby booms" in the 1950s that produced comparable demographic structures. And both developed broadly similar income security and labor market regulations over the course of the twentieth century. But against this backdrop of similarity are "small differences" in policies, institutions, and economic outcomes. . . .[29]

For example, although differences between the two nations' business cycles often complicate cross-national comparative research, the United States and Canada shared similar rates of economic growth from 1979 to 1990[30] (see fig. 2.1). Such similarities between the United States and Canada help us isolate and learn about the impact of their differences.

And the social policy differences between the United States and Canada are significant; however, the current research is not precise or in-depth enough to show what these differences mean for the lives of low-wage workers or the urban poor. Thus far, studies have almost exclusively relied on quantitative analyses of large-sample surveys beset by problems of limited availability of accurate and comparable data, particularly for those households at the bottom of each

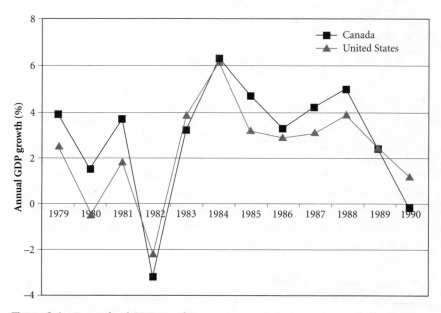

Figure 2.1   Rates of real GDP growth, 1979–1990

nation's socioeconomic hierarchy.[31] These problems limit the current literature to broad discussions of poverty rates, differences in levels of inequality, and union-coverage differences; economists and political scientists complete most comparative research with little or no attention to sociological issues.[32]

U.S.-Canadian Household Poverty and Inequality Trends

In the mid-1970s, the United States and Canada looked almost identical with respect to relative poverty and inequality. For the next thirty years, the United States and Canada experienced diametrically opposed trends in relative household poverty and inequality, according to data from the Luxembourg Income Study (LIS). LIS provides the highest quality, accessible, and comparable data for cross-national comparisons, harmonized so that they have the same meaning across data sets.[33]

Pre–tax and transfer, or market-driven, poverty increased in both countries at about the same rate (see fig. 2.2). In Canada, the pre–tax and transfer relative poverty rate increased from 28.1 percent in 1975 to 35.5 percent in 1994; similarly, in the United States it increased from 28.6 percent in 1974 to 33.9 percent in 1994. Thus, Canada actually had a marginally *higher* rate of household poverty in 1994 compared to the United States before taxes and transfers.

Yet after taxes and transfers Canada had a significantly *lower* poverty rate than the United States (see fig. 2.3). The relative household poverty rate in Canada declined from 15.6 percent in 1975 to 10.6 percent in 1994. In the United

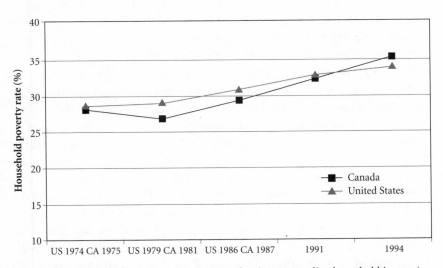

Figure 2.2 Poverty rates before taxes and transfers ($< 50\%$ median household income); as an artifact of the harmonization of the data, comparable U.S. and Canadian data are a year apart)

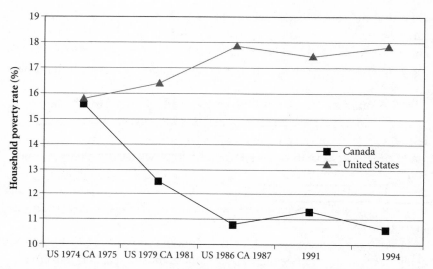

Figure 2.3 Poverty rates after taxes and transfers ($<$ 50% median household income); as an artifact of the harmonization of the data, comparable U.S. and Canadian data are a year apart

States, on the other hand, the household poverty rate increased somewhat over the same period from 15.8 percent in 1974 to 17.9 percent in 1994.

Three decades ago, the United States and Canada also shared similar levels of household inequality. After taxes and transfers, U.S. and Canadian households at the ninetieth percentile (P90) of the income distribution had approximately five times the amount of household income that households at the tenth percentile (P10) had. In the United States, this P90/P10 ratio—one of the standard measures of inequality—increased steadily from 5.16 in 1974 to 6.42 in 1994. In sharp contrast, Canada's P90/P10 ratio of inequality dropped steadily from 5.01 in 1974 to 3.93 in 1994. So, by 1994, those households in the ninetieth percentile of the income distribution in Canada had approximately four times the income of those at the tenth percentile.[34] Although the wealthy got wealthier over this period in both countries, the poor in Canada marginally improved their relative position while the poor in the United States became worse off.

The U.S.-Canadian comparative institutional literature has identified certain policy differences as impacting macro-level trends in poverty and inequality. For example, Rebecca Blank and Maria Hanratty demonstrate in a simulation using Census data that poverty would be dramatically reduced in the United States if the Canadian public-assistance and unemployment policies were implemented. If the U.S. rules of these programs were applied to Canada, poverty would rise dramatically.[35]

In the *Warmth of the Welcome*,[36] Jeffrey Reitz compares the impact of institutional differences in Canada, the United States, and Australia on the labor-market fortunes of immigrant groups. Although the existing U.S.-Canadian comparative literature provides evidence that policy and institutional differences do matter for macro-national-level outcomes, they fail to explain how the complex interactions of these differences are experienced by individuals themselves.

As I learned in my fieldwork, comparing Canada to the United States is a national sport in Canada, second only to hockey. I thought it was something Americans—including myself—could use a little more of. I decided a new sociological study on the urban working poor would add to both the U.S.-Canadian comparative institutional literature and the urban poverty literature. In the tradition of Georg Simmel,[37] the urban sociologist, I wanted to better understand the impact of these differences from the perspective of the subjective experiences of individuals. U.S.-Canadian comparative research helps advance our understanding of the ways that policy matters in the lives of low-skilled workers in advanced industrial nations.

My study of hotel workers located at the lower end of the labor-market hierarchy in both cities examines the impact of macro-level social forces—including economic and local and state policy regimes—as well as micro-level forces.[38] Through in-depth interviews with workers and participant-observation research in their workplaces and urban neighborhoods, the Global Hotel study views both cities through the experiences of one segment of their populations.

Both the United States and Canada have experienced similar macro-social and economic transformations. Cross-national comparative analysis helps disentangle the impact of coterminous structural factors. It remains difficult to study the impact of policy differences on the working poor through the quantitative analysis of large-sample data sets because of limitations on truly comparable data. Comparing the lived experiences of workers in the same jobs with the same multinational corporations in similar cities in two different countries allows us to examine both the macro- and micro-level differences that shape the quality of life and material hardships experienced by these workers and their families. The similarities and differences in their experiences shed light on the broader social forces and micro-level institutions that shape not only Seattle and Vancouver but also the postindustrial city globally.

CHAPTER 3

The Story and the Setting

The Global Hotel Study

During the past several years, I have told the story of my research project—which in academia we formally call our study methodology—many times: to professors, to fellow students, to family members, to union leaders, to hotel general managers, to hotel workers, to security, and to editors. And now I am pleased to share my story with you. (If you are interested in even more detail, check out my favorite part of every book based on a qualitative study—the appendix section on methodology.)

One of the first questions I am often asked is, "So, why hotel workers?" The main reason I chose to study hotel workers is that large multinational hotels have similar branches in many cities around the world, including Seattle and Vancouver. A second reason is that hourly workers occupy the lower rungs of the service-industry labor force in each country. From the other side of the new service sector, hotel work often exemplifies what Saskia Sassen in her book *The Global City*[1] refers to as the support staff of the new global elite, who jet-set around the world for conferences, meetings, and business deals.

I also chose to focus on the hotel industry because many hotel employees are ethnic minority immigrants, often coming from the same or similar countries of origin before settling in the United States or Canada. Contrasting the experiences of immigrants from the same countries of origin—sometimes from the same town or region of China or the Philippines—currently living in Seattle and Vancouver reveals the importance of macro-level policy and institutional differences for shaping the resources available and context for immigrant incorporation.[2] In addition, hotels are part of the large and growing hospitality industry. According to Annette Bernhardt, Laura Dresser, and Erin Hatton, in the United States, "Hospitality is an $86.5 billion dollar a year industry that employs roughly 1.9 million workers in more than 40,000 establishments nation-wide."[3]

One academic inspiration for my research design was Ronald Dore's *British Factory—Japanese Factory*,[4] in which he compares two similar manufacturing plants in the United Kingdom and Japan. Another came from David Card and Alan Krueger, both economists, whose Princeton Study compares changes in the number of restaurant jobs in two contiguous counties in New Jersey and Pennsylvania before and after one state raised its minimum wage. They find that more new jobs were created in the state that increased the minimum wage —contradicting predictions based on neoclassical economic theory and proving that worker-friendly policies do not necessarily hurt job creation. Instead, they may, in fact, create job growth because better-off workers have more money to spend.[5] My research design also takes Seymour Martin Lipset's insights about the value of U.S.-Canadian comparison from *Continental Divide*[6] to the next level of methodological focus—the city.

My study is the first to compare the experiences of workers in the same job positions, working for the same multinational firms, in two similar cities in different countries. Part of what made this study so compelling for me was that given the similarity between Seattle and Vancouver—which some even refer to colloquially as "twin cities"—we might expect that, despite small differences in policy at the federal level, the experience of the working poor would not be all that different between the two cities. I was interested in looking more closely at these differences and how they affected the quality of life and material hardships experienced by hotel workers and their families.

Comparing Seattle and Vancouver

The close proximity, social and economic similarities, and different social policy regimes of the cities of Seattle and Vancouver create a unique opportunity to explore the impact of social policy differences cross-nationally. By comparing family experiences in similar cities, we can overcome some of the difficulties faced by cross-national policy researchers due to major variations between states or regions within a country.

Located only two hours driving distance from one another in the Pacific Northwest, Seattle and Vancouver are the U.S. and Canadian cities most similar to one another. They share a qualitatively similar feel and many social and economic similarities. Both are considered prospering cities that have experienced population and economic growth over the last decade. At the same time, they are also both known for their slower pace of life and incredible natural beauty of the Pacific Northwest region, including the mountains, forests, and lush vegetation.

Historically, Seattle and Vancouver developed as frontier cities. Both cities began as small lumber settlements in the mid- to late 1800s and grew dramatically, in part as a result of their selection as the last stop of transcontinental railroads; they both grew to be major regional hub cities. Other historical similarities are truly remarkable. Both cities even experienced anti-Chinese riots at similar times: in 1886 in Seattle and 1887 in Vancouver. They also shared very similar boom-and-bust economic cycles over the course of the twentieth century.[7]

Seattle and Vancouver continue to share demographic similarities. They have virtually the same population size (approximately 520,000) and number of households (approximately 110,000).[8] Residents of cities that are the same size—particularly those also in the same region—are more likely to experience similar challenges and opportunities. Certainly, Seattle and Vancouver are more similar along critical dimensions than other potential comparable cities near the U.S.-Canadian border, such as Detroit and Toronto or Boston and Montreal.

Different challenges exist for and different coping mechanisms are used by urban poor families in cities, even within the same country. For example, low-income families in San Antonio in Edin and Lein's *Making Ends Meet* had more problems and much higher expenses for transit than similar Chicago families, where heating bills and proper winter clothing were more important issues.[9] Comparing Seattle and Vancouver—two cities with similar size, history, climate, and region—should control for some of these differences.

Seattle and Vancouver differ in ways that might impact a comparative study of working-poor families. For example, the two cities have somewhat different ethnic compositions, with Seattle having a higher proportion of African Americans and Afro-Caribbeans than Vancouver and with Vancouver having a larger Asian population than Seattle. After World War II, Seattle also experienced a unique increase in military-based economic growth.[10] Although this might be an important difference in terms of the general economic health of each region, there is no clear reason that it should impact a comparative study of the lives of hourly workers in the hotel industry who are not in that sector.

Other differences between the two cities are important for comparison, but arise out of the complex interaction of market and government policy differences. Seattle residents have a higher educational attainment compared to Vancouver, with a substantially higher percentage completing a bachelor degree or higher, 44.5 percent compared to 29 percent.[11] Although these differences reflect country-level differences in the attainment of higher education, the higher-education gap has rapidly shrunk over the past decade with a massive increase in the percentage of young people enrolling in university in Canada. In addition, more Canadians than Americans have a skill-based certification other than a bachelor's degree.[12]

In terms of income, the median household income in the late 1980s was higher in Seattle, at $29,343 compared to $22,667 in Vancouver (in U.S. dollars, based on the currency exchange rate at the time).[13] The higher median household income suggests that workers in Seattle are better off than in Vancouver.

Table 3.1 Average expenditures in metropolitan Vancouver and metropolitan Seattle (US$)

	Seattle expenditures	Vancouver expenditures[a]
Food	5,241	4,345
Shelter	8,820	6,685
Clothing	1,952	1,479
Transportation	7,712	4,195
Health care	1,557	803
Personal insurance payments; pension contributions	3,827	1,691
Total	**40,440**	**35,861**

Source: Family Expenditures in Canada, 1996; U.S. Current Expenditure Survey, 1996–1997 (http://ww.stats.bls.gov/).
[a]Conversion: US$1 = CA$1.50.

Yet metropolitan-level data suggest that Canadians also spend less on essential items in matched areas (see table 3.1). Although the median and average incomes for households in Seattle may be somewhat higher than in Vancouver, the level of expenditures in Vancouver compared to Seattle reflects the lower cost of living and the fact that the median- and average-income differences are overstated. Comparing these incomes using a Purchasing Power Parity (PPP) Index to convert the Vancouver averages reveals similar median and average incomes for the two cities. This similarity improves my case that comparisons between the two cities in terms of incomes and expenses of working-poor families (discussed in chaps. 4 and 6) are valid.

City-level statistics reveal that the rate of home ownership was higher in Seattle than in Vancouver and that the median rent, after currency conversion, was slightly lower (based on data from the early 1990s; see table 3.2). The high median housing value in Vancouver reflects the dramatic increase in property

Table 3.2 Housing statistics[a]

	Seattle	Vancouver
Owners (%)	48.9	40.8
Median value (US$)	136,500	209,223[b]
Renters (%)	51.5	59.2
Median rent (US$)	463	472[b]
Built pre-1940 (%)	36.2	N/A
Built pre-1946 (%)	N/A	26.5

Source: 1990 U.S. Census CD-ROM; 1991 Canadian Census Databooks (Sample — 100%).
[a]N/A, not available.
[b]Conversion: US$1 = CA$1.50.

values through the late 1980s and 1990s. Although the average rent did not increase very much (only 2.25 percent), the number of families paying more than 30 percent of their income for gross rent quintupled during this period. Even the number of homeowners paying more than 30 percent of their income for mortgage payments tripled.[14] Hence, without social policy differences, we might expect lower homeowner rates and increased housing hardships among Vancouver employees compared to Seattle. (These differences are discussed in greater detail in chapter 6.)

The Study Design

I designed the Global Hotel study to elucidate how social policy differences between the United States and Canada impact the lives of one group of the working poor in the new global city—low-income service-sector employees. In the study, I address the following research questions.

- What government policies are particularly important for the well-being of working-poor families in the United States and Canada? Do the working poor experience less hardship in Canada than in the United States?
- How do labor policy and unionization matter for hourly service-sector employees?
- How does the provision of universal health insurance and services impact the working poor?
- Do more generous social programs, assistance, and unemployment benefits affect the lives of the working poor, and in what ways?
- How do neighborhood and public infrastructure differences impact the quality of life of working poor?

The goal of my research design was to try to control as much external variation as possible, including job and corporate policies, in order to gain a better understanding of how social and labor policy differences matter for these employees and their families.

The hotel industry spans the U.S.-Canadian border and uses the same division of labor. I selected franchises of the same two multinational chains (which I call here Globe Hotel and Hotel Deluxe) in the two countries to control for firm variation. While I completed twenty-four formal employee interviews at the non-unionized Globe Hotel Seattle, I interviewed twenty-one hotel employees at the unionized Globe Hotel Vancouver. I formally interviewed fifteen employees at the unionized Hotel Deluxe Seattle and seventeen at the non-unionized Hotel Deluxe Vancouver. I intentionally selected one unionized and one non-unionized hotel in each city. The impact of the union difference is discussed in the chapter 4.

Table 3.3 Number of in-depth employee interviews conducted with employees from each general division

	Housekeeping department	Maintenance engineering	Guest services	Total interviewed by city
Seattle	18	5	16	**39**
Vancouver	23	5	10	**38**
Total interviewed, by division	41	10	26	**77**

Hotel Employee Interviews

From January 2001 to October 2002, I met with over one hundred hotel employees and several hospitality union representatives. These meetings and interviews took place in homes, in offices, in coffee shops, in restaurants, and in my favorite place, over coffee in the small café on the ground floor of the older hotel where I lived while completing part of my study. I formally interviewed seventy-seven lower-level employees, who worked in the Housekeeping, Maintenance Engineering, and Guest Service departments in the four hotels. These three departments are the foundation for the smooth operation of any major hotel (see table 3.3). The proportion of employees interviewed in each department roughly reflects the relative size of that group of employees within a hotel's hourly workforce. Most employees interviewed were in Housekeeping, the largest department in most hotels. Overall, the sample of employees interviewed is quite similar, despite not being perfectly matched.[15] (Later in this chapter, I describe the characteristics of each department in more detail.) I asked each employee detailed questions about his or her life story, family, work history, income, expenses, health, networks, hardships, and future outlook (the formal interview protocol is described in greater detail in the appendix methodology section).

The Employee Interview Sample

Who were the workers and what sets them apart? Similar to city-level population differences, my sample includes more Asians in Vancouver and more blacks in Seattle (see table 3.4). The largest group interviewed in both cities was Asian/Pacific Islander, which included employees with Chinese, Filipino, and Indian origins. The next largest ethnic group interviewed was white employees, some of whom had emigrated from Europe.

Larger differences existed in the immigration status of the samples between the two cities. The Vancouver interview sample included a higher proportion

Table 3.4 Ethnicity of hotel employees interviewed

	Seattle	Vancouver
White	15 (38.0%)	11 (29.0%)
Asian/Pacific Islander	17 (44.0%)	23 (60.5%
Hispanic	2 (5.0%)	4 (10.5%)
Black	5 (13.0%)	0 (0%)
Total	39 (100%)	38 (100%)

of immigrants (87%) than did the Seattle sample (54%). A larger proportion of the Canadian population overall is foreign-born compared to the U.S. population, which partially explains this difference.[16]

Certain characteristics set this sample of hotel employees apart from other studies of the working poor. For example, virtually all the employees interviewed who had children were married at the time of the interview (see table 3.5). Of course, some of the "married with children" employees had previously been divorced and had remarried. Yet the vast majority had remained married to their original spouse in long-term stable marriages, with most reporting that they had been married between ten and twenty-five years. A few of the "single childless" hotel employees had been married and divorced without having children.[17]

Why did my sample include so few lone parents? Hotels may be gravitating toward hiring either single childless individuals or people who are married with children. Several employees indicated that they were asked if they had children during their interviews. At the same time, it also probably reflects the more traditional values of ethnic minority immigrants who are often hired for many of these behind-the-scenes positions in the hotels.

This lack of lone parents among the employees interviewed sets my sample apart from the other studies of the working poor in the United States. With marriage promotion being prioritized by the current U.S. government administration as a means of reducing poverty, the findings of my study are illustrative. Hotel workers with children were most often married to spouses working

Table 3.5 Marital and child status of workers interviewed

	Married with children	Single childless	Married childless[a]	Divorced with children	Total
Seattle	17 (44%)	15 (38%)	5 (13%)	2 (5%)	**39 (100%)**
Vancouver	18 (47%)	11 (29%)	6 (16%)	3 (8%)	**38 (100%)**

[a]Includes three common-law childless couples.

in job positions of a similar class.[18] In Vancouver, spouses worked as electricians, handymen, cooks, data-entry clerks, cloth cutters, gas station attendants, registered nurses, janitors, car repair technicians, room attendants, and cab drivers.[19] In Seattle, they had a similar range of occupations, including night janitor at a downtown office tower, dishwasher, restaurant cook, server, dental assistant, bus driver, night houseman at a hotel, and firefighter. Most of the children over sixteen in these households also worked in low-wage service jobs, frequently in the fast-food industry. Many of the hotel workers qualify for David Shipler's culturally "heroic"[20] status: they are married and employed (some with more than one job). Yet many families in both Seattle and Vancouver still have not achieved financial security.

Accessing the Hotels

How did I generate my sample? My first interview was with the president of the union that represents most hotel employees in Vancouver. After receiving his permission to complete my research on hotel employees, I sent letters about the study to the general managers of the branches I selected.[21] In Seattle, my first interviews were with employees in the non-unionized hotel; I waited to interview the president of the union representing most of the hotel workers in Seattle until I began research at the second, unionized hotel. In most cases, I began by interviewing the general manager and securing his or her permission to complete my study at the hotel. Starting at the top of the hotel hierarchy prevented future problems.[22] After obtaining permission from the relevant union and management, I used a combination of sampling techniques—including snowball sampling—to find hotel employees to formally interview. In addition to asking people directly or requesting workers I interviewed to encourage their co-workers or friends to contact me, I also posted a sign-up sheet in the employee areas of the hotel sites. This sheet included my contact information and space so interested workers could put down their names, phone numbers, or e-mail addresses so I could contact them for an interview. I compensated each worker interviewed out of my research funds: CA$50 per interview in Vancouver and US$40 in Seattle.[23]

My research includes interviews with managers at all levels in the hotels. I took insider tours, ate in the employee cafeterias, and completed hotel-site and neighborhood-based participant-observation. In the months following the terrorist attacks on September 11, 2001, in New York City and Washington D.C., a severe recession gripped the travel industry in North America. Tourists and business travelers canceled plane tickets and hotel reservations en masse as major conventions were postponed indefinitely or scuttled altogether. The hotel industry was hit particularly hard, even hotels far from the northeastern United States. I phoned many of the hotel workers I had interviewed previously in Van-

couver in order to assess the impact of this external shock on the hospitality industry and to examine how the social safety net deployed during this time of
crises for many of the hotel workers.

To supplement the employee interview data, I completed additional open-
ended interviews with managers and union leaders, selecting questions to answer my specific research concerns as well as to gain permission and access to
gather more data for my study. Both employees and lower-level supervisors in
each division of the hotel showed me what tasks employees in that department
complete in a typical day. The participant-observation revealed a surprising
similarity between the policies, procedures, hierarchies, and organizational
structures of the branches of each multinational hotel chain and also between
the two hotel chains. It also shed light on how difficult, repetitive, and stressful
many of these jobs actually are, as well as the factorylike conditions under
which the employees, supervisors, and management toil during their shifts.
The observations focused on the qualitative dimensions of these types of jobs,
including daily work routines, how workers relate to one another, and how the
employees interact with management and customers. I analyzed the data collected—thousands of pages of interview transcriptions, notes, and material—
with the help of the Qualitative Social Research's N6 software. The software
helped me analyze the data by identifying patterns of responses and allowing
me to informally test hypotheses.

The Hotels

Many people have asked me, "What were the hotels like that you studied?"
Although they are similar in many respects, the four hotel sites involved in this
study have unique backgrounds, stories, and atmospheres. What was similar
was the sharp contrast between the guest and public areas, which I character-
ize as the "show," and the employee and administration areas, which I char-
acterize as the "backstage."[24] Although they share the same building, the
luxuriousness of the public areas stands out against the institutional atmosphere of the employee area in all the hotels. The lack of windows in the employee areas seem designed not to prevent employees from looking out but,
rather, to keep guests from looking in. The hotels place a high level of importance on creating an extremely clean and perfectly maintained public space
in order to live up to the standards of the discriminating international global
traveler.

Globe Hotel Vancouver

The first hotel I chose to study is the Globe Hotel Vancouver (see table 3.6).
It is a large, unionized three-star hotel, similar to most major downtown hotels in Vancouver, that serves mostly business travelers. The branch in Seattle is

Table 3.6 Key comparative dimensions between hotel branches

Hotel (owner)	Seattle	Vancouver
Globe Hotel (Lexicon International Inc.)	Over 550 rooms Non-unionized workforce More business-travel oriented Typical of Seattle hotels Recent mass firings and security orientation	Over 400 rooms Unionized workforce More business-travel oriented Typical of Vancouver hotels Part of hotel-employee strike summer before interviews
Hotel Deluxe (Rosemont International Inc.)	Nearly 900 rooms Unionized workforce Upscale hotel Nice employee cafeteria	Over 200 rooms Non-unionized workforce Upscale hotel New hotel Tense management-employee relations

similar. Located in the heart of the downtown business district, the Globe Hotel Vancouver is surrounded by other major international hotel chains and near the Vancouver Convention and Exhibition Centre. The hotel has twenty stories, and many of its over four hundred rooms have magnificent views of Vancouver's waterfront, Stanley Park, the North Shore mountains, and the seaplanes that regularly take off to surrounding island destinations.

Past the costumed doormen and bell staff and through automatic sliding glass doors, luxurious gray slate tiles line the floor and dark oak wood trim lines the walls. Up a small set of stairs, the check-in desk sits immediately on the left, and straight ahead is a sophisticated lounge with a stately black grand piano. The Lobby Lounge and a smaller wood-paneled bar located next to it share forty-foot floor-to-ceiling windows with a breathtaking view of Coal Harbor and the Coast Mountains. On the right, a small shop, *Merlin's,* sells chocolate, cigarettes, and bottled water for well over double what you would pay at the convenience store across the street. A tourist information desk is located by the bank of elevators next to the shop. One of the two restaurants, *Belle,* is located to the right of the entrance, complete with crystal chandeliers and an expensive art-deco design motif. On the twentieth floor, *Sunsets,* a rooftop restaurant, serves expensive continental fare.

Most of the guest rooms at the Globe Hotel Vancouver are quite luxurious, featuring amenities such as Internet access, cable TV, a morning newspaper delivered during the week, and free in-room coffee. The proximity of the hotel to the Convention Centre attracts many business and other conference clients. Because the Globe Hotel Vancouver has a unionized workforce, it secures contracts for bulk room reservations for the meetings of large national and international progressive organizations, such as the Council of Canadians. The hotel even (bravely) hosted many young people visiting Vancouver for a World Skateboarding Convention. The guests of the hotel are generally business travelers in town for work meetings, conferences, or deal closings. The lounge and restaurants at the hotel are filled with white middle-age men dressed in suits or shirts and ties discussing finance and other business deals. There are also many tourists who stay at the Globe Hotel Vancouver.

Located several floors below the main floor, next to the underground parking garage, there is a set of employee backrooms, all connected by the back elevator. The floors of this labyrinth of tunnels and rooms are scoffed linoleum. Dirty off-white concrete cinder-block walls, harsh fluorescent tube lighting, and exposed pipes dominate the areas behind the unmarked beige doors guarding these areas. Lower-tier employees often complete their assigned tasks in isolation, except for the communal coming together at the employee cafeteria during rotating lunch breaks.

Although they are service workers, these employees are involved in what feels like a Taylorist organization of the labor process. As Fredrick Taylor envisioned for the factory floor in *The Principles of Scientific Management*,[25] the tasks required for the process of creating the hotel experience for guests have been broken down, scientifically optimized, and proscribed into management and training binders. Specialist skills are not wanted for these behind-the-scene jobs; in fact, previous hotel work experience for room attendants and other positions was described as a potential *liability* by the human resources director because "bad habits" and "incorrect" procedures may be hard for employees to unlearn, making it more difficult to train them to follow the specific work procedures mandated by the hotel. Each employee task has been broken down into discreet steps, to be completed in the correct order by the assigned worker.

Uniforms are washed, cleaning fluids are refilled, and carts are stocked in the main Housekeeping office. Scheduling, "crises," and other personnel tasks, including employee hiring, training, discipline, and guest- or room-related incidents, are managed by the hourly supervisory employees and departmental managers. Messages on the wall remind employees of the number of days the hotel has gone without employee injury. They provide admonitions about worker safety, procedures, or guest-service tips — such as "Smile" in large letters.

The executive administrative offices are somewhat nicer, with offices and cubicles located in large rooms under paneled ceilings, with thinning gray institutional carpet. They are located on the upper floors of the employee area and have windows looking out over the water, unlike the windowless areas inhabited by the rest of the employees.

Globe Hotel Seattle

The Seattle branch of the Globe Hotel has a non-unionized workforce and is representative of a typical multinational hotel in downtown Seattle (see table 3.6). The thirty-story hotel has over five hundred rooms and is located at the top of a hill in the downtown corridor near the heart of the city. The hotel is a seven-minute walk from the Seattle Convention Center. Several other major international hotel chains and some of Seattle's largest corporate office skyscrapers are nearby.

On a clear day, the location of the hotel at the top of a hill provides a spectacular view. Facing west, down past the piers on the waterfront, guests can watch ferries sail off through Elliott Bay to the nearby islands. On the east side of the hotel, a major Seattle hospital complex is located across a car and pedestrian overpass for the I-5, the ten-lane interstate highway that slices through the center of Seattle. A few blocks over is the Westlake Mall complex, a large tourist shopping mall and an entrance to the underground city bus station (many of the city buses operate almost like an underground subway system in the fare-free downtown corridor).

A costumed doorman greets guests outside the Globe Hotel Seattle and ushers them through the circular door and into the main lobby, where the check-in desk is located just past a sitting area with some comfortable leather couches and seats. A bar and overpriced shop selling candy, gum, cigarettes, and drinks is located on the main floor near the elevator banks. An escalator leads up to the meeting rooms and a cafeteria-style restaurant. On the top floor of the hotel, a luxurious restaurant, *Eclipse*, with white starched tablecloths, affords a stunning 360-degree view of Seattle.

The Globe Hotel Seattle's rooms are quite luxurious, with high-speed Internet access, two phone lines, a mini-bar, and a newspaper delivered in the morning. The hotel tends to attract mostly business travelers attending meetings either at one of the hotel's fifteen meeting rooms or at the Seattle Convention Center. Typical hotel guests are mid-level sales executives of medium-size corporations. The hotel also attracts a fair share of tourists—some visiting Seattle from other parts of Washington state.

The walls of the Globe Hotel Seattle's employee area feature many posters decreeing the vital importance of the international Lexicon Corporation—the umbrella conglomerate to which the Globe Hotels belong—and the human resources training theme of the moment, for example, "Super Service." Other "Safety First" messages line several hallways.

One notable difference between the employee area at the Globe Hotel Seattle and the other hotels studied is the significant presence of a massive security system. After entering the main employee area through a card-access door, you see a long hallway that leads to the hotel's windowless human resources office, the employee cafeteria, and the security center. Many times every day, employees walk past a large room off this main hallway containing a bank of nearly thirty screens—feeding rotating images from all public areas of the hotel—which allow for the complete surveillance of the workers and guests in all the public and employee areas of the hotel. The aim of the head of Human Resources and Security was to construct a mini-version of a panopticon[26] in this hotel, explicitly in order to reduce employee theft. Although presumably some theft has been prevented by the system, the Human Resources director explained that the security system was important because rumors of theft could be substantiated and incontrovertible evidence could be produced if employees stole supplies.

As an ex-federal law-enforcement agent, Seth Michaels, the head of Human Resources, runs a tight ship at the Globe Hotel Seattle. Lower-level managers frequently defer decisions to him for approval. For example, when a housekeeping attendant decided that he wanted me to interview him in the Club Lounge on the thirtieth floor of the hotel where he worked, we first went to the security office to get the appropriate access key. A very suspicious security guard instructed us to ask the security boss for permission. The security boss, an older white man in his fifties, had a lot of difficulty understanding the house attendant because of his thickly accented English. Frustrated, he quickly barked at him that we needed to get ourselves immediately to the Human Resources director's office. Seth Michaels finally gave the house attendant permission to take me to the Club Lounge.

This atmosphere of mistrust, employee and supervisor distance, and ethnic group self-segregation was not as pervasive at other hotels. Perhaps it relates, in part, to the mass firing of 75 percent of the Housekeeping staff the previous March for working without the proper employment papers. In general, the low pay and employment conditions of this non-unionized hotel attract a vulnerable workforce and foster a high turnover rate among lower-end employees. Many employees speak little or no English. Recent recruitment has focused mostly on refugee community organizations that serve newly arrived refugees from African countries as well as on network hiring.

Hotel Deluxe Vancouver

The Hotel Deluxe is a bit more upscale; it is a four-star hotel. It serves a mix of tourists, celebrity clients, and business travelers (see table 3.6). The Hotel Deluxe Vancouver (part of the larger Rosemont International group of hotels) is located in the shopping and cultural heart of Vancouver, known as the entertainment district. Close to two shopping streets and a booming yuppie neighborhood, the hotel is convenient to many of Vancouver's tourist attractions. The hotel's hip image attracts well-known celebrities as well as wealthy tourists.

The newly renovated thirty-one-story building features distinctive reflective windows. Guest balconies provide views of downtown, the mountains, and the waterfront. The main level of the hotel is elevated above the ground floor. On one side, cars pull in off the main street and enter under a small covered awning, where bellmen, valets, and guest-services employees receive guests and ensure an easy check-in. Once relieved of their bags, guests proceed up a marble staircase to the main-floor lobby area. An understated door off the main street also opens to the same set of stairs. At the top of the stairs, the hotel lounge and main restaurant, *Solstice,* sits immediately to the right and the check-in desks are located on the opposite side. At *Solstice,* the servers wear white shirts and black pants, matching the black marble tabletops and white tile. Water is served in elegant blue glasses. A wall-to-ceiling window looks out on some of Vancouver's most famous buildings and beyond. The food prices range from about $9 for a sandwich to $15 to $25 for an entrée. To the left, there is a bank of phones and a hallway leading to some of the six conference rooms and the elevators.

Luxurious blue velvet covers the chairs in the lobby. Classical music is piped through ceiling speakers into the public areas, which are delicately lit with yellow incandescent bulbs. There is a very distinct style of modern but understated art used in the hotel. Each room has two small blue paintings, in the same style. The rooms also have floor-to-ceiling windows with a range of incredible views.

On the third floor, there are more conference rooms and the large health-club facilities, with treadmills, bikes, and weights. This fitness area also features a sauna, steam rooms in both the men's and women's bathrooms, and an outdoor heated roof-deck pool and hot tub. The ceiling and floor of the pool area are heated to keep any snow or hail from sticking and to make it a pleasant experience for guests to swim outside, even in the middle of winter. The two hundred plus rooms in the Hotel Deluxe Vancouver all have high-speed Internet access and two phone lines. A convenience kitchen includes a microwave, toaster, mini-fridge, coffee maker, and kitchenware.

As a smaller hotel, the Hotel Deluxe Vancouver has a more modest employee area than the other hotels. One assistant manager described it as being poorly designed because it does not provide enough space for the staff. Employees are actually not called "employees" but, similar to other multinational service-sector workplaces, are euphemistically called "associates." Despite the recent major renovations to the hotel, the employee area looks run-down and institutional, an atmosphere abetted by the harsh fluorescent lighting, the concrete floors, and cinder-block walls. The Hotel Deluxe Vancouver employee cafeteria is a small, windowless room with a few tables covered by cheap plastic table-cloths. The employees share a rather large communal fridge. A sign on the wall explains that bread, peanut butter, juices, coffee/tea, and any leftovers are free to all employees.

The walls of the hallway heading back to the offices are covered by many gray lockers, with their own padlocks. The employees can store their valuables and street clothes in their lockers. Down the hall from the employee cafeteria and lockers, the chief engineer works from a small office. Next door, the House-keeping supervisors share a larger room containing rows of uniforms and boxes of cleaning chemicals. The property manager's small office is located in the back of this Housekeeping area. These offices are far from luxurious. They are cramped, windowless rooms containing a computer, desk, and bookshelves. The employee areas are sterile—lacking the style, warmth, and character so carefully constructed for guests in the rooms and public areas.

The office of the property manager, who officially acts as head of House-keeping and Engineering, has a dark-colored floor and two large florescent lamp rods, with vents and exposed pipes across the ceiling. Her wood book-shelves are filled with binders about quality assurance and training binders with other procedure materials from Rosemont International headquarters.

Labor-management relations are more tense at the Hotel Deluxe Vancouver than at other hotels studied. The general manager, James Caldwell, is vehe-mently anti-union. He successfully blocked an organizing drive by the House-keeping Department staff, arguing to the British Columbia Labour Relations Board that the department was not a "viable" bargaining unit because em-ployees in other departments also complete Housekeeping tasks. He chose keeping the workforce non-union as the number one priority of the current Human Resources director. In fact, at the end of each year, she gets thirty points (out of one hundred) in her work performance evaluation for successfully keeping the workforce non-union. He told me that there had actually been sev-eral defeated union drives at the Hotel Deluxe Vancouver and exclaimed that as long as he was there, he would do everything in his power to keep it that way. He pointed around and said derisively that union organizers would sit in the restaurant passing out union cards, trying to recruit the Hotel Deluxe Vancou-ver employees.

The women in the Housekeeping Department used to be almost exclusively immigrants from the Philippines. The hotel's first general manager used per-sonal networks and network hiring to fill the open staff positions when the ho-tel first opened. James Caldwell has been trying to break up what he sees as an unhealthy ethnic "cartel" among employees at the hotel. He said that when he arrived "99.9%" of the housekeeping staff were immigrants from the Philippines. He reported that he has been successfully using "diversifying" hiring practices to create an ethnic mix in Housekeeping.[27] He also expressed a preference for hiring employees from the interior of British Columbia, the Maritimes, or Atlantic Canada rather than from Vancouver because he thinks they have better values and work harder.

In an unusual practice, Caldwell personally interviews every single candidate. During the interview, he puts them in a pressurized environment, similar to what they would experience when dealing with a demanding guest. He looks for many details, such as how they plan ahead to shake his hand, how they walk, whether they make eye contact, and how they hold themselves. He does not like "wimpy, limp" handshakes. He asks them all the following three questions:

1. Why do you want to work for the Hotel Deluxe Vancouver?
2. What would make this a successful job experience in two years for you, looking back?
3. Why should we hire you?

He also judges how the candidates are dressed. He asks them about their career aspirations during the interview to see if they are realistic. He wants to avoid "bad attitudes" caused by unrealistic expectations. For example, if an applicant for a room attendant position tells him that she wants to be in sales in a few years, but her "English is terrible" and she has the "social skills of a wilted flower," he tells her that the Hotel Deluxe Vancouver is "not the right place for her." He thinks it is better to be honest and upfront rather than to allow unrealistic expectations.

In order to recruit new employees, Mr. Caldwell personally visits the Vancouver Community College (VCC) hospitality training program to give a talk every year. He arrives ten minutes early to observe students as potential job candidates. He notes who comes in late, who makes eye contact, and who sits up front. He said his goal is to recruit candidates who are detailed oriented, plan ahead, have excellent social skills, and are articulate. He has tried skills testing before and finds it to be a waste of time, except to fill technical positions; it is all about attitude. In terms of hiring, he says that, although you can teach skills, you cannot teach employees "presence and style" or "ability and ambition" or "common sense." Although it costs money to train new employees, Caldwell believes a 20 to 25 percent annual turnover in workforce is healthy in Vancouver's economy. He said he believes in succession planning, so he hires about two staff members per year who begin in entry level positions with the expectation that they will move up into management roles over time.

Hotel Deluxe Seattle

The Hotel Deluxe Seattle is among the largest hotels in Seattle. Located in the center of Seattle, the hotel is over forty stories high with a large base (see table 3.6). The hotel has several entrances off the main pedestrian street. Down one level on the other side, the main entrance is designed primarily for guests arriving in automobiles, taxis, and limousines. Guests enter under a massive atrium, lit with thousands of small incandescent bulbs, where a costumed bell-man and valets assist them with check-in. The guests then go up the escalators to the enormous main-floor area of the hotel. There are several restaurants, a sandwich shop, and overpriced gift store on the main concourse as well as the check-in desks. A separate area handles VIP arrivals. Two small concierge help desks by the pedestrian foot entrances are located almost a full city block apart. In the center sits a huge grand piano and a lounge area for the guests to relax in while perhaps having a drink or snack from the bar. Escalators lead up and down to the many large conference rooms located on several floors above and below the main floor. Display areas throughout these floors exhibit hand-crafted crystal art pieces, blown glass, and jewels.

The Hotel Deluxe Seattle has over eight hundred rooms, all containing mini-bars, coffee makers, and voice mail. The rooms also feature a specialty bed of the Hotel Deluxe chain. The hotel attracts a diverse range of wealthy guests. It hosts corporate and organizational conventions, political meetings, and celeb-rities. As one of the few hotels in downtown Seattle with a unionized workforce, the Hotel Deluxe Seattle also attracts large left-of-center organizations for meetings, including meetings of the state and national Democratic Party. The hotel was also at the heart of the storm around the 1999 World Trade Organi-zation (WTO) talks and protests in Seattle.

As the largest hotel site, the Hotel Deluxe Seattle also has a correspondingly large employee area. From the side employee entrance, I usually entered through a secure door and then went down several flights of stairs. The em-ployee area spans four stories under the hotel, stretching the full city block. I often found myself completely lost, meandering through what at times seemed more like a large factory floor or hold of a freight ship than a hotel.

Located on the third floor, the employee cafeteria is the nicest of the four hotels sites, similar to a newly renovated attractive college dorm cafeteria. Ma-chines dispense juices, coffee, and soda. A buffet-style set-up features a choice of entrées, including delicious desserts. The cafeteria has a Mexican-style decor with fancy white paper and cylindrical-shaped lamps hanging on the walls. In contrast to the safety messages and information sheets posted in the employee cafeterias at the other hotel sites, paintings and mirrors adorned the wall of the cafeteria. At the time of one of my interviews, I noted that there were approx-imately fifteen employees sitting at the cafeteria tables. They were mostly black or Asian, with a few younger white people and older white men. They were not segregated by race or gender and seemed to be having a good time chatting at the tables. In the background, two new large-screen televisions were turned to CNN, and many chatted about the news of story of the day, the Washington, D.C. area sniper. Most of the managers and other hotel executives also frequently eat in the employee cafeteria with the other employees.

These descriptions reveal some of the unique characteristics of each hotel. What was amazing to me, however, were the similarities among these four hotels. They all had the same procedural handbooks and similar routines. Hotels, like many of the large workplaces of the new economy, are quite standardized in their overall functions and procedures, with many differences in small details, such as the thread count of the bedsheets. The hotels must aim to please the highest common denominator of the well-traveled global businessperson. The standard greeting may vary by chain, but the move to multinational franchise operations in the hotel industry, as in the fast-food industry, is a move toward convergence. The convergence creates a research opportunity to examine the impact of policy and institutional differences, which begins in the next chapter. But, first, let us consider what the departments in which these employees work are like.

Portrait of the Departments

After knocking loudly twice on the door, Marianna Lakon, a forty-three-year-old immigrant from the northern Philippines and room attendant at the Hotel Deluxe Vancouver, shouts, "Housekeeping," waits a moment for no response, and then opens the door to reveal her job for the next thirty to forty minutes. As she opens the door, she hopes the room will be empty and neat. She really hopes the guest has left a "be environmentally friendly" card on the bed. When guests who are staying more than one night display this card, it means that the room attendant does not need to change the linens. These rooms are called "shortcuts"; not having to change the linens saves the room attendants valuable time that they can use to complete the other cleaning tasks required by messier rooms. A messy room that takes more than thirty minutes to clean can cause a mini-crisis, requiring the room attendant to call her supervisor for an emergency backup.

The first thing Marianna Lakon does is walk in and spray the bathroom with an all-purpose cleaning solution. Each room attendant has a basket stocked with different kinds of cleaning products for different surfaces. After the mirror, toilet, sink, and shower walls have soaked for twenty minutes or so, she returns to the bathroom and wipes it down. She then strips the bed and makes it

—placing a clean cotton sheet on the bottom, followed by the first flat sheet, a blanket, and a top cover. After changing the pillowcases, the four pillows and two pillows with shams must be fluffed. She is responsible for checking that all the lamps are working, all the glasses are clean, and even that the inside of the microwave oven is clean. The carpets are expected to be spotless. If she sees a spot, she is supposed to use a medium-strength detergent cleaner to remove stains. If the stains do not come out, she is expected to call a houseman. She is also supposed to check the phones to make sure they are clean and working— and it is explicit that she must pick up the receiver and check every time she cleans a room. She then vacuums the room, dusts the sills, and cleans the windows. After some tidying up, she cleans the bathroom: wiping down the mirror, sink, and shower and scrubbing the toilet. These are only some of the tasks required for a typical room cleaning. Every day, one or two of the rooms cleaned by each room attendant at the Hotel Deluxe Vancouver are inspected by a Housekeeping supervisor.

The head of Housekeeping has created a very detailed 100-point inspection sheet for the hourly supervisors to use. Room attendants are expected to score at least a 95 out of 100 or face sanction. The inspection begins as soon as the door is open, with an examination of the door frame for black oil marks or smudges. Second, the inspector checks the large air vents above the door. While the room attendants probably only have to vacuum the air vents once a week to keep them clean and dust free, they are required to check the vents every time they clean the room. Next, the inspector checks the mini-kitchen part of the room to make sure that everything is organized and that all the sets of dishes are appropriately set up and clean. She checks that the room attendant has set the temperature controls correctly on the room monitors. The bathroom is always closely inspected. One Housekeeping supervisor at the Hotel Deluxe Vancouver confirmed what an employee told me during her interview: the inspectors are especially strict about stray hairs left in the bathroom. One hair results in an automatic 5- to 10-point penalty. The reason for this strictness is that the hotel can lose a rating star if a hair is found in the shower, sink, or bathtub. The inspector also checks to make sure all the bathroom products are replaced in the correct order. Ironically, there is a structural flaw in the design of the Hotel Deluxe Vancouver that the room attendants cannot fix despite the hotel's goal of perfect cleanliness. The gold-leaf wallpaper in all the bathrooms evidently is defective and is prone to spots and other pretty serious markings. Although the room attendants are expected to try to clean any toothpaste marks, for example, from the walls, they are not held liable for the often quite dramatic marks on this wallpaper; in one room, it looked like acid had been splattered against the wall.

Housekeeping

The Housekeeping Department includes room attendants, housemen, and laundry staff. Room attendants are the largest single group of staff at any hotel. They focus primarily on cleaning rooms, although they also clean common areas, conference rooms, and corporate offices. Generally, room attendants are assigned sixteen rooms to clean per eight-hour shift at each of the four hotels. The difficulty of accomplishing this task varies significantly day by day for room attendants, depending on the cleanliness and condition of the room as left by the guest. Some room attendants found cleaning rooms to be both arduous and demeaning work, especially cleaning other people's toilets. It is unusual for room attendants to get tips. When I toured the Hotel Deluxe Vancouver with a Housekeeping supervisor, we went into one "check-out room" that had beer cans strewn about. The place reeked of cigarette smoke, and the guest left lots of dirty dishes and trash all over the place. The Housekeeping supervisor said that the smoking rooms, which occupy three floors of the hotel, do tend to be messier, but that she did not consider this particular room—which I found revolting—to be messy enough to warrant calling for backup. Classically, the guest had left a dime on the bed as a tip or perhaps it was merely change that had fallen out of his or her pocket. On the rare occasions that the room attendants do get tips they are supposed to submit them to the pool that is then distributed to all of them.

Housemen or house attendants assist the room attendants with heavy-duty room-cleaning jobs and major cleaning tasks, such as shampooing the hallway carpets. Each has standard duties and is expected to be available for special assignments, including providing support for room attendants facing a messy room. The housemen are responsible for keeping the hallways clean. They vacuum, dust, and polish the public areas. At the Hotel Deluxe Vancouver, the housemen bring the clean sheets, towels, and other linens up to each floor's storage closet every morning. One houseman is responsible for checking the big blue bins in the basement room and moving them whenever they get full of dirty laundry. The night housemen are responsible for refilling all the supplies, including the housekeeping buckets. If there are any marks on the walls in guest rooms, room attendants are first expected to try to rub them out. If they cannot clean the marks, they are expected to report it to the Housekeeping supervisor, who then compiles a list for the housemen who will be assigned to clean the walls of 5 to 10 rooms at a time with stronger cleaning agents.

The laundry staff handles the outsourcing and receiving of sheets, towels, and other laundry, as well as the tailoring and dry-cleaning. In the hotels that continue to wash most of the laundry in-house, working in the laundry department is considered one of the most physically difficult jobs because of the back-straining repetitive tasks, heavy machinery, and harsh chemicals involved.

At all four hotels, most of the Housekeeping Department employees had limited English proficiency. In general, there was a surprising uniformity in backgrounds and demographic characteristics of the employees in housekeeping jobs. Of the employees interviewed in the Housekeeping Departments in Vancouver, nine were immigrants from China and five were from the Philippines. Two others were ethnic Chinese who had immigrated to Canada from Vietnam and South America. Two were immigrants from Russia. One had emigrated from India, one from Sri Lanka, and one from South America. Only one was a native-born white.

In Seattle, the Housekeeping Department employees interviewed had a similar mix of ethnic backgrounds. Four employees had emigrated from China and four from Taiwan. Three had emigrated from the Philippines, and two came from Vietnam (one was Sino-Vietnamese). One had emigrated from Guam and another from Fiji (ethnic Indian background). My interview sample also included one Korean immigrant, one Mexican immigrant, one Somali immigrant, and one Ethiopian immigrant. Two employees were African American.

Most of the room attendants interviewed were ethnic minority women between the ages of forty and fifty-five who had immigrated to Vancouver or Seattle from China or the Philippines. Although they had arrived with a range of education and work experience (from servers to accountants), their lack of English language fluency greatly limited their job prospects in their new city, even within the service sector. Most of the employees interviewed had taken advantage of beginner English courses offered free of charge to newcomers in each city, either completing the free program or quitting when they began to work.

Most room attendants reported finding their first jobs in North America through their social networks. They often worked as seamstresses in garment factories, piecework sewers at home, house cleaners, nannies, or servers in ethnic-food restaurants. Because the hotels also rely heavily on network hiring, many learned about their current room attendant jobs through friends or relatives.

Housemen were either ethnic minority or white men, ranging in age from twenty-seven to fifty. Their backgrounds included previous work experience in areas such as construction, carpentry, repair, and maintenance fields, and many had some vocational training.

The laundry staff members tended to be almost exclusively ethnic minority immigrants and non-immigrants. The laundry departments employed a mix of men and women, generally from ages thirty to fifty. For some jobs, tailoring experience was important because the laundry staff completed on-the-spot fabric repairs. In other jobs, strength, perseverance, and a compliant personality seemed to be the main requirement to move, load, sort, press, and fold large mountains of towels, sheets, uniforms, and other linens generated by the hotel.

Maintenance Engineering

The Maintenance Engineering Departments employ engineers, who complete a diverse variety of essential tasks to maintain the physical infrastructure of the hotel. They are responsible for the more technical side of the hotel, although many of the more serious repair jobs are outsourced, including television, fire system, and elevator repairs. For some maintenance engineers, duties include monitoring the heating and electrical systems as well as the chemical levels in the swimming pool and Jacuzzis. Others focus on the operation and maintenance of the major air, heating, and electrical systems and equipment running the hotel. More novice maintenance engineers tend to be assigned to painting rooms and public spaces and to making minor repairs in the guest rooms and public areas.

The maintenance engineers tend to be thirty- to fifty-year-old men. In Vancouver, they were a diverse mix of ethnicities and immigration backgrounds. The maintenance engineers I interviewed included one Egyptian immigrant, one Indian immigrant (ethnic Chinese), one South American immigrant, one Filipino immigrant, and one native-born white. In Seattle, they were all native-born whites. Because many of these jobs require a technical background, some employees had completed electrical or plumbing training programs and/or had construction experience. Several maintenance engineers continued their education while working at the hotel, upgrading their skills for the job.

Guest Services

The broadly defined Guest Services Department includes doormen, bellmen, room service staff, concierges, banquet staff, servers, stewards (dishwashers), and bartenders.[28] Guest Services employees generally have a lot of contact with guests staying at the hotel, which can make these jobs both more enjoyable and more stressful when the employees must deal with difficult clients. Doormen and bellmen greet the guests as they arrive at the hotel and assist them with their bags. They often hold doors open, hail taxis, and take care of special requests for the guests. Concierges help arrange guests' evenings on the town and answer questions about events. They arrange outings and rental cars, give directions, secure tickets, and provide other special services requested by guests. Banquet servers, room service staff, servers, and bartenders also interact with guests as they work in and around the hotel restaurant, bar, and food service facilities.

The demographic backgrounds of the employees on the frontline in the

Guest Services Departments were more diverse than in the other departments. Generally, the Guest Services Departments included both immigrant and non-immigrant whites and ethnic minorities. They ranged in age from eighteen to seventy-two, with a bias toward young people (this was more evident at some hotels than others). In Seattle, there was a similar pattern among Guest Service employees interviewed. Nine employees were native-born whites. One employee, of Chinese descent, had emigrated from Vietnam at the age of fifteen. Another had emigrated from Moldova (in the former Soviet Union) at age eleven. A third had emigrated from Ethiopia when only four years old. In Vancouver, the Guest Service employees interviewed included four native-born whites, and three white European immigrants (from the United Kingdom, Norway, and France). Of the three ethnic minority immigrants interviewed, one had emigrated from China in 1972, the second had moved from Vietnam when young in 1982, and the third had moved with his family from Nicaragua in 1987, when he was only eight years old.

In general, recently arrived ethnic minority immigrants do not work in Guest Service positions. This is most probably because the main requirement for these positions is strong social skills. Above all, employees in these jobs are judged on their ability to socialize comfortably with the hotel guests, for which English language proficiency remains a prerequisite. Guest Service employees are most likely to spend the bulk of their time in the public areas of the hotel. In a way, they are some of the main actors in the production of the hotel experience for guests. Hence, their physical appearance, manners, grooming, and uniforms are much more important than those of the employees of the other departments.

The Guest Service employees I interviewed tended to have previous work experience in the tourism industry or other service-sector jobs, including serving in restaurants. Only a few had completed hospitality-training programs after high school. Several were part- or full-time university students. Many of the younger employees planned to work in their current jobs temporarily while they spent a few years skiing or trying to figure out a career path. The older employees often had started out that way but then never moved on. Employees in these jobs often relied heavily on gratuities from guests to dramatically raise their generally low hourly earnings.

Although the hotel branches are remarkably similar on both sides of the border, each hotel has its own unique characteristics. As described in further detail in the following chapters, the similarities and differences between the individual hotel sites relate in part to corporate policy and in part to government policy. For example, although the employee training handbooks are the same in the Housekeeping Department manager's office in the Globe Hotel Seattle and Globe Hotel Vancouver, the employee compensation and benefit packages in the Seattle and Vancouver hotels are very different because of government policy differences. These policy differences also affect the lives of employees outside the workplace. In the next several chapters, I describe the impact of these differences—in labor, health, social welfare, and urban public-investment policies—on the hotel workers and their families.

CHAPTER 4

The Union Difference

Jason Fielding would like to see his hotel job unionized. He is a twenty-eight-year-old Hispanic man who lives with his aunt's family in Seattle and currently works in Room Service at the Globe Hotel Seattle. When he was younger, he worked at McDonalds and as a grocery-store shelf stocker. Then, he switched to a job at a courthouse: "It was janitorial. It was cool, but a lot of people, my friends appear in court and stuff be like, 'you doing community service.' And I'm like, 'no I'm not doing community service.' Meanwhile you are polishing the brass and stuff like that, but no it's not community service, it's to make some money."

He decided to change sectors and began working in the hotel industry. He got his first job as a banquet houseman. Jason Fielding's second job was as a banquet steward at the Globe Hotel Seattle:

> Yeah, I looked in the paper, and then went and applied. . . . I started out doing the graveyard thing. . . . I was just cleaning all the kitchens. All the kitchens . . . cleaning all the grills and mop the floors and then when they got a new cleaning company coming in, that's when, after that I started doing the banquet [job]. Yeah, they let us know [about the new company] and then I helped train them for a little bit, and then I just started doing the banquet stuff, morning, swings and nights.

Jason Fielding worked as a banquet steward for three years at the Globe Hotel Seattle:

> It was just getting hectic. It wasn't the hours, I didn't mind working the hours, but it just got stressful at times. You're doing banquets for 400 people at least, that's all the [conference] floors basically depending on how many parties it is. It got stressful because you are getting things ready, but then you got Service coming telling you need this, you got to try to find that, plus you have the cook saying, "Hey I need this, go get this." You are just running and running and running and it gets stressful to the point where you are like, "leave me alone, for a while" or something. But it was reasonable, you know. It wasn't that hard for me. Plus you got to make sure you get the dishes done and the kitchen cleaned up.

I mean there was times where I doubled back [shifts], I'd come back until 11:30 [p.m.] and then come back at 8 [a.m.]. And then, I started Room Service graveyard. The graveyard guy would have two or three days off and I would do his shifts, plus then sometimes I'd have to work in the afternoon for stewarding.

When I asked how many hours he was working, Jason Fielding explained:

If I worked at 6 in the morning, and then I'd do it until 2:30 [p.m.]. Sometimes I would take an hour off, but it always depended on the business, and it was like until 10 at night. When we had our real big crisis, when our manager left, we didn't have a manager, but a sous chef and banquets were taking care of us, we had these events called culture events and it was like breakfast, lunch, and dinner, see, and let me tell you: I'd be there all day long. I mean my sous chef would pick me up over by my house, I'd be there by 5 in the morning, work 5 in the morning to at least 5 at night.

With the occasional twelve- to sixteen-hour workdays, it is no surprise he wanted to transfer from stewarding to Room Service, but he had to wait. When I asked him why, he explained:

JASON: Yeah, I've been trying to transfer for a while. I couldn't do it because I had a couple situations where I had a couple of write-ups, and I couldn't transfer, I had to wait like six months.
ME: Oh no, what kind of write-ups for what kind of things?
JASON: One was, oh, I can't even . . . one was about not polishing all these things, and it just, the manager said, ooh, "we had [to do it] . . . it took us time." It was just basically dumb, so I just signed it and was like ok, whatever. . . . The other one, I knew I messed up.
ME: What was it?
JASON: I think it was just kind of like, yelling at one of the managers. It was like, ok. I mean, I have done everything at the hotel. I have done banquet houseman, when they needed it, bussed tables, especially through WTO [the World Trade Organization meeting] and stuff. I was working long hours there, and you know, and then none at all.

After a waiting period he finally got his transfer and now works Room Service where "Even order taking, you still gets tips. It all depends on how you upsell too. If you upsell on things, if you have a special you try to get them to order the special, order drinks, order dessert at the same time, that way if it is a nice amount, they will get a nice tip, then you are going to end up getting a nice tip later on."

He is happy he changed to a new job position:

Yeah. I liked it. It was something different. Something new to learn. Another experience underneath the belt. It's pretty calm, I mean you have to deal with guests. It's like you can't really, you want to say something but you can't. You just keep it cool. You just talk among yourselves, "that guest is . . ." As much as the guest can irritate you, you got to let them do it. It's a win or lose situation. So you know when they phone and they are drunk and they are like "I want, no I don't want to. . . . no wait I want to order this, no I want to change," and its like, "what do you want already?"

At the same time, Jason Fielding said he thought it would be better if his job was unionized. He explained:

> JASON : Like some of the benefits would be like let's say something happen where they can say that you are fired and you don't think that its worth firing over, then you can take it to the union and the union can investigate it whether or not. Plus, [with] the union you can also get paid a little bit more. It all depends. I've dealt with the union. The thing about the union is that you've also got to pay them money too for that.
>
> ME : So is that the negative side, the dues and things?
>
> JASON : Yeah, but I mean they are always there for you, I've heard good things about unions, that were there, you need the help. If you are in a situation where you need help, they can do it. They can always investigate.

Many more hotel jobs are unionized in Vancouver than in Seattle. This difference—which relates to differences in the union-organizing rules in Canada and the United States—both directly and indirectly improves job security, benefits, and working conditions for employees in the hotel industry in Vancouver compared to Seattle. Union membership confers substantial advantages on hotel workers, although this surfaces more in terms of stability and benefits than in wages. The major differences between the two cities have to do with the much higher proportion in Vancouver of hotel-industry workers who have union cards and who therefore reap the benefits of collective bargaining.

U.S. and Canadian Labor Policy Differences: Driving the Divergence

The United States and Canada part company when it comes to employees' right to organize and the rights given to management to obstruct organizing drives. These legal differences explain the current differences in union labor-force coverage between the two countries. My position differs from that of scholars who point to cultural differences between Canadians and Americans or to differences in the structure of the labor force as explaining the patterns of union labor-force coverage.

In Canada, workers who desire collective representation or unionization have a much easier time organizing and joining a union than do workers in the United States, mainly because Canadian labor laws do not grant nearly as much power to management to challenge unionizing efforts. The evaluation of the literature by Joseph B. Rose and Gary N. Chaison concurs with this finding:

> The American system of labour board certification of unions relies on elections among workers and typically results in protracted campaigns in which employers use union-avoidance tactics ranging from procedural delays to discrimination against union supporters. In contrast, certification in Canada normally is based on signed membership cards (and occasionally expedited elections), thereby minimizing the opportunity for employers to resist unions.[1]

W. Craig Riddell, an economist, finds that differences in government policies and enforcement with regards to union organizing and collective bargaining, as well as somewhat lower levels of management opposition in Canada, help explain the Canadian-U.S. unionization gap.[2] In the *Paradox of American Unionism,* Seymour Martin Lipset and Noah Meltz challenge these findings that management opposition is greater in the United States: "Contrary to the opinion of many in the field of industrial relations who attribute lower U.S. membership to greater managerial hostility, survey data have consistently found similar or lower rates of stated hostility in the United States compared with their Canadian counterparts."[3]

The trend data for union-coverage rates support the argument that labor policy barriers to union organizing in the United States compared to Canada are largely responsible for the current differences in union coverage of the labor force. In both the United States and Canada, approximately 30 percent of the nonagricultural labor force were members of a union during the period 1950–1970. After 1970, union-coverage rates in the United States began to fall steadily every year, particularly after 1975. By 1985, union coverage had declined to 20 percent of the labor force and continued to fall to just under 14 percent by 1999. In sharp contrast, Canada's rate of union coverage of its workforce increased steadily after 1970 to a high of 40 percent in 1985 before dipping slightly to 35 percent in 1990 and then increasing again slightly through 1994.[4]

Efforts to explain the differences in union density rates have also considered other factors, such as structural shifts in employment and public support for unions. Neither of these factors offers a satisfactory explanation for the divergence in U.S.–Canadian union density rates. Public opinion data about workers' attitudes about unions and their desire to join a union do not support arguments that Americans are less likely to want to join a union than Canadians.[5] Indeed Lipset and Meltz found that "In most cases, social surveys, including our own, actually show that unions are more approved of in the United States than in Canada."[6]

Despite greater approval of unions in the United States—after thirty years of divergence—Canada's union coverage currently is at least double that of the

United States across all economic sectors. The divergence between U.S. and Canadian levels of union coverage is largest and growing fastest among traditionally non-unionized workers—including women and part-time workers—in the service sector.[7] The divergent trends in unionization occurred during a time in which the United States and Canada experienced virtually identical economic sector shifts away from manufacturing and agriculture and toward the predominance of the service sector.

Union Coverage of Hotel Industry Employees

The current cross-national difference between the United States and Canada in the rates of union coverage of the labor force is mirrored in the difference found between Washington state and British Columbia and magnified in the difference between the hotel industries of Seattle and Vancouver. Whereas 30.4 percent of the entire labor force in British Columbia belongs to a union, only 18.2 percent of the labor force in Washington state is unionized, despite the fact that Washington state is considered a labor-friendly U.S. state.[8] Yet the difference between the union coverage of hotel-industry employees in Washington state and British Columbia is much larger than this and more in line with the national rates of union coverage for service-sector employees.

The vast majority of hotel-industry employees who are unionized in British Columbia and Washington state are members of what I call the Service Industry International Union (SIIU).[9] The major difference in the rates of union coverage of the hotel-industry labor force can be seen from the list of unionized properties in British Columbia and Washington state. Vancouver Local 5 of the SIIU represents workers at thirty-two hotels in downtown Vancouver, twenty-nine additional hotels in the Greater Vancouver Regional District, and eighty-four other hotels elsewhere in the province of British Columbia. Seattle Local 99 of the SIIU represents workers at only ten hotels in Seattle, one additional hotel in the Metropolitan Seattle Region, and four other hotels in the rest of the state.[10]

Vancouver Local 5 has nearly ten times the number of hotel properties unionized than Seattle Local 99 (145 hotels compared to 15 hotels). The SIIU has unionized three times the number of hotel properties in the city of Vancouver as in Seattle, and the unionization of these thirty-two hotel sites in Vancouver represents a significant majority of the major hotels in downtown Vancouver. In contrast, the ten hotels unionized by the SIIU in Seattle include branches of only three major chain hotels; they are only a small proportion of hotel properties in downtown Seattle.

Recent trends in unionization of the hotel industry in Seattle and Vancouver mirror the national U.S.-Canadian divergence. Vancouver Local 5 of the SIIU currently represents approximately 10,000 workers throughout British Columbia. Whereas most of the hotels in Vancouver have been unionized since the 1970s, Seattle has experienced a significant drop in the percentage of hotel rooms covered by unions (union density) over the past thirty years. According to Michael Findley, the president of Seattle Local 99, the union had 8,500– 9,000 members as of the late 1980s. At the time of my study, there were approximately 4,600 paying members and 600–700 event workers and casual workers. A wave of decertifications by members in the late 1980s caused SIIU to lose several major downtown chains and other historic properties. Seattle Local 99 has not even attempted to organize a hotel site in many years. As a result, the union density in Seattle in hotels is currently only 16 percent of full-service rooms and is slipping as a result of the construction of additional non-unionized hotels.

Labor policy differences between the United States and Canada clearly help explain the significant differences between the union representation of hotel-industry employees in Seattle and Vancouver. The federal and state labor laws in the United States and Washington state erect barriers to unionizing, including generous opportunities for management lobbying against unionization and the extended time period required for the process. Employees with a desire to unionize in Vancouver are much more likely to be able to unionize their workplace because of the rules of union organizing.

Unions in the United States now rarely use the traditional organizing process because of the barriers created by the current National Labor Relations Board (NLRB) rules for organizing. The process, based on the current U.S. and Washington state labor policy, includes waiting periods and several opportunities for management legal appeals, which can extend the process up to two years. According to Michael Findley, the national office of the SIIU allows the process of organizing a work site in the United States through the NLRB procedure to begin only after 70 percent of the employees sign authorization cards. Even with that precaution, the barriers prevent the successful unionizing of a workplace in 60 to 65 percent of cases. So, the SIIU union locals in the United States have moved away from traditional organizing and are focusing instead on the special cases where Card Check organizing rules apply.

Under the Card Check system of organizing, the union follows rules similar to British Columbia's organizing procedure. But in the United States, very few work sites qualify for a Card Check. For example, the next Card Check organizing drive by Seattle Local 99 will be one Hotel Deluxe branch in Bellevue, Washington. This hotel branch has union pension funds invested in it, so it has become a special case requiring a Card Check. Seattle Local 99 will spend two years trying to organize this one property because the Card Check is much more likely to succeed. Michael Findley estimated that the SIIU nationally has experienced a 95 percent success rate in unionizing a workplace once they can get a "card check agreement."

In sharp contrast, workers in British Columbia can be certified in ten days, and the union can become their legal bargaining agent. According to Robert Graves, the president of Vancouver Local 5, it also helps that workers, rather than lawyers (as is the case in the United States), present their cases to the British Columbia Labor Relations board. The rules allow a more human element to be included. The labor policies of British Columbia are among the most progressive in North America. Anti-scabbing legislation, which prevents the hiring of strikebreakers, is particularly powerful and is the key to leveling the playing field between management and workers during disputes. Although Robert Graves characterizes the hospitality industry as the "hostility" industry when it comes to labor organizing, Vancouver Local 5 has managed to successfully organize a majority of hotels in Vancouver and its metropolitan region.

Union Membership: Improving Benefits, Job Security, and Work Conditions

Unionized hotels do not always pay more than non-unionized hotels. Yet comparisons between these two hotel chains do reveal patterns about some of the direct and indirect benefits of union membership for hotel workers. Membership in a union generally accords hotel workers better benefits, including a higher base pay and regular wage increases; greater job security by providing clear grievance procedures and representation; and better working conditions for most hotel employees.

Better Benefits

Strictly comparing union and non-union hotels in each city does not demonstrate clearly that union membership is associated with higher hourly wage rates. In nonsalary positions, the non-unionized Hotel Deluxe Vancouver often pays the same hourly wage or even slightly more per hour for many job positions than does the unionized Globe Hotel Vancouver. In Seattle, on the other hand, union representation does result in somewhat higher wage rates for hourly employees in many departments in the hotel industry. At the same time, hourly wages were higher for Housekeeping Department employees in both hotels in Vancouver than in Seattle (see fig. 4.1).[11] Workers in the Guest Services Divisions also earned higher base hourly wages. In the Maintenance Engineering Departments, the picture is more mixed. Workers received similar or higher hourly wages in Vancouver compared to Seattle. The highest hourly wages were paid to the unionized engineers (who belonged to a Skill Specific Union) at the unionized Hotel Deluxe Seattle.

The collective agreements negotiated annually by Vancouver Local 5 set standard hourly wages, overtime rates, and raises for all employees in a department within a hotel, regardless of the employee's experience (after a standard three-

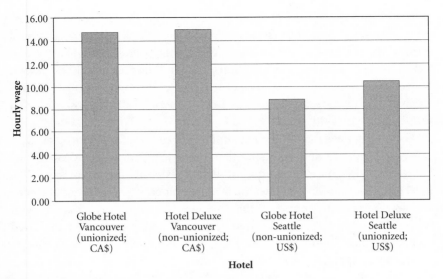

Figure 4.1 Hourly wages for room attendants

month probationary period at lower wages). All room attendants, laundry attendants, and housemen who I interviewed at the Globe Hotel Vancouver earned $14.84 per hour after a 3 percent raise the previous March, whether they had worked there for five years or twenty years. In comparison, the British Columbia provincial minimum wage is approximately $7.50 per hour.

On the other hand, in Seattle many hotel workers were not earning much more than Washington state's $8.00 per hour minimum wage. At the Globe Hotel in Seattle, many of the non-unionized hotel employees in the Housekeeping Department were earning only $7.50 per hour during their probation period and $8.75 per hour after probation. After two years on the job, the wage increased to $9.50 per hour. In the Laundry Department, employees started at $7.75 per hour and went up to $9.75 per hour after two years. The Housekeeping inspectors (hourly supervisors) earned $8.50 per hour to start and after two years earned $10.50 per hour. Only unionized maintenance engineers, who had significant technical skills and were in fields with high union density, got paid more in Seattle than in Vancouver. Joey Harrison, Hotel Deluxe Seattle maintenance engineer and member of Local 15 of the Skill Specific union, said that the union helped get them "higher wages, we have the highest wages in Seattle as engineers." Management at the non-unionized Globe Hotel Seattle decided to freeze wages after the hotel-industry downturn caused by the 9/11 terrorist attacks. So, for employees such as Kay Chiang—a Chinese immigrant working as a room attendant at the Globe Hotel Seattle—the last raise had been received almost two years before we met.

Union membership also guarantees yearly wage increases for most job categories. At the unionized Hotel Deluxe Seattle, wage rates and raises are agreed on for three or four years at a time during the contract agreement. The new collective agreement between Seattle Local 99 and the Hotel Deluxe Seattle, which includes wages, benefits, grievance procedures, and conditions of work, also specifies yearly wage rate increases for nearly all nongratuity job positions from June 1, 2002, to May 31, 2006.

The hourly wage rates at the non-unionized Hotel Deluxe Vancouver were generally similar to or even higher than those at the unionized Globe Hotel Vancouver. Why? The evidence suggests that the extensive union coverage of the hotel industry workforce in downtown Vancouver creates what economists call a "union wage effect" for many of the hotel-industry employees in the city. With thirty-two hotel properties unionized by the SIIU and several others unionized by the Technical Industry Union (TIU), non-unionized hotels in Vancouver must offer competitive pay comparable to that at union hotels to attract and retain high-quality employees and prevent the unionization of their hotels.

Union membership does appear to be associated with more comprehensive and generous job benefits for hourly hotel-industry employees in both Seattle and Vancouver. The increased job security of union jobs improved the quality of benefits for hotel-industry employees in the sample of employees that I interviewed. Many detailed benefits of union membership are written into the collective bargaining agreements, which specify rules that improve the work environment for employees, such as mandatory extra pay per room for room attendants who have to make up guest cots in the unionized Hotel Deluxe Seattle hotel.

In terms of specific benefit advantages, Seattle Local 99 allows employees easier access to higher-quality health insurance coverage for them and their families (although access to benefits was problematic for new employees at both hotels in Seattle due to mandatory waiting periods). Workers can receive more expansive health insurance coverage with fewer qualifying hours at union hotels, and this insurance extends to the entire family without extra cost.

Other benefits from being unionized include course reimbursement and other perks. For example, the Technical Skills Specific Union, which represents some workers at the Hotel Deluxe Seattle, also provided the additional benefit of helping to pay for courses to improve its members' skill set. Joey Harrison has taken advantage of these benefits, including taking Boiler Certification courses. In addition, the collective agreement at the Hotel Deluxe Seattle requires that employees get a pseudo-weekend—two consecutive days off per week.

Hotel workers at the unionized hotels in both cities had more average paid vacation time than at the non-unionized hotels.[12] This is partially attributable to the longer vacation time accorded in union negotiated contracts, but it also results directly from the longer job tenure of workers in unionized hotels compared to those in the non-unionized hotels. More vacation time can be seen as extra salary because it could be paid out if it had not been used by the employee. Paid vacation time also acted as a cushion for employees in cases of temporary low-season lay-offs and illness.

Vancouver's Local 5 provides more comprehensive member services than Seattle's Local 99 because it has a larger resource base (it has more members). These services include a quarterly newsletter and an informative website. The fall 2000 issue of the newsletter includes detailed information about how to apply for Employment Insurance benefits and articles about members and labor issues. Mark Heung, a thirty-two-year-old immigrant from Saigon, Vietnam, works as a houseman at the Globe Hotel Vancouver. He described the services of the Vancouver Local 5 Employees Assistance Program as "Well they provide a host of gambling addiction, substance abuse addiction, stress counseling, marriage breakdown, all that services."

Vancouver Local 5 also supplements sick pay, as Sven Johannsen, a Globe Hotel Vancouver server and union shop steward, found out when he was diagnosed with cancer. "I got about $448 per week," he said, from a sick leave negotiated on the basis of the collective agreement. "I was off 13 weeks." With fewer resources because of a smaller membership, Seattle's Local 99 has no work referral hall, job training, or member newsletter. According to Mark Corbain, a Hotel Deluxe Seattle doorman and union shop steward, "We have a union food bank down at the Labor Temple. And when families are laid off or their hours are cut, [we} make sure they know where the food bank is."

The differences that exist in terms of wages and benefits between unionized and non-unionized hotel jobs emerge from the interaction of regular wage increases and the somewhat higher wages and benefits that come with long job tenure. The longer job tenure is associated with job security, better working conditions, and other positive benefits of union membership for hourly hotel employees.

Job Security

In Vancouver, the unionized hotel employees at the Globe Hotel ardently defended the job security afforded by union representation. Michael Anthony McDonald, doorman and union shop steward at the Globe Hotel Vancouver, has worked at the hotel for nine years: "[The union] is very good. It's, I mean, it is a safety belt for us, it's like the protection man, like the Mafia man, you go and see the Godfather and he helps you, you know. It's our way of protecting ourselves. Without the union, we'd be lost. We really would." As George Chan, a fifty-year-old recent immigrant from Fujian, China, who works at the Globe

Hotel Vancouver as a houseman, described it, "In the union, the union protects; the boss not able to fire you. Here you never make mistake, the boss cannot fire you."

Many employees describe job security as the most important benefit of working in a union hotel. Sven Johannsen, a fifty-three-year-old who immigrated to Vancouver from Norway in the early 1970s, has worked at the Globe Hotel Vancouver for twenty-five years. He describes the security as especially important for older workers: "I've always done union jobs, nothing but union jobs. I truly believe in the union . . . because new managers we get. They really bug me, because they come in and they think they know the world and they somehow, they don't like older people in the service industry and the first thing they try is to fire them." The job security afforded by union membership means that union employees cannot be arbitrarily fired and that there is a standard grievance procedure for workers who are unhappy with management actions or sanctions.

The hotel workers in unionized hotels in Seattle and Vancouver enjoyed greater job security and longer job tenure compared to the employees of non-unionized hotels.[13] The long employee tenure in union hotels reduces the overall employee turnover compared to non-union hotels. At the unionized Globe Hotel Vancouver, job-turnover rates are quite low, especially for entry-level service employees. Many workers who I interviewed at the Globe Hotel Vancouver and Hotel Deluxe Seattle are "lifers" and plan to stay in the same company and job until retirement. Some have worked at the hotel site longer than the current company has owned the hotel. The benefits of the union-based seniority confer such big advantages in terms of benefits and hours that only a few mentioned planning to change careers or companies.

Over 50 percent of the employees at the unionized Hotel Deluxe Seattle had worked at the hotel for more than five years. Many of the employees are ten-, fifteen-, or twenty-year veterans. One employee had just celebrated fifty years working at the hotel, and a second was honored for forty years of employment. Margaret Fielding, the general manager of the Hotel Deluxe Seattle, estimated the turnover rate for all staff at 30 percent per year (including job changes and promotions within the hotel).[14] The variation in turnover does not depend as much on department as it does on seniority, with a higher turnover among employees with less seniority; some employees quit because they cannot secure enough hours.

In contrast, the non-unionized Globe Hotel Seattle had almost twice the rate of employee turnover, as calculated by its Human Resources director, Seth Michaels, who estimated a 6 percent employee turnover rate for the previous month and a 53 percent year-to-date rate, including a 57 percent rate for the hourly staff.

In the non-unionized hotels, particularly the Hotel Deluxe Vancouver, some employees viewed their job as more temporary than employees at the union-ized hotels. For example, two Hotel Deluxe Vancouver employees planned to leave their current jobs and temporarily move to Peru and Australia at the end of the summer. Some had well-researched plans for their next career moves. One planned to become certified in ESL teaching, and another talked about qualifying for a firearms permit to become a driving courier. The non-union-ized hotels in both cities also relied more on recent immigrants and refugees for behind-the-scenes job positions.

At the Globe Hotel Seattle, several of the employees cited greater job secu-rity as one reason that they would like to see their workplace unionized. Kin Wa Lee, a fifty-eight-year-old Vietnamese immigrant who began working as a room attendant eight years ago and had moved up to Housekeeping inspector, explained, "You know sometimes union take care of people, sometimes if you have mistake, little mistake, you need the protection. Sometimes, employees have little mistakes but no have union, no protections. Get in trouble. But I think if I have company, I have the union. It's fair. It's fair. Sometimes employ-ees they need protection, but no have union."

The greater job security for unionized hourly hotel employees results from the collective agreement contracts that specify a standard grievance procedure management must follow when an employee is disciplined. Mark Klein, the Vancouver Local 5 business representative for the Globe Hotel Vancouver, re-ported that many times companies make errant dismissals based only on the feeling that something is "going on" with a worker rather than on work per-formance problems. The union has successfully reversed errant dismissals for hotel employees. Without union representation, workers have to wait until af-ter dismissal to file a complaint with the British Columbia Labour Relations Board, which can move slowly.

The collective agreement also allows the union to represent the employee in disciplinary and appeal proceedings in the case of dismissal. Michael Findley of Seattle Local 99 said that, if a union employee has a grievance over a dis-missal, they can go straight to the worker advocate. Whether or not the firing was unfair depends on the union contract. The union meets with the supervi-sor, department head, Human Resources director, and then the general man-ager, if necessary, and it may even take the case to arbitration. This process happens frequently, and often the union succeeds in getting an employee's job back. The union is generally more successful if the employee was fired for "work performance" reasons rather than for "behavioral or attendance" issues. The views of the hotel management in union hotels vary in terms of the costs and benefits of the grievance procedure for the hotel operation. Although the long-term "lifers" are more expensive to employ in terms of benefits and salaries, they provide advantages to the hotel, including lower training expenses, professionalism, and lower expenses in terms of fewer job inspections and reduced theft. Ted Jensen, Human Resources director at the Hotel Deluxe Seattle, described the benefits of a unionized hotel as having a "more professional workforce" as opposed to employees who are "there as a transitional stop to somewhere else." On the other hand, Johanna Larson, the chief housekeeper at the Globe Hotel Vancouver, felt that the process of termination in a unionized hotel was so difficult that her "hands are tied" in a lot of cases; that is the downside of having a union workforce. There are few terminations, and the main causes for termination are poor attendance and consistently not meeting standards. She said that the union contracts require a "lot of documentation" for disciplining an employee. An employee is entitled to a verbal warning, a written warning, a one-day suspension, a three-day suspension, and a five-day suspension before he or she is terminated. And any improvement by the employee during any step of this process can reset the discipline process. There are some exceptions; for example, theft is grounds for immediate termination. Johanna Larson admitted that, although she finds this process "burdensome sometimes," it results in infrequent employee dismissals.

Although most hourly hotel-industry employees do not get promoted into supervisory or management roles, the longer job tenure created by greater job security appears to increase the odds of employee advancement. The current head of the Housekeeping Department at the Hotel Deluxe Seattle moved up from working as a room attendant. In addition, most of the assistant managers and hourly supervisors at the Hotel Deluxe Seattle also started as room attendants and worked their way up the ladder into their current jobs. On the other hand, because of the wages, benefits, and hours offered by high-seniority unionized positions, many hourly employees choose not to accept promotions, even to lower-level salaried managerial roles.

Better Working Conditions

There is a qualitatively different feel when working in a unionized hotel compared to a non-unionized hotel. The relationship between management and employees is certainly different. Employees in unionized hotels were more confident and less afraid of management. The employees have more opportunities to freely voice their opinions and participate in the process of improving the quality of their work environment. The rules provide them with procedures to "tame" bad managers, address their concerns, and request changes to improve their working conditions.

Kendra Smith, a forty-three-year-old African-American mother who works in the Laundry Department of the Hotel Deluxe Seattle, explained, "I think it is good to have them [the union] in order to prevent having to do all kinds of wild, crazy things that you would normally not have to do. . . . We don't have mandatory overtime because of the union, which is good. Some of the women in my department are like sixty-eight years old, and they don't really need to do overtime." In Seattle, for example, unionized hotels provide strict limits on the number of rooms that can be cleaned by room attendants per shift.

Florence McDaniels, a thirty-seven-year-old immigrant from Taiwan, was recently demoted during lay-offs from Housekeeping supervisor to coffee service attendant at the non-unionized Globe Hotel Seattle. She thought that union representation would improve the employees' position relative to the management: "Yeah, I think the employees do need some representative to, who can speak fluently and communicate with the employer. It can be healthy thing, doesn't mean always fighting. Sometimes it's just a wish of employees and can make environment better that they would like to stay. . . . You know hotels have high turnover."

The union also allows workers to provide feedback about their working conditions and other complaints through meetings and the employee shop stewards. The greater degree of employee rights and protection from dismissal allows them to "speak out," which, for example, can help protect them from abusive departmental managers. Julia Rodgers, the Hotel Deluxe Seattle chief housekeeper mused, "Personally I have to say that I think working in a union house keeps the managers good. Managers can't do really outrageous things or they will be called to account for it real quick. I wonder about managers who complain a lot about the union, I wonder what is wrong with their leadership style."[15] One of the union shop stewards at the Globe Hotel Vancouver, Michael Anthony McDonald, described how a union-sponsored employee satisfaction survey resulted in the removal of particularly reviled manager from the hotel.

Mark Corbain, a fifty-one-year-old doorman and union shop steward at the Hotel Deluxe Seattle, reported that the subcontracted valet company that runs parking at the hotel recently tore up the SIIU union contract halfway through its term and fired all the workers. While the case proceeds legally, the subcontracted company employed new non-unionized valets, mostly young men, who work next to and together with the unionized hotel door staff. The consequences of not being represented by a union are clear during every shift: the valets now have no control over hours, no two consecutive days off per week (the pseudo-weekend), no health benefits, no job security and no protection from abusive managers. One of the Hotel Deluxe Seattle non-union valets, Ivan Karissov, a twenty-one-year-old immigrant from Moldova, said, "Yeah, the only negative thing is the management sucks, really, really bad management. . . . [I think getting a union would get us] better wages, get benefits, all the vacation stuff, and probably some better management."

Unions provide employees with representatives who can act as their advocates or represent their claims to management and negotiate a solution, especially when management is breaking its part of the collective agreement. Joyce Lee, a forty-three-year-old immigrant from Hong Kong who works as a room attendant at the Globe Hotel Vancouver, briefly described an incident in which management stopped respecting seniority in scheduling: "The supervisor no fair for us. For example, the schedule. They don't go by seniority and you have to talk to the union. And the union to talk to the supervisor. And then they, yeah. It worked." Employees can talk to the union representative about situations at work that they feel are unfair or violate their employment contract; the union can intervene and fix the situation. Joyce Lee is one of several employees who mentioned this specific instance of successful union intervention. Gee Yong Chow, a fifty-one-year-old maintenance engineer at the Globe Hotel Vancouver, concurred with Joyce Lee's sentiments: "[The benefits of] the union? Well, settling grievances, no? If you have any problem with the management and you can't solve, then you call the union and they come and they try to solve for you."

Although union membership clearly confers benefits to hourly hotel employees through greater job security, clear grievance procedures, and opportunities to improve their own work environment, many employees and managers express serious concerns about unions in the hotel industry in Seattle and Vancouver.

The Benefits Outweigh the Costs

Although there are several clear patterns of complaints or negative comments about unions made by employees at all four hotel sites, ultimately these arguments reveal trade-offs and do not persuasively demonstrate that union membership is truly harmful to hotel-industry employees. The negative comments made by employees and management in Seattle and Vancouver largely consisted of complaints about dues and an ideological perspective that deemed unionization to be fundamentally incompatible with the hospitality industry. In terms of the quality of life provided by unionized hotel employment, in both Seattle and Vancouver the evidence is clear. Despite the concerns raised, the balance of the evidence demonstrates that unionized hotel employees are better off than non-unionized employees.

Concerns about Dues

Several union employees complained about the cost of monthly union dues. Membership in the SIIU union, or any union for that matter, is not free. Dues, which largely support the union, are required from members each month and are deducted from each employee's paycheck. For Vancouver Local 5, union dues are now $47 per month for all employees, regardless of seniority or hours, and these dues are tax deductible. For Seattle Local 99, dues are paid based on classification and geographic area; Seattle room attendants, for example, pay $29.80 per month.

In Vancouver, ethnic minority immigrant employees often complained the most about the union dues, especially the lower-seniority room attendants, who do not receive many shifts during the winter but must continue paying a monthly flat fee to the union. Tse Leung, a fifty-four-year-old immigrant from Shanghai, China, works as a room attendant at the unionized Globe Hotel Vancouver and generally expressed positive views of the union, except, "I think is not good, because if I work four hours, two weeks . . . they charge me $25 right . . . Because not charge a percent." After nine years working as a room attendant at the Globe Hotel Vancouver, Kerry Wong a forty-seven-year-old immigrant from Shanghai, China, explained, "We don't like the union. Oh we don't like, because not worth it. Every month they pay, I just pay every month too much. . . . Like for example, if the winter time, three months no job, like January, February, no work, March [no] going to the work." And Kathleen Leun, a fifty-year-old Chinese immigrant who works as a room attendant, argued, "every year we pay about $500 but I use nothing for me. But we must to pay it. So nothing for me, so I don't like the union."

In Seattle, a few of the hotel employees at the unionized Hotel Deluxe Seattle also complained about the monthly dues. Ben Bishof, a twenty-five-year-old white man born in Seattle, works as a bellman at the Hotel Deluxe Seattle. He complained, "Well the final straw was that they're taking $35 a month out of your paycheck and giving nothing back."

Note, however, that the majority of unionized hotel workers interviewed in Seattle and Vancouver did not complain or even mention the cost of the union membership.

The Incompatibility Argument

Many managers and employees who were opposed to unions framed their opposition as an ideological argument, referring to the incompatibility of unionization and the hospitality industry. James Caldwell, general manager of the non-unionized Hotel Deluxe Vancouver, vociferously argued this claim. He stated that there are optimal terms of employment in a hotel that vary by department, from two years at Guest Services to five to eight years for Housekeeping. His view of limited tenure for most employees is impossible to square with union job security, job-role rigidity, and seniority benefit system. He also felt that unionization "dampens the spirit of the workforce" and "complicates communication between the management and employees" and that it "prevents management from rewarding stars."

Some employees also expressed similar ideological opposition to unions in the hospitality industry. More often than not, these responses came from older white men, some of whom have benefited from the job security provided by the union but who have neoconservative political values. Nathan Roberts, a thirty-nine-year-old white man, works as an engineering coordinator for the Hotel Deluxe Seattle, a non-unionized position. He has worked in several unionized and non-unionized jobs within the hotel over the last twenty years and was opposed to the union: "Unions were meant back when there were sweatshops and stuff like that, not now. . . . I think the union hides too many slackers. People who shouldn't be working those jobs sometimes have those jobs, when there are good people out there who should have those jobs who deserve those jobs, can't get the jobs because of people who are slackers or when you had to hire minorities and stuff." Peter Keyes, a thirty-eight-year-old single white man with a bachelor of arts degree in business from a midwestern college, works as a doorman at the non-unionized Globe Hotel Seattle. He expressed this ideological disdain for unions based on his bad experience as a unionized employee selling women's shoes at a major downtown department store:

> [A union] interrupts the idea of free enterprise . . . and so you get some people who are there for the pay and not for the work. . . . you have people that either are incompetent, or don't want to work to be competent, then they can survive on the job and the other people pick up the slack. . . . they also fight for, for the incompetent people too. . . . I'm a hard worker and I don't like some of my coworkers, I don't like working with, because they don't work hard, they are not ethical. . . . I guess its one of those sink or swim attitudes, and I guess I think if you can't swim, you shouldn't be there.

A few of the other hotel workers expressed concerns about a lack of union activity, low levels of strike pay, and job role rigidity.

The general managers and other lower-level managers at the unionized hotels, on the other hand, tended to espouse either neutral or more balanced perspectives on unions and the hospitality industry. Timothy Downing, the general manager of the unionized Globe Hotel Vancouver described the benefits of unions in terms of employee professionalism and pointed out that overall the guest-satisfaction reports put his hotel in the top five among Globe hotels, that is, out of over fifty Globe hotels worldwide and of the over 2,000 hotels owned by the Lexicon Corporation. He discussed the cost savings of not having to inspect rooms after they have been cleaned by mostly high-seniority room attendants. Margaret Fielding, general manager of the unionized Hotel Deluxe Seattle also described the benefits of unionization as attracting a more professional and higher-skilled workforce.[16]

The Indirect Impact of Higher Levels of Unionization

The higher rates of hotel unionization in Vancouver, compared to Seattle, also have a political institutional impact that indirectly benefits all lower-wage service-sector employees in the city. The high rates of pay and generous benefit packages negotiated by Vancouver Local 5 for its employees appear to have a union wage effect, improving wages and benefits for both union and non-union hotel workers in the city. Organizationally, unions represent a countervailing political institutional force that combats the rising influence of corporations, which often act through chambers of commerce, other lobbyists, and wealthy individuals to influence politics and policy in both Seattle and Vancouver.

In Canada, unions have more power to negotiate more generous wage and benefit packages for their members than in the United States. Michael Findley, president of Seattle Local 99, described his envy at the power of unions in the hotel industry in Vancouver. In Seattle, contracts have been negotiated individually with each hotel since the collective contract was ripped up in 1991. This reduces the power of the union to increase employees' wages and benefits because the managers compare notes across hotels and use the bargaining victories of other hotels to limit their own concessions to workers. On the other hand, in Vancouver, there are two big groups of hotels that negotiate joint collective agreements with the union. These two standard agreements provide more generous terms for the hotel workers than the hotel-by-hotel collective agreements negotiated by Seattle Local 99.

The local, national, and international offices of unions allow them to lobby for progressive worker-friendly legislation at the city, state/province, and national levels, and even internationally on vital issues such as international trade agreements. Until recently, the British Columbia legislature was dominated by the union-backed left-of-center New Democratic Party (NDP), which helped enact strong anti-scabbing legislation. This legislation forced management to run the hotels during Vancouver's hotel strike in summer 1999. Progressive labor policies mandate employment benefits such as paid vacation, regardless of their union status, and set clear guidelines for employee grievance procedures. Further, the labor code legislates many union job protections for all employees in British Columbia. Robert Graves, president of Vancouver Local 5, also mentioned the greater access that unions have to the media in Canada compared to the United States, as well as the more favorable coverage they receive during labor disputes. On the other side of the border, Seattle Local 99 played an important role in mobilizing workers and putting pressure on the Washington state government to successfully defeat new "tip credit" legislation that would have allowed corporations and restaurants to pay subminimum wages to employees who received gratuities.

❖❖❖

Labor policy in the United States and Canada dictates the process by which workers can organize for union representation; the differences in these rules are largely responsible for the divergent trends in unionization between the two countries over the past thirty years. Canada's significantly higher national rates of unionization, particularly in the service sector, compared to the United States, are replicated in the substantially different levels of unionization in the hotel industry in Vancouver and Seattle. A hotel-industry hourly employee is much more likely to be covered by a union contract in Vancouver than in Seattle. The Seattle hotels that are non-unionized have opted for a "low road" of high turnover, whereas the unionized hotels are "high road" shops that value employee stability, provide workers with better benefits, and experience cost savings from reduced turnover.

An analysis of employee, management, and union leader interviews demonstrates that union membership provides hotel workers better benefits, improved job security, and better working conditions. In Vancouver, the rates of unionization in the hotel industry are high enough that they create a union wage effect that also increases the wages and benefits offered to employees in non-unionized hotels. Although some hotel employees certainly discussed some negative aspects of unionization in terms of dues or ideological opposition to unions in the hospitality sector and other complaints, the evidence is clear that unionization, in general, improves the work experience and lives of hourly employees in the hotel industry in both Seattle and Vancouver. In order to improve the quality of life for the large and growing ranks of service-sector employees, policy reforms should reduce the barriers that prevent the organizing of service workplaces.

CHAPTER 5

Health-Care Differences

Money is important, health is more important. If you are mil-
lionaire, but you are poor in health, you are not good. Your
health is more important.

—George Chan, fifty-year-old Chinese immigrant and
houseman at the Globe Hotel Vancouver

Canada and the United States have developed very different health-care systems over the past fifty years. The Canadian universal system of health insurance mitigates the financial stress around health care, whereas the current U.S.
system keeps financial considerations linked to health care, with deleterious
consequences for the working poor and their families. Accessing health care
and treatment creates much greater financial stress for the working poor and
their families in Seattle than in Vancouver. The problems with the current
health insurance system in the United States go well beyond people simply lacking insurance. The financial stresses surrounding health care in Seattle also
translate into lower levels of preventive care and higher levels of health hardship among hotel workers. Because of the many interacting factors that contribute to health outcomes, we should be cautious about attributing poorer
health outcomes among Seattle workers to differences in health policy; however, it is no doubt an important factor.

Cross-National Comparative Research
on Health and Health Care

Previous U.S. and Canadian research on the topics of health and health care
has focused on several issues, including comparative health quality and outcomes; policy lessons for the United States based on Canadian policy; and
health-care development, care, and outcomes within each country.

Public health and medical researchers have completed a number of studies

Table 5.1 U.S. and Canadian comparative health-care statistics

	United States	Canada
Individuals without health insurance[a]	41 million (14.6%)	None (0%)
Individuals without health insurance for some period in 2001–2002[a]	75 million (26.7%)	None (0%)
Infant mortality, 1995 (per 1,000 births)[b]	8	6
Health expenditure per person, 1998 (US$)	4,270	2,250

[a]From McLellan (2003).
[b]Before one year old. From Marmor and Sullivan (2000).

comparing health outcomes, such as avoidable mortality, life expectancy, infant mortality, and mortality from specific diseases, in Canada and the United States.[1] The lack of health insurance coverage, even temporarily, has developed into a major crisis for many Americans. Canada's universal health insurance system, in contrast, covers all residents at lower per-capita cost. Many national-level statistics show better health outcomes for Canadians in general compared to Americans,[2] with lower infant mortality and higher life expectancy[3] (see table 5.1).

Much of the cross-national comparative literature discusses the current problems with the health system in the United States, with a focus on the increasing number of Americans lacking health insurance and the skyrocketing costs of the system. These works discuss how Canada's single-payer (government-funded) universal system of health insurance covers all residents and controls health-care costs.[4] Many "health policy lessons from Canada" books and articles have been published in the United States over the past twenty years.[5] These works encourage U.S. policy makers to learn from the successes of the Canadian health system.

There have also been a large number of noncomparative studies on many aspects of each nation's health-care system.[6] These studies cover a diverse range of issues, including the development of the current system, potential directions for reform, investment in new health technology, spiraling prescription medicine costs, and private provision of health services.

Health Insurance and Care in the United States

The current U.S. health insurance system is a complex mix of public and private insurance and services. The defeat of the Clinton administration's proposed universal health insurance legislation in the early 1990s has been followed by a wave of incremental health policy reforms. These reforms include the regulation of private insurance providers through Consolidated Omnibus Budget Reconciliation Act (COBRA) legislation in an attempt to increase the portability of private insurance for those between jobs.[7] Many states have also implemented their own health insurance legislation, such as Children's Health Insurance Programs (CHIP), aimed at providing health insurance for currently uninsured children. These reforms have failed to stem the increase in the percentage of Americans lacking health insurance. The current mixed system in the United States is among the most expensive per capita in the world, and the U.S. government spent more per capita on health care in 1998 (excluding the huge private expenditures) than the Canadian government spent to provide the entire universal system of insurance and provision.[8]

At sixty-five years of age, all Americans become eligible to apply for Medicare, relatively high-quality, publicly funded health insurance. Even though they have Medicare, many elderly purchase extended health insurance privately to ensure that they are covered in case they require long-term care. Public-assistance recipients in the United States can apply to receive more restricted public health insurance from the Medicaid program, which also provides some coverage for basic dental and vision needs. Some U.S. states now have child health insurance programs, which provide health insurance for children under eighteen who lack insurance.

Most Americans get their health insurance through workplace benefit packages. Often they must pay a subsidized monthly premium for these services. Some Americans also purchase private health insurance independently from insurers. The premiums for coverage range dramatically in cost; they are based on an individual's previous medical history and can be extremely expensive for those with preexisting medical conditions. Those without health insurance risk having to pay for extremely expensive health-care services, especially for emergency or chronic care. According to Katherine Newman in *No Shame in My Game*, "Kids in working poor families go without health insurance at a much higher rate than any other group of American children. In 1994, 27 percent of the kids from working-poor families had neither public nor private medical insurance."[9]

The problems with the current U.S. health system go well beyond the large percentage of American's who lack insurance. Spiraling health-care costs threaten the financial well-being of even insured families. According to Elizabeth Warren and Amelia Warren Tyagi in *The Two Income Trap*, "Over the past twenty years, the number of families declaring bankruptcy in the wake of a serious illness has multiplied more than twenty-fold, or *2,000 percent*."[10]

Growing evidence points to the severe costs in terms of the overall health of Americans under the current health-care system. Ichiro Kawachi and Bruce P. Kennedy in *The Wealth of Nations* find that "The poor are also denied access to screening and preventative services that could make the difference in terms of the early detection and treatment of cancer and a host of other serious conditions."[11] The health system in the United States is in crisis. A nonpartisan committee of the National Academy of Sciences recommended that the U.S. government create universal health-care coverage by 2010 because noncoverage is killing 18,000 people per year in the United States and resulting in tremendous economic costs.[12]

The Health-Care System in Canada

Canada's universal system of health insurance evolved after World War II. The universal single-payer Canadian health system developed incrementally through waves of reform—and not without initial opposition from the medical profession, providers, private insurers, business organizations, and even trade unions. Although the federal government proposed a cost-sharing universal program for health insurance in 1945, it was the creation of a "universal, comprehensive system of tax-financed hospitalization insurance" in the province of Saskatchewan by Premier Tommy Douglas, elected by the farmer-dominated Co-operative Commonwealth Federation (CCF) party, that inspired other provinces to begin to implement their own cost-sharing tax-financed systems. By 1961, the nine provinces had similar hospital insurance programs. The current Medicare program was established after the Royal Commission on Health in 1964 led to the Federal Medicare Program in 1966, which all provinces and territories in Canada had joined by 1972.[13]

The current Canadian Medicare system is not a national socialized health system. The health services are provided by nonprofit providers, and each province runs a publicly financed health insurance plan.[14] The current system continues to operate as a mixed public-private system, but with physician and hospital services largely covered by the public system. The public sector covers nearly 100 percent of physician services and most hospital care expenses.[15] The system works to minimize administrative overhead through a single-payer (the government) system, price controls on physician fees, and the bulk purchasing of prescription medications. The savings are substantial: whereas 1 percent of health-care funding goes to overhead in Canada, 15 to 30 percent goes to overhead in U.S. private insurance companies.[16] Lower overhead and the provision of services through not-for-profit organizations have created a health-care system that provides comparable care for all Canadians and is far less expensive per capita than the U.S. system.

The Current State of the Health-Care System in Canada The Canadian health-care system is not without problems, many of them the result of a declining federal financial commitment to health-care expenditures. Recently, the

Canadian health-care system came under the scrutiny of a Federal Commission on Health Care, headed by ex–Saskatchewan Premier Roy Romanow. The Romanow Report makes it clear that the Canadian system is under fiscal strain.[17] The provinces, for example, have picked up a growing percentage of medical expenditures in the past ten years, and the system as a whole is suffering from the federal cutbacks made in the 1990s, the failure to expand home care, and problematic patterns of access in remote rural areas. There is the also growing problem of waiting lists, especially for noncritical services.

> Last summer, Statistics Canada produced its first national look at access to health services, ranging from specialists to non-emergency surgery. StatsCan estimated that 4.3 million Canadians had difficulty accessing so-called "first contact" services such as family doctors, and 1.4 million Canadians had difficulty getting specialized care over a 12–month period. Most cited waiting times as the specific problem, ranging from 55 per cent of those who had difficulties getting non-emergency surgery to 72 per cent of those trying to get a diagnostic test. Almost 60 per cent of those affected by delay in seeing a specialist talked about wrenching stress; more than 30 per cent said their health deteriorated.[18]

Because the health-care system in Canada is public, the complaints and debate around it are also very public. The federal government currently appears set to legislate some of the proposed reforms outlined in the Romanow Report and infuse a significant surplus of cash into shoring up the system. Despite its weaknesses, the Canadian health-care system clearly provides a level of care for average Canadians, and most especially for the poor, that is more dependable than is available to their counterparts in the United States, who lack health-care coverage.

The differences between living under a universal system of health coverage in Canada and a mixed non-universal private-public system in the United States go beyond standard measurable indicators of health and health-care access. Adam Gopnik, debating Malcolm Gladwell—both Canadians living in the United States—in a *Washington Monthly* article on universal health insurance coverage, sums it up as follows: "The crucial point is, I think, the difference in social tone between a society in which universal access to medical care is taken for granted and one in which it is something that weighs constantly on all of us, even though some of us are lucky to have good insurance, and becomes an omnipresent preoccupation to the lower middle classes and to the working poor. It's enormous."[19] Gopnik relates his sister-in-law's experience having a premature baby to illustrate the impact of the difference between the health-care systems in the United States and Canada:

> My wife's sister had a very, very premature baby born in Edmonton six years ago, the kind who normally lives in about 20 percent of cases—and they had eight

months of intensive care. I mean really intensive care. And the baby ended up living. It was a pound and a half at birth, the smallest baby that survived in western Canada in that year. The one thing they never thought about, the one thing they never considered, the one thing they never had to pay a moment's attention to was: How much will this cost? When does our insurance run out? It simply was not in the agonizing equation of worry and concern that they had to face. That seems to me, in itself, the most powerful argument you can make for socialized medicine, to put it in the bluntest possible terms.[20]

A universal system of health-care changes the experience of health care by eliminating worries about the cost of care; health crises alone generally create enough worry.

A comparative analysis of data collected on hotel workers in Seattle and Vancouver confirms the essential point of Gopnik's argument: the Canadian health system greatly limits financial stress around health insurance, care, and treatment compared to the United States.

Health Care in Washington versus British Columbia

Because the hotel workers in this study live under the policies not only of their country but also their state/province, the differences between health-care systems in Washington state and British Columbia are also important. Generally, national-level differences between U.S. and Canadian health policies and outcomes are replicated when we compare Washington state and British Columbia.

Every resident of British Columbia is covered 100 percent by the government insurance for medically needed care in physicians' offices and hospitals.[21] Along with health insurance, the province also provides some prescription drug coverage, although the program was recently changed to become more means-tested. The old Pharmacare system paid for medications for low-income people and seniors, as well as prescription expenses over $800 for most other British Columbia residents. For their health insurance, British Columbia residents pay a small monthly premium for their health benefits under the Medical Services Plan (MSP) program.[22]

The new provincial government in British Columbia recently cut income taxes across the board, which has reduced revenues available for health care, and the past two years have seen many unpopular decisions to close hospitals and long-term senior-care nursing sites, particularly in more rural communities. Because 39 percent of British Columbia's budget went to health care in 2000, the largest expense for the provincial government, it is no surprise that the recent tax cuts have led to hospital closures in British Columbia and other cost-saving measures.[23] At the same time, British Columbia residents are expected to pay for more health-related expenses out of pocket or with extended health benefits.

In recent years, pressure has mounted for Canadians to cover an increasing number of health-related expenses out of pocket (or through workplace extended benefit plans), ranging from physiotherapy to prescription drugs. British Columbians spent an average of $891 per person on private health care in 2000, the fourth highest level of private health expenditures among the provinces, and up from $685 in 1997. Overall, BC is also in the middle [compared to other Canadian provinces] in terms of the share of total health expenditures (71.5%) paid for by the public system.[24]

While the provincial government of British Columbia may have scaled back funding for health care, the Canadian federal government's latest commitment to increasing funding in targeted areas, such as homecare, will probably shore up the current system for some time.

In Washington state, 910,000 people (15.8 percent) lacked health insurance coverage in 1999 (see table 5.2)—slightly higher than the U.S. national average. The state experienced one of the fastest rates of growth in the number of non-insured residents during the late 1990s in the United States.[25] Why is the number of people without health insurance in Washington state increasing? Mirroring the national trend in the United States identified by Ichiro Kawachi and Bruce P. Kennedy, a decreasing percentage of employers in Washington state are providing health benefits to employees.

According to the WA [state] based Economic Opportunity Institute, seven of 10 of the uninsured are members of working families. The proportion of private employers with 100 or more employees providing health benefits dropped from 97 percent in 1980 to 76 percent in 1997. Increasingly, employers are replacing

Table 5.2 Washington state and British Columbia comparative health-care statistics

	Washington state	British Columbia
Individuals without health insurance, 1999[a]	910,000 (15.8%)	None (0%)
Infant mortality, 1998 (per 1,000 births)[b]	5.7	4.03
Average family expenditure on private health care, 1998 (CA$)[c]	2,267	1,499

[a]From U.S. Census Bureau, *Health Insurance Coverage by State: 1997–1999*, in Vogel (2001, 17).
[b]From British Columbia Vital Statistics Agency, *The State of Washington's Children*, in Vogel (2001, 17).
[c]Includes medical services and supplies, drugs, and medical insurance. Canadian dollars based on 1.3 Purchasing Power Party (PPP). From Vogel (2001, 15).

permanent staff with temporary workers in order to avoid responsibility for providing health benefits and other benefits.[26]

Despite the increase in the number and percentage of people lacking health insurance, it appears that the government of Washington state does not plan to address the issue due to a revenue crunch: "Facing a revenue shortfall this year, Washington's legislators have proposed a budget that would cut health funding. The number of people receiving state subsidies for basic health insurance would be reduced from 133,000 to 100,000 over the next two years. Federal funds that were supposed to go to hospitals that treat the uninsured would be diverted to other purposes."[27] Thus, the current trend of increasing levels of noninsured Washington state residents is not likely to change in the short term.

Comparative Analysis of Health Insurance, Health Care, and Outcomes

I analyzed the data on health and health care for hotel workers for three interconnected domains: access to health insurance, access to preventative health care, and health outcomes. These measures are based on commonly used measures in public health research and the health economics literature.[28]

Health insurance coverage is intricately linked to household financial security and psychological well-being, as, for example, when a family has a medical crisis requiring extremely expensive catastrophic care. Some of the measures used to compare access to health insurance are percentage lacking insurance, monthly financial outlays for medical care, financial stress related to health care, and percentage reporting lack of dental and vision benefits.

Health insurance coverage also increases access to the second domain, preventative health care (e.g., regular physical exams). Those without health insurance coverage generally avoid going to the doctor, except when there is a health emergency. Some measures used to compare preventative health care are frequency of visits to a doctor, time since the last visit to a doctor, distance to providers, and sleep deprivation.

The quality of preventative care is generally enhanced by consistency of care, which is improved by having a personal physician or regular doctor. A regular doctor can examine an individual's medical history for patterns to detect, prevent, or provide early treatment for health problems. Other potentially problematic long-term health behaviors, such as smoking, high stress, and sleep deprivation, can be counseled against and possibly addressed by preventative health care. Preventative health care for children can set the stage for lifelong healthy behaviors.

Because high-quality preventative care is associated with better health outcomes, access to this care is an important contributor to individual quality of life. Some measures of health outcomes are life expectancy, self-assessed health status, and reports of health problems.

The following analysis uses comparable data in these three domains, collected through the interviews, to evaluate the impact of health policy differences between Canada and the United States on workers in the hotel industry and their families.

Health Insurance Findings

In my study, I found hotel workers in Vancouver were better off in terms of the percentage with health insurance and regular access to care and they experienced much less financial stress concerning health emergencies. Whereas all the workers interviewed in Vancouver had medical insurance coverage, a significant percentage of Seattle employees lacked health insurance coverage. This was a problem among employees at both the Globe Hotel Seattle and the Hotel Deluxe Seattle, where approximately one in four (25 percent) hotel workers interviewed lacked health insurance coverage.

In both Seattle and Vancouver, workers received benefit packages with health, dental, and vision benefits from the hotel after a certain probationary period, as long as the employee had worked a certain minimum number of hours over a set period of time. In Seattle, the probationary period was for receiving basic health insurance coverage, whereas in Vancouver the probationary period was for extended health benefits, which go beyond the government-provided basic health insurance. Because of the high rate of turnover in the hotel industry, the probationary period for basic health insurance coverage in Seattle results in a significant proportion of employees lacking health insurance coverage. In contrast, in Vancouver employees cannot lose the government-provided universal health insurance and only low-seniority workers can temporarily lose their employee extended health benefits, if their hours are reduced below a certain level or if they are laid off during the slow winter season. Some of these employees simply go without the extended health benefits temporarily; others temporarily purchase extended health coverage for their families for approximately $35–50 per month to cover prescription, dental, and vision expenses.

Despite the surface similarities between the U.S. and Canadian branches of the two multinational hotel chains in my study in terms of health benefit policy, the experiences of the hourly employees appear to differ systematically cross-nationally with regards to health insurance, health-care access, and particularly the financial stress surrounding accessing health care. For example, hotel workers in Seattle report paying higher regular expenses for medical care and insurance than employees in Vancouver, including spending more per month, on average, for medical care and medical insurance.

Whereas only one hotel worker in Vancouver reported having regular medical expenses, 69 percent of Seattle employees reported spending money every month on health expenses, including insurance costs deducted from paychecks, co-pays, and treatment expenses. These reported expenses varied dramatically. Although most were around $50 per month, one hotel employee's household expenditure on medical care and medical insurance averaged $350 per month and another reported spending an average of $750 per month. In contrast, in Vancouver hotel employees were covered by government-provided universal health coverage and also received extended health benefits as part of their employee benefit packages with no premiums deducted from their paychecks.

Conditions such as having to work a minimum number of hours and being subject to probation periods left some Seattle workers without health insurance coverage. The lack of a universal health-care system in the United States has created substantial gaps in health insurance coverage, and these gaps impact nonsalaried hourly employees particularly. The most vulnerable, such as those receiving public assistance, often qualify for government Medicaid programs, and recently arrived refugees receive special health benefits. Alma Meteko, an eighteen-year-old refugee from Ethiopia who works full-time as a room attendant at the Globe Hotel Seattle while attending high school full-time, is covered by a government health program. According to Kevin Johnson, a twenty-eight-year-old maintenance engineer at the Globe Hotel Seattle, as a former member of the U.S. military he is eligible for Medicare coverage for his family through the Veterans Administration (VA) programs if he does not have access to subsidized health insurance through his job: "if [we] had no other health insurance, I think you could go to the VA." James Allan, a forty-five-year-old African-American banquet houseman at the Hotel Deluxe Seattle, is fortunate to get Social Security Disability for schizophrenia, which provides him with $600 a month (as an income supplement) as well as medical care and coverage through a government program. His co-worker, thirty-four-year-old Amy Luminov, who works as an on-call banquet server in the same department, had a much more difficult time accessing necessary mental health care, therapy, and medication for her bipolar disorder until she became an experimental patient for University of Washington Hospital psychiatry students.

Several of the hotel workers in Seattle who I interviewed were either waiting to get health insurance coverage or do not work enough hours to qualify. Even within families, a husband may be covered by his employer, but his wife and/or children are not. In some cases, a Washington state program temporarily provides health insurance for children, leaving the parents uninsured. Whereas in Canada hotel employees enjoy the protection of the government-provided universal health system as a critical safety net, in the United States workers are one bad work day away from being uninsured medically and extremely vulnerable financially in the event of a major health catastrophe.

Most of the employees who lacked health insurance in Seattle discussed it as a stressful situation, as did Sujita Hassam, whose story is presented in Chapter 1. Instability of coverage can also cause stress. Hue Chung is a thirty-seven-year-old recent immigrant from Guangdong, China, who works as a room attendant at the Globe Hotel Seattle.[29] She said that she would like to see her job unionized because of "Health care. [We] pay for the kids, the bills, a lot of burden, it's a lot of money." Although Hue Chung and her husband were covered by her hotel benefits, her children were still in a waiting period. "For some reason, the insurance only cover adults, then [I] have to wait for a year to have the kids. Appreciate. Cannot join for one year. [I] thinks [my] income is not that much already, in fact, even with that, it is going to take out more, and [I] think it will become a problem eventually." At the time of the study, her children were covered temporarily by a Washington state government health program because, "the school, the school actually ask them to apply."

A few workers commented that health insurance coverage prevented them from switching jobs or retiring early. Jane Donaldson, a fifty-nine-year-old Hotel Deluxe Seattle Housekeeping supervisor stated, "I probably still working [five years from now], because now, we really need the insurance. I was going to retire at sixty-two, because my husband is a lot younger than I am, can continue to work, but now he can't work, I don't know, I can never retire at sixty-two."

Even the younger employees who did not have health insurance or who were waiting for coverage reported feeling some stress. Mark Frulo, a twenty-one-year-old banquet houseman at the Hotel Deluxe Seattle and his nineteen-year-old live-in girlfriend Rita Hall, a manager at a major retail store, moved to Seattle from the U.S. territory of Guam to attend Seattle Community College and experience life in the continental United States. Even though both of his parents work at a hospital, Mark Frulo and Rita Hall lack health insurance coverage. He complained that doctor's visits in Seattle without health insurance are "pretty expensive. You pay a sitting fee, and then later on you get billed. . . . The sitting fee is like $40, and then when they bill you, [it's] like [another] $60."

Many on-call banquet servers do not work enough hours to qualify for continuous health benefits and cycle through periods of being on and off coverage. Carrie Fitzpatrick, an on-call banquet server at the Globe Hotel Seattle, described the stress of not having health insurance during probationary periods: "It is kind of stressful, because when you don't have insurance, if something happens. . . ." At the same time, she said that health insurance coverage can be inadequate: "But then also sometimes when you do have insurance, you feel at ease because you think they'll take care of you and then something happens, and it turns out, they're like, oh, we don't cover that."

Samantha Beck is a thirty-three-year-old Ethiopian immigrant who only recently began working in the food service as a barista (or coffee server) at the Hotel Deluxe Seattle. One day she spilled a pot of boiling water on her arm while cooking at home, but did not go to the doctor or emergency room because she did not have health insurance. Samantha Beck felt she could not afford it, especially since she was already past due on paying for a previous hospital visit. She showed me her serious scar on her arm and reflected that she should have gone to the doctor because now it would probably be permanent: "Yeah, I burn it with hot water and I was a mess, I didn't have money to go to the doctor. . . . It's about a second degree burn. It was like all blistered and it was really bad. . . . I didn't have the money. I owed Uptown Hospital still, I couldn't go there." The cycling through periods of being on and off health coverage appears to encourage employees without coverage simply to avoid going to the doctor, if at all possible, and hope that they do not require any medical care.

Problems with the health-care system in the United States go well beyond the number of people lacking health insurance. As Elizabeth Warren and Amelia Warren Tyagi report, "Many families have discovered that the exclusions, co-payments, and caps on health insurance mean that they are on the hook for far more than they anticipated, while others have learned that much needed services such as physical therapy or mental health treatment are scarcely covered at all."[30]

The insufficient coverage provided by some health insurance plans—particularly by 80/20 plans—also causes financial stress for several of the Seattle hotel workers I interviewed. Kevin Johnson, a maintenance engineer at the Globe Hotel Seattle, discussed his previous experience with an 80/20 health-care plan, explicitly emphasizing the financial dimension of health and health care.

> Like unfortunately when I worked for Major Soda Company in Indiana, when we had our daughter, the only health care they offered . . . [was] the 80/20 [plan]. You pay, they pay 80 [percent], you pay 20 [percent].
>
> Well that's the kind of plan we were on in Indiana. And it cost us thousands of dollars to have our child. . . . Because like when you get an epidural, it's like $1,000. We had to pay $500 of that. Actually it was so we ended up paying thousands of dollars to have our daughter, which if we would have had managed care or whatever it's called, it would have been you know, $15 for every doctor's visit and then like once you went in to have the baby, it would have been like $15.

An 80/20 health insurance plan may sound acceptable to a healthy individual and family, but when a health crisis strikes it can turn out to be inadequate coverage to prevent major financial hardship. Alfred Jones, a long-time maintenance engineer at the Hotel Deluxe Seattle, was diagnosed with terminal prostate cancer that had recently spread to his bones. He was forced to switch to an 80/20 plan:

> So they wouldn't offer it [to stay in the General HMO plan] to me. You know, tried, I asked them to make an exception, especially because having the cancer and all that, and plus the fact that I had been on General HMO for all that time [over twenty years]. And they said, we can't do it. . . .
>
> Before . . . if I had a monthly treatment for my cancer infusion that I get every month, it was twenty bucks. And that went up from ten because the co-pay used to be $10 and then it went to $20. Now, I have to pay, 20 percent of like $3,500. . . . I know that essentially I am going to end up either not paying the bills or I'm going to just pay all my savings away to where I don't have any anymore, which is essentially what they want you to do when you are ill with a terminal disease anyway. They want to bleed you till you don't have any assets so they can stick you in the nursing home and put you on Medicare, at that point.
>
> Trying to arrange your will and stuff too is real hard, because you are trying to give your kids something. And they are waiting to recoup any losses that they make or have. So they can even go back after the fact, and try to recoup it from your kids.

Recent changes also forced Alfred Jones to keep working full-time despite having terminal cancer because the Hotel Deluxe Seattle reduced the amount of pay an employee could receive during extended sick leave from $2,000 to $1,200 per month, a level that is too low for Alfred Jones to make ends meet.

Dental and vision benefits do not differ between Seattle and Vancouver in the same way as medical insurance and prescription coverage. The province of British Columbia does not currently provide dental and vision benefits for residents, except for public-assistance recipients. Until two years ago, British Columbia health insurance covered annual eye examinations, but now residents who are not covered by a work-based or a private dental and vision plan must pay for insurance or pay directly for these services themselves. The Vancouver workers expressed their disappointment at not having the same protection when it comes to vision and oral health care that they do for health care more generally. Americans face the same problem for all health services.

Dental expenses came up frequently during the interviews as one of the main health-related hardships in both countries. In Vancouver, many of the lower-seniority room attendants had lost their extended health, dental, and vision benefits when their hours were cut or when they were laid off in the winter slow season. Whereas all the workers I interviewed at the Hotel Deluxe Vancouver reported having dental benefits at the time of the interview, four out of the twenty-one hotel workers interviewed at the Globe Hotel Vancouver reported they did not have dental benefits because they did not work enough hours to qualify for coverage. These benefits cover the cost of dental visits every six months and 80 percent of other dental expenditures. Tse Leung, a fifty-four-year-old Chinese-immigrant room attendant at the Globe Hotel Vancouver was not able to access dental care because it was too expensive. Kerry Wong, also a Chinese-immigrant room attendant at the Globe Hotel Vancouver, said that dental care was so expensive in Canada that she waited and visited the dentist during her visits to Shanghai.

The subject of vision coverage came up less frequently, although some respondents had also lost access to vision benefits during the slow season. One employee, Hassam Mansour, a maintenance engineer at the Globe Hotel Vancouver, reported that even with the vision benefits provided by the hotel, his wife could not afford to get herself a new pair of glasses. He remarked, "Yeah, my wife actually wanted to get eyeglasses, but we could not afford it, so she didn't get it. She had to use her old ones instead." Until recently, many of the hotel employees could still visit the eye doctor regularly even without extended health benefits from work. Also, perhaps because regular vision check-ups seem less important and are required less frequently than dental cleanings, hotel workers interviewed did not report losing vision benefits as being much of a problem.

In Seattle, 29 percent of the employees interviewed at the Globe Hotel Seattle and 26.7 percent at the Hotel Deluxe Seattle reported not having dental and vision benefits, a slightly higher percentage than for those lacking health insurance. Sheila Chang, a forty-seven-year-old immigrant from Guangdong, China, works as a room attendant at the Globe Hotel Seattle. She said that she spent an average of $220 per month—over $2,000 per year—on dental expenses to fix her "bad teeth." Kevin Johnson, a maintenance engineer at the Globe Hotel Seattle, reported serious problems with the inadequacy of the dental coverage: "Well, even if it is [covered by the employee dental plan], it's like 50 percent of a root canal, which is $1,000. So that's still $500, $500 I don't have." Kevin Johnson's comments were echoed by Sheila Chang, the Globe Hotel Seattle public space supervisor, who emigrated from China and ended up spending thousands of dollars for dental work, despite having dental coverage through the employee benefit plan. Although dental benefits cover preventative work in Seattle, they also leave employees vulnerable to paying a substantial percentage of potentially very expensive dental bills due to the structure of benefits.

Health-Crisis and Financial-Stress Findings

Financial stress as it relates to health care and health crises was virtually nonexistent among Vancouver hotel employees I interviewed. A car accident, sudden illness, or a sports injury can in a single moment create a major crisis for an individual and his or her family, but the physical consequences are not compounded by financial trauma in Canada. Although Vancouver hotel workers had their share of injuries and illness, their positive experience with the Canadian health system and freedom from health-care expenses relieved them of the burdens—psychological and financial—that Americans in the same jobs must constantly bear in mind. For example, Mark Heung, a Vietnamese-immigrant houseman at the Globe Hotel Vancouver described a typical Canadian story about a trip to the emergency room:

> Oh, we had a family fondue, you know the Chinese set-up and it was a big family gathering and the dining table wasn't big enough. So what we did, was we cleared the living room floor and we ate on the floor. . . . And after we were eating, drinking and things, like my oldest daughter, she was monkeying around. And she somehow fell and she rolled into the center of the dining set-up. . . . And the soup that was in the center of it, were hot, not boiling hot, but hot, okay and it was enough to scald her on the side of the thigh. So that was a major, major crisis. . . . Boy, was it stressful. . . . that was one event that we had to go to the hospital under extreme stress.

When I asked him if he had to pay a large medical bill for the visit, Mark replied, "No, it was all covered." His story was typical among Vancouver workers—most reported not having to pay anything for emergency health care.

Tara Wang, a forty-year-old immigrant from Guangdong, China, who works as a room attendant at the Globe Hotel Vancouver, has three boys: twelve-year-old Wa-Jun, eight-year-old Gerry, and four-year-old Alan. One day, she had to take Gerry to the emergency room. When it rains, it pours—after being treated, Gerry broke his leg the next day skating. Tara Wang said, "Two days [in a row] go the same doctor." Despite the misfortune, Tara Wang explained that they did not have to pay anything for the medical care. Health-care emergencies in Vancouver are covered under universal coverage and, thus, do not cause serious financial stress for hotel workers.

Insurance coverage and medical costs were the most frequently mentioned hardships by Seattle employees in terms of accessing health care. A medical crisis can set off a chain of events that can completely undermine a family's financial security as a consequence of uncovered medical costs (deductibles and co-payments) and lost wages. Joey Harrison a long-time maintenance engineer at the Hotel Deluxe Seattle owns his home, but piled up significant credit card debt due to lost wages and expenses related to his mother-in-law's cancer, his wife's kidney cancer, and the births of and medical expenses for his children.

> JOEY: Well, medical you know. Maybe like the mom has medical problems. My wife needs to take a lot of time off work and we are a two income family and we need that extra income and that's when the credit cards start saving us. So maybe we start charging $1,000 a month on credit cards so she can get to the hospital with her mom. So you know that's kind of a sad deal. . . . Yeah, yeah, its saving you, its keeping you to do things, and then all of a sudden like bang, your minimum payment is more than you can afford.
>
> ME: It sounds like you have a lot of debt . . . and it's because, so your wife's mom got sick?
>
> JOEY: Yeah, and then she passed away. After she passed away, my wife was diagnosed with cancer. . . . Yeah, she has to go through the whole works, for the rest of her life. . . . Yeah, she gets a CAT scan every three, I mean, six months. . . .
>
> ME: You said at one point, you almost had to declare bankruptcy but you had to cash out your pension?
>
> JOEY: Yeah, that was hard times.
>
> ME: This is when you had one child?
>
> JOEY: Yeah, I had to look at ways we could save money. Should we cancel our AOL, our cable, our cell phones, our storage, you know, should we use less heat. How are we going to save money here and there?
>
> ME: And meanwhile maximizing the amount of hours you worked?
>
> JOEY: Yeah, taking a credit card that's got really high interest rate, 25 percent some of them and looking for one that will handle like 6 month, one that's like 3 percent, and that will handle for 6 months. You know, playing the credit card game, transferring everything over to new different credit cards so they can have less minimum payment, so you can make the minimum payment. And trying to do Home Equity Loans. Have you ever been denied on getting a credit card? Well, you get a credit card and you get denied for it. And then you get credit cards that come that will take you no matter what.
>
> ME: Yeah, its almost surprising.
>
> JOEY: And then you get denied, someone wants to help you with your minimum payments, like those companies.
>
> ME: Yeah, the consumer credit companies.
>
> JOEY: And they look at you and they shake their heads and say you got to be nuts, I'm not doing that for you. Your minimum payments are $2,500 per month and you make, without food and utilities or anything like that, and you make $2,600 per month. How are you going to make that happen, you know. I say, I just make it happen and they don't understand that. They don't understand

that I'm not just going to be sitting on the side of the road, I'll just go do gutters, I'll change, I'll go do something to make it happen. Like this interview, I'm making it happen. This will probably be a costume for my son for Halloween.[31]

Joey Harrison's story is both unique and illustrative; a large proportion of the workers interviewed in Seattle described major financial stress resulting from medical crises.

On the other hand, some Seattle hotel employees, particularly younger ones, reported not having any problems in terms of health or health-care, dental, and vision benefits. In Seattle and Vancouver, health and health care were often more of a concern for older workers and those with children. Unless forced to deal with a health crisis, younger hotel workers did not often think about the health system.

Preventive-Care Findings

The higher costs of accessing health-care services in Seattle provide disincentives to seeking preventative treatment, such as regular doctor visits. A greater percentage of employees interviewed in Seattle (20.5 percent) than in Vancouver (7.9 percent) said they had delayed or not received care they thought they needed for themselves or a family member because of difficulties getting medical care. Because they had little or no concern about the financial aspects of accessing health services, hotel workers in Vancouver reported going to the doctor more frequently for regular check-ups and preventative care than similar employees in Seattle. Fewer workers in Vancouver than in Seattle also reported hardships in terms of accessing preventative care.

A higher percentage of workers in Vancouver than in Seattle reported having a regular doctor. Most hotel employees I interviewed in Vancouver had a family doctor that they visited in a non-hospital-based office located less than fifteen minutes driving distance from their home.

Overall more employees in Vancouver than in Seattle said they saw one doctor regularly for care (85 percent compared to 67 percent). The differences are magnified for the children of hotel workers: 100 percent of children in Vancouver had a regular doctor compared to only 56.6 percent of children in Seattle.

Cross-national differences also emerged as to where hotel employees accessed medical services (see table 5.3). Seattle workers reported relying on a wider range of health-service providers than did Vancouver employees, who almost exclusively saw the doctor in a doctor's office or private clinic, arguably the best option because of the preventive benefits of consistent care.

Hotel workers in Seattle reported visiting the doctor less regularly. They had

Table 5.3 Health-care providers of hotel employees

	Seattle	Vancouver
Doctor's office	11 (28%)	31 (82%)
Private clinic	8 (21%)	3 (8%)
Community health center	3 (8%)	4 (11%)
Hospital-based doctor's office	4 (10%)	None (0%)
HMO	7 (18%)	None (0%)
Hospital emergency room	1 (3%)	None (0%)
Don't know	5 (13%)	None (0%)

not visited the doctor as recently, on average, as employees in Vancouver. A higher percentage reported visiting the doctor in the past year: 92.1 percent in Vancouver compared to 79.5 percent in Seattle. Hotel workers in Vancouver also reported more visits to the doctor on average in the past year. There was also a small group of hotel employees in each city who had not visited the doctor in the two years before their interview, in Vancouver 5.3 percent and in Seattle 12.8 percent—more than twice the percentage.

As another dimension of preventative care, hotel employees interviewed in Vancouver reported sleeping longer per night on average and a lower percentage of respondents suffered regular sleep deprivation than in Seattle. A proxy measure of how well employees take care of themselves, a sleep deficit can also lead to deleterious health effects as well as to increased incidences of fatigue, depression, and rage.[32] Many more Seattle hotel workers reported sleeping fewer than six hours per night—25.6 percent compared to 10.5 percent in Vancouver. Although a combination of personal life stress and preferences may be contributing to this figure, sleeping fewer than six hours per night may contribute to poorer overall physical and mental health in the long term among the respondents in Seattle compared to Vancouver.

Health-Outcome Findings

Based on my interviews, hotel workers in Vancouver appear to have somewhat better health outcomes than those in Seattle, but, given the complex interaction of factors that shape health outcomes, it is extremely difficult to draw definitive conclusions about causality from the data collected. It does make sense that differences in the health-care systems make a difference in health outcomes of populations. At a national level, life expectancy is higher and infant and young-child (one- to five-year-olds) mortality rates are lower in Canada than in the United States; this is suggestive. Hotel workers in Vancouver reported having somewhat better perceptions of their own health, physical as well as mental and emotional, relative to others of the same age than did their counterparts in Seattle.[33] They also appear to have slightly better health outcomes based on their answers to questions about health problems and auxiliary measures of health.

Although the results of the Global Hotel study cannot prove that a universal health insurance system results in better health outcomes than the present U.S. health-care system, it does provide evidence of some of the pathways by which these policy differences could translate into outcome differences. For example, early detection is critical to the successful treatment of cancer and other life-threatening diseases. If Americans are delaying going to the doctor because of a fear of the financial consequences of medical care, then more will die prematurely—and unnecessarily—than would under a system that guarantees universal health insurance coverage.

Canada's universal health insurance system decouples health insurance from employment and reduces the financial stress that surrounds health-care insurance and treatment for working-poor families compared to the current mixed public and private system in the United States. The two health-care systems differ in similar ways on the national level and on the state/province level. The U.S. mixed public and private system leaves many—especially the working poor—without health insurance coverage; despite the provision of health insurance benefits by the hotels, a significant percentage of hotel workers in Seattle lack health insurance. In the realm of dental or vision insurance, however, few differences exist between hotel workers in the two cities.

The universal system of health coverage in Canada strongly mitigates the financial stress surrounding health care, even in health emergencies, for hotel workers in Vancouver. The differences in health policy also appear to foster conditions in which employees in Vancouver and their families are more likely to access preventive health care and have lower levels of health-related hardships than in Seattle.

The current health-care system in the United States leaves a growing number of Americans vulnerable to stressful periods without health insurance and many more susceptible to financial collapse due to inadequate health coverage in the event of a health emergency. The Global Hotel study findings suggest some of the many ways that the United States could benefit from its own version of a universal health insurance system.

CHAPTER 6

Social Welfare Policy Differences

Government programs provide protection against material hardship for hotel employees in Vancouver during economic downturns, but in Seattle employees rely more on extended family or personal resources as well as on working multiple jobs simultaneously in order to make ends meet. This chapter focuses on a broad conception of social welfare policy that includes more than public-assistance programs and also examines unemployment policy, training, income tax benefit programs, child-care policy, and government-subsidized savings programs. Although many of the adult, non-elderly, poor hold formal employment positions, little research has been done on how social policy matters in the lives of working-poor families. In the United States, urban poverty and even welfare reform studies have begun shifting their focus to examine this aspect, but more research needs to be done.[1] From the perspective of working-poor employees, what resources are there to support them if they are laid off or lose their job? How do social policies shape their quality of life and the hardships endured by their families?

Social Welfare Policy

The Canadian government spends significantly more of its tax revenue on social programs and income supports than does the U.S. government.[2] These additional expenditures on social supports and programming make the Canadian government more effective at lifting families out of poverty, especially lone parents with children, and at generally providing a stronger social safety net compared to the United States.[3] The same general pattern exists between Washington state and the province of British Columbia. Hotel employees in Vancouver have access to more generous and easily accessed social programs, including unemployment and public assistance, than do employees in Seattle.

Unemployment Benefits

In Canada, the Employment Insurance (EI) system is a federal program that is provincially administered. In the United States, the federal Department of Labor sets basic guidelines for state-designed and administered unemploy-

Table 6.1 Unemployment benefit program rules for residents of Seattle and Vancouver

	Seattle	Vancouver
Qualifying hours	680	630[a]
Benefit percentage/ replacement income	48% average insured earnings[b]	55% average insured earnings
Benefits paid	30 weeks	40 weeks
Waiting period for benefits	1 week	2 weeks
Family supplement for low-income families with children	No	Yes[c]
Maximum benefits	US$510/week	CA$413/week
Minimum benefits	US$109/week	None
Work while on benefit?	Approximately 75% of part-time earnings are deducted from weekly benefit amount	$50 or 25% benefits per week, whichever is less are kept (on top of weekly benefit); beyond that, dollar for dollar deduction

Source: Human Resources and Development Canada website (http://www.hrdc.gc.ca); Washington Employment websites (http://www.wa.gov/esd/ui/; http://access.wa.gov/)

[a]From 420 to 700 hours, depending on local unemployment rate in region. As of August 2003, 630 hours in Vancouver. From Human Resources and Development Canada website (http://www14.hrdc-drhc.gc.ca/ei-ae/ratesc.htm).

[b]Washington State Employment Insurance provides weekly benefits equaling 4% of a person's average of the two highest quarterly earnings from the qualifying base-year of earnings. Therefore, Weekly benefits = 0.04 (12 weeks in a quarter × Weekly earnings), or, more simply, weekly benefit amounts equal 0.48 or 48 percent of average weekly earnings in the highest two quarters of the qualifying base year of employment.

[c]Up to 80 percent replacement wage for low-income families with children. From Human Resources and Development Canada website (http://www.hrdc-drhc.gc.ca/ae-ei/pubs/219017.shtml).

ment insurance programs; Washington state sets both the benefits and regulations for unemployment benefits and administers the program that governs hotel workers in Seattle (see table 6.1). At first glance, the programs do not seem very different. Although the waiting period is shorter and maximum benefits higher for employees in Seattle, the EI program in Vancouver pays a larger replacement rate of income as benefits and for a longer period of time. Fewer completed working hours are required before an employee can qualify for unemployment benefits in Vancouver than in Seattle. Most important for hotel workers with children, in Vancouver a family supplement provision targets low-income workers with children and provides a major boost to their unemployment benefits, bringing their benefits up to a maximum of 80 percent replacement income.

Public Assistance

Public-assistance benefits are minimal and difficult to access in both Washington state and British Columbia. They continue to be more generous in

British Columbia; although the provincial government recently failed to implement two-year time limits, they successfully toughened program requirements and cut benefits.[4] Public assistance provided $13,660 per year for a single parent with one child in British Columbia, compared to $8,500 per year for a single parent with one child in Washington state.[5] British Columbia also continues to provide minimal benefits for single adults, unlike Washington state.[6]

Labor Policy

Workers in Vancouver are more protected from material hardship indirectly by strict British Columbia provincial labor standards than workers in Washington state. These labor standard differences include paid maternity leave, sickness benefits, vacation benefits, government-subsidized retirement savings programs, and dismissal protection. Together, these standards act as a buffer against material hardship in economic downturns and other situations in which hotel employees and their families became vulnerable. Specifically, Canada mandates fifty-two weeks parental leave for a new parent, during which time eligible mothers receive EI benefits based on their hours worked and income. Generally, the maternity benefits are 55 percent of a worker's average weekly earnings, capped at $413 per week.[7]

In Washington state, only the public sector and employers with over fifty employees—only 45 percent of the workforce—are obligated to provide maternity leave. It is often unpaid and of comparatively short duration (twelve weeks).[8] Private-sector employees in firms with fewer than fifty workers receive maternity leave only if their firms provide it voluntarily; firms are not required by law to do so.

Labor standards mandate more paid holidays and vacation pay in British Columbia than in Washington state. According to Donna Vogel's report *In Search of the Good Life*, "In BC, workers are entitled to nine statutory paid holidays a year and at least two weeks annual [paid] vacation [after one year, and three weeks after five years]. In WA, there are no laws providing either paid holidays or annual vacations."[9] British Columbia labor standards also require that employees who have worked for one year must be given two weeks notice or severance pay if there is no just cause for their dismissal; no such employee protection exists in Washington state.

We understand the macro picture. Benefits are easier to obtain and more generous in Canada than the United States; hence, poverty is less ubiquitous in Canada. But this tells us relatively little about working poverty "on the ground," about how policy differences impact the lives of poor workers, especially when they seek the support of a safety net. To whom do they turn? How effective is that net in cushioning the impact of unemployment on poverty? To answer these questions, we must compare the circumstances under which the working poor use government social welfare programs in each country.

The Effects of Social Welfare Policy in Vancouver and Seattle

Employment Insurance Benefits in Vancouver

In Vancouver, the EI program had the greatest impact mitigating material hardship by providing financial support for room attendants and their families during the annual slow season from November to April. As the rainy season approaches, tourism plummets and, as hotel occupancy rates follow, many room attendants working in Vancouver hotels lose some or all of their shifts.[10] It becomes difficult even for room attendants with relatively high seniority to get more than three 8-hour shifts per week. A substantial proportion of room attendants at downtown hotels are systematically laid off every winter, so finding another cleaning job becomes extremely difficult during this period.[11]

When room attendants learn that their hours will be significantly reduced or that they will be temporarily laid off, they visit the local Manpower office and apply on computer terminals to receive EI benefits. Many employees remain on-call and will receive a shift or two per week through the winter. Others supplement their income through private housecleaning or serving tables at a restaurant.

Although EI benefits provide some important replacement income, the uncertainty of the winter slow season still creates a lot of stress. Kerry Wong, a forty-seven-year-old immigrant from Shanghai, China, who works as a room attendant at the Globe Hotel Vancouver described the yearly downturn: "But for me is no time [available hours to work]. Like this time, or everyday, stay home like last three months. I was two days work. Five days off. But off in the home, oh, I am very worried. And it's difficult to find another job, because everyday have to [be] on call. Yeah, so after 8:00 a.m. and they no call me, so I stay home. Oh very worried. No happy."

EI benefits provide critical support that allows hotel workers to continue to make ends meet during the slow season. Kerry Wong's friend Kathleen Leun, a forty-nine-year-old immigrant from Guangdong, China, also works as a room attendant at the Globe Hotel Vancouver. Kathleen Leun has applied for EI benefits every winter she has worked at the hotel and received about "$200 something" per week. By combining her benefits with her husband's income, they have not had a hard time making the monthly payments on their home.

The EI system in Canada is far from problem-free; eligibility has been drastically reduced and tougher work-search requirements and monitoring policies have been implemented. Elizabeth Hubar, a thirty-seven-year-old, refugee from Tamil, Sri Lanka, arrived in Vancouver three years ago and works as a room attendant at the Hotel Deluxe Vancouver. She and her forty-seven-year-old husband, Farsham Hubar, are awaiting the processing of their refugee application. Their four children, seventeen-year-old Amy, ten-year-old Anand, seven-year-old Reginald, and three-year-old Rohit are currently staying with her mother in Sri Lanka. As a recently hired room attendant, Elizabeth Hubar had a difficult time accessing EI benefits when she was temporarily laid off during the slow winter season. In the end, she received about $250 per week, but felt that the government representative at the Manpower office was extremely rude to her. She picked up an occasional shift at the hotel and then reported her earnings to Manpower. Some of her work earnings were deducted from her EI benefits, but working shifts also helped extend her eligibility. Elizabeth Hubar had a particularly difficult time coping after the terrorist attacks of September 11 caused an economic recession in Vancouver's hospitality industry. Both she and her husband were laid off simultaneously. During a follow-up interview, she described the situation: "They were really very slow there [after September 11, 2001]. But in between, they will call me whenever they need. Like I got four hours, six hours, sometimes, yeah, eight hours. . . . [But] no, not 20 hours. [So] I'm going to lose my benefits. Yeah. It [the benefits] last until 14th of . . . this month. That's it. . . . Of course we never expect, you know . . . but what to do. I can't blame the hotel, right?"

Hotel occupancy rates plummeted across Vancouver after September 11, not just at the Hotel Deluxe Vancouver. The financial squeeze caused the hotel to change guest-service policies to save money, including limiting the formerly universal turndown service to VIP customers only.[12] These changes further reduced the need for room attendants.

At the Hotel Deluxe Vancouver, the general manager, James Caldwell, convened a meeting of the Housekeeping staff to discuss and vote on work sharing, an optional government program for coping with economic crisis. Under this complex system, high-seniority employees give up some shifts so low-seniority workers can get some hours, and the government provides some tax relief on employment benefits to increase the incomes of the most affected employees. Elizabeth Hubar expressed disappointment that the vote failed because if it had passed this labor policy provision may have allowed her to work more shifts and extend the period of time that she could survive on a combination of EI benefits and part-time work hours.

The economic situation hurt Elizabeth Hubar's husband's janitorial subcontracting business, as well. As a subcontractor, he did not qualify for unemployment EI benefits and so immediately took a new janitorial cleaning subcontract with a hotel at lower pay. Elizabeth Hubar said she had to begin receiving unemployment benefits much earlier than the year before:

> Maybe there are people who want to go on EI, but not me, I prefer to go work, I get more money if I work. And but I still, like Thursday, when I applied for my EI, I still got my last year [remaining eligibility]. Yeah, so I continue, so I still got two or three weeks. I have to go and reapply on the 17th. I don't like that.
>
> And it's not easy to get jobs anywhere else too. Because everything is affected, unexpected. . . . And we are in here, we don't know what is going to happen. . . . We never know. . . . It's very hard to get a job.

To make matters worse, Elizabeth Hubar's grandfather passed away in Sri Lanka on September 7, 2001. Given her refugee status in Canada, she could not travel to be with her children for the funeral while her claim is being processed. She and her husband had no savings or personal network in Canada to fall back on. When I asked her in our follow-up interview if the situation was stressful for her, she said:

> Is it going to last like this? For me, it's very difficult. Because once you get big money and then when you, when they really really minus some money, it's very hard for you to go back . . . and I don't know how much money I'm going to get.
>
> So, I don't know what's going to happen. But it's very hard for me to send back some money [to my children in Sri Lanka]. I can't get so much I can send. Like last time I know how much I can send [now]. I can't afford it, I have to pay my own bills. Like telephone and I have car insurance and insurance is starting to go up. It's going to go up, I don't know. For us we're really badly need the car. And um, no security [jobs], that's all. . . . All the house is clean. . . . Even we could go for a government job, they are cutting out. Cutting down on the government jobs, too. What can I work, if I want to go back to school, maybe someone can give me loans, but how sure they will give us, the job. [The] situation is like that. You know. If I want to find another job, 'what job?' Everything is bad. If you want to open a restaurant also, people don't have money, how they can go to a coffee shop and drink a coffee or something like this? . . . so it's very difficult. Whole world . . . suffering because of . . . September 11.

Many room attendants I interviewed in Vancouver would have experienced more hardship if they not been able to receive unemployment benefits during the winter slow season.

Many employees interviewed in Vancouver described periods of unemployment before working in the hotel industry, and the critical role of unemployment benefits in helping them make ends meet when they were temporarily out of work. Often, these benefits prevented them and their families from experiencing major hardships during those difficult economic periods. Marianne

Lakon, a forty-three-year-old immigrant from the Philippines, works as a room attendant at the Hotel Deluxe Vancouver. She described how EI benefits helped her family. First, she received maternity benefits through the EI system and then continued to receive EI benefits for eight months while looking for work. She received $620 every two weeks while her husband earned a small commission-based salary. She paid to attend classes and considers this to be one of the most difficult times her and her family went through:

> No I didn't borrow any money. I used my credit card, but I only use it if I know that I have [the money to pay it off]. . . . But the children understand, because we've been in a poor family, you know. So I tell to my children that we don't have anything, extra, so we don't go shopping. They don't ask me for money. As long as they have bus fare and they will pack their lunch from the house. But I don't feel bad for them, because they're healthy, that's the best thing. They're healthy, they're good in school.

Programs that provide workers with replacement income during unemployment prevented material hardship among many Vancouver hotel workers.

Unemployment Insurance Benefits in Seattle

The combination of low hourly wages and replacement rates sharply reduces the effectiveness of the Washington state unemployment insurance system in mitigating material hardship caused by unemployment for the working poor. The ratio between weekly benefit amounts relative to the cost of living proves critical for understanding why more hotel employees use the unemployment insurance system in Vancouver than in Seattle.

When asked about the previous five years, fewer hotel workers in Seattle reported being unemployed or temporarily laid off compared to workers in Vancouver. The hotel industry in Vancouver experiences larger seasonal fluctuations between the winter and summer seasons than in Seattle. Yet a much higher percentage of Vancouver hotel workers who were unemployed or temporarily laid-off accessed unemployment benefits in the past five years than did Seattle workers (64 percent compared to 22 percent). The more restrictive requirements and lower benefit levels in Washington state help explain the lower percentage of employees accessing unemployment benefits in Seattle.

Whereas EI benefits for Vancouver employees allowed them to continue to make ends meet without major hardship during temporary periods of unemployment, the weekly benefit amounts from unemployment for Seattle hotel workers were so low that many employees did not bother applying for them when they were temporarily laid off or unemployed. The hassle—it is far from an easy process—of signing up and reporting for unemployment benefits was not worth it for many laid-off Seattle employees, who could expect unemployment benefits of approximately $170 per week or $680 per month.[13] The formula used to calculate unemployment benefits in Washington state causes the program to not work for the working poor. When people earning low wages are unemployed or laid off, the meager amounts provided by unemployment are barely enough for a single person to make ends meet, much less a family with children. Instead of applying for unemployment, many workers reported simply taking whatever job or jobs—no matter how poorly paid—they could find, even if temporary or paying minimum wage, until they could find something better paid. Working full-time, even at minimum wage, provides $300 per week in income, or $1,200 per month—significantly more than the potential unemployment benefits most Seattle hotel workers would receive if they were laid off.

The unemployment system in Washington state has recently been reformed to simultaneously become even more stingy in terms of benefits and tougher on recipients. The new Washington Unemployment Insurance Employment Security program website describes how the state has dramatically raised the work-search expectations for unemployment benefit receipts.[14] On the screen, a large circular button links to a new web page warning of dire consequences for those who do not live up to the new stringent work-search requirements. Potential applicants for benefits are warned of random interviews, at which unemployment recipients will have to provide proof that they have satisfied these work-search requirements—similar to the WorkFirst program for public-assistance recipients. At the same time, the new benefit determination formula reduces the already low percentage of former income received as unemployment benefits, again hurting low-wage workers the most.[15]

Very few hotel workers living in Seattle reported *ever* using unemployment benefits or other government programs to get through hard times. Instead, the two major coping strategies employed by out-of-work employees were quickly finding other work—even if it was not well-paid or secure—or relying on personal and family resources.

Only a few Seattle hotel employees discussed receiving unemployment benefits at any time in their past. It was not a fond memory.[16] Kevin Johnson, a twenty-eight-year-old from Tennessee who works in the Engineering Department of the Globe Hotel Seattle, was formally employed at a major soda company factory. Only a few months after relocating from Washington state to Indiana to work at the factory, he received the dreaded pink slip—he had been laid off. For three months, he received $300 per week, or $1,200 per month, from the Washington state unemployment system—he had not switched his residency—but even though his earnings at the factory translated into higher unemployment benefits than he could have received based on his hotel earnings, he still had a hard time making ends meet.

I had [been] looking for a job [unsuccessfully] . . . and was like well, "we have to get out of here because, we can't keep doing this." So we were just going to move back [to Washington state], job or no job.

And then we got screwed on that too, because we had to break our lease [to move] and they [the landlord] said [we] couldn't. I said "You know, look dude, I don't have a job anymore, I can't pay the rent." But, he's like, "I'm sorry, I don't care. You have to pay out the rest of your, you have to pay three [expletive] months, you have to pay $650 per month for three months, I don't care if you're living here or not."

Fortunately, Kevin Johnson's in-laws came to the rescue and loaned him the money to pay the landlord off. Many hotel workers described occasions when they had relied on family resources to save them from financial crises.

Kay Chiang, a thirty-eight-year-old immigrant from Guangdong, China, works as a coffee service attendant at the Globe Hotel Seattle. She discussed temporarily receiving unemployment benefits after being laid off from a former job. When Kay Chiang immigrated to Seattle fifteen years ago, her family shared crowded accommodation with her husband Ming Chiang's relatives for five years. She got her first job at the Mountain garment factory, while Ming Chiang worked in the kitchen of a Chinese food restaurant. After five years, the Mountain garment factory shut down and the employer arranged for the employees to receive unemployment insurance benefits. In Kay Chiang's case, she received about 50 percent of her salary for six months. During this period, Kay Chiang reported she "spend less." "You know, [I] has yard, so [I] plant some veggies. A while back, [we] even have a chicken. So poultry." She found it very difficult to find another job searching the want ads; fortunately, her friend Julie Chu recommended her for a job at the Globe Hotel Seattle.

Herbert Michaels is an on-call banquet server at the Globe Hotel Seattle as well as several other downtown Seattle hotels. He was one of the few Seattle hotel employees to report temporarily using unemployment insurance benefits. He received unemployment benefits for brief periods four times in the past few years, receiving an average of only $150 per week. He could survive on this amount only because he did not have to pay rent for his basement apartment, which is in a house owned by a friend.

Government-Paid Education and Training

Many hotel employees in Vancouver—particularly ethnic minority immigrants—benefited from training programs paid for by the government while they received unemployment benefits. These employees reported frequently finding their first jobs in Canada through social networks, often as seamstresses in garment factories, maids cleaning homes, nannies, pieceworkers, or servers in ethnic restaurants. Although many had a post–secondary school education and/or professional training and work experience in their home country, their poor English language skills and the lack of recognition of their foreign credentials limited their job opportunities. After working in these very low-wage jobs for some time, many found themselves unemployed or laid off due to economic downturns. While they collected unemployment benefits and looked for work, government programs paid for their training and/or certificate programs, often in the hospitality industry. During the internship portion of these programs, many of them ended up securing their first hotel jobs.

Joyce Lee, a forty-three-year-old immigrant from Hong Kong, used the training to move up from unstable and poorly paid jobs in food service to secure employment as a room attendant at the Globe Hotel Vancouver: "Oh, the first time, I only [found a job] in a restaurant. For the waitress. And then after waitress, I go some job, this job is very short time, you know, like for selling the clothing. And then to do the bakery. Bakers is good. And then back to the restaurant. So again, and then after restaurant, I take the course the training course [for eight months], and then I go to the hotel." She found the job through an internship placement by the Vancouver Community College (VCC) hospitality program. Joyce Lee has worked at the Globe Hotel Vancouver for ten years. She is single and does not have any children. As her salary went up from $8 to $14.84 per hour, she managed to save quite a bit of money to help buy a four-bedroom house—with a two-bedroom apartment in the basement—that she shares with her brother's family. They recently paid off the mortgage.

Tse Leung, a fifty-four-year-old immigrant from Shanghai, China, and her sixty-year-old husband Liu Leung both took advantage of the government-provided English language courses and retraining. Liu Leung immigrated to Vancouver in 1989 and Tse Leung joined him with their two children one year later. After arriving, she took English classes, paid for by a government program for new immigrants, for six months while working part-time in the kitchens of a Chinese restaurant and a Japanese restaurant. She continued to work in the kitchen of one restaurant for three years until it closed. During this time, Tse Leung tried to pass the accounting certification exams (her previous profession) twice and failed because of her difficulty in reading technical English. So she was encouraged to take a hospitality-training course, and the government paid for her tuition while she received unemployment benefits for eight months. Liu Leung continued to work at a restaurant until he too lost his job. The government then paid for Liu Leung to take a Building Services certification course while he was receiving unemployment benefits. Although Tse Leung remembered those times as difficult ones, the unemployment insurance benefits were a critical safety net:

> Yeah, we always got EI because we want to find some job, that's why. So we always learn English in the night, it was difficult, yeah. . . . But we still pay for

everything. Because we don't buy some clothes, don't buy some [things]. Friends help us, giving [us a] bed or giving some things so I don't [have to] buy. Only buy food. We, want loan, [and to] make more money but [it's okay] because my kids never ask me for . . . buy shoes, the expensive things, they never ask for that.

In Seattle, immigrants took advantage of the free basic English as a Second Language courses offered by Seattle Central Community College (SCCC) (when there were places available). In both cities, these English courses only provided basic English language skills; in general, immigrants were on their own to acquire technical English or other advanced English language reading, writing, and speaking skills that would enable them to take advantage of their former work experience or training.

Supplemental Benefits for Families with Children in Vancouver

With the addition of the low-income family supplement, EI benefits compensated for a higher percentage of many of the employees' income than the standard 55 percent. This program recognizes that there are significant costs to raising children and so helps ease the potential hardships of unemployment for low-income parents experiencing temporary unemployment. Hernando Reys is a forty-seven-year-old immigrant from Quezon City in the Philippines. He joined his wife, Carla Reys, who immigrated to Vancouver by being sponsored through the live-in caregiver program. She said, "It was a big sacrifice. I had to go." As a result of program regulations of the caregiver program, she had to move to Vancouver alone and was separated from her husband and four children for two years. When I asked if she could have brought her children, she said, "No. It wasn't allowed by the government. I had to finish my two years program. Although I could go home every year, but still I couldn't sponsor them yet. So three years later, I applied as immigrant, together with them. That is the lawyer, said you should apply with your family. So it was approved." After long years apart, they had a happy reunion and Hernando Reys went looking for work. After only one week, he got his first job in Canada analyzing soil samples: "We are dealing with the soil samples from all over the country. So what we did is to put it in the separate conveyors and poured some chemicals, what will be the reaction there. Then we put it in the oven, what we call furnace, and heat it almost 45 minutes, and if it will be melt into liquid, and after that we will take it out, pour that in the one containers and let it dry, almost 25 minutes." He started at somewhere between $10 and $11 per hour and worked in this job for two years. When I asked why he left this position, he said, "Oh, because of my hand get burned." With four children to support — Eric, Julio, Anthony, and Maria — the Reys could have faced a major financial crisis, perhaps even losing the condominium they had purchased in Port-Moody, an inner-ring suburb of

Vancouver. After recovering from the burn, Hernando Reys received unemployment benefits for three months. As a low-income parent, he estimated that he received 75 percent of his previous weekly income as unemployment benefits during this period—20 percent more than the maximum replacement rate for a childless claimant. While receiving benefits, Hernando Reys took advantage of a government-subsidized training program in hospitality. The training program helped him secure a job at the Rose Hotel in Vancouver as a houseman. His supervisor at the Rose Hotel then moved to the Hotel Deluxe Vancouver when it opened (they are part of the same larger Rosemont hotel group). She hired Hernando to work as a houseman at the Hotel Deluxe Vancouver,[17] where he works full-time at $15 per hour and picks up occasional extra shifts at the Rose Hotel.

Unemployment Benefits and Training

In Vancouver, the interaction of the EI family supplement for low-wage workers and government-subsidized training programs helped many hotel workers to secure stable positions in the hotel industry. George Chan, a fifty-year-old immigrant from Fujian, China, arrived in Vancouver in 1998 with his wife Chi Yin and daughter Alice Chan. In China, he had managed a large department store.

> I was manager of a large department, because in China I work long time, many many year. In these many years, no any problem, so it is sure for me to work. But here, the language broken and less local [understanding] and no local [connections]. Certainly, no one is going to hire you as a manager. This a new country. It's a different culture, different language, that's a big problem. So much struggle and improved for many many years.
>
> At the beginning, when I arrived in Vancouver, because I don't have enough friends and I know little about the situation, so it was a little hard to find something [a good job]. Then I stay here for a long time, I have a lot of friends and I know how to get information about employment. I don't think it difficult to find job. I have job [at a bakery for $8 an hour]. But you, you have to find good job, high payment, it's hard. . . . Yeah, we just look for advertisement from newspaper, and try to find job. It's not easy.

When he was laid off from the bakery, George Chan received $880 per month from unemployment for one year, with the EI family supplement. His benefits from the EI insurance program were not much less than a full-time minimum-wage employee salary in Vancouver. During this time, George Chan completed a hospitality-industry training course at North Vancouver Community College in five months. While he finished the requirements to receive his hospitality certificate, the government paid for his tuition, books, and expenses. He began working as a houseman at Globe Hotel Vancouver about a year before, after a practicum through the program at a hotel near the Vancouver airport. His probation wage of $10.77 per hour increased after he completed his probation period and increased again with a 4.3 percent raise last April to his current wage of $14.77.[18]

In contrast to the experiences of workers in Vancouver, only one Seattle employee reported receiving government-subsidized training while collecting unemployment insurance benefits.[19]

Public-Assistance Benefits

Despite the focus of much poverty research on public assistance and welfare benefits, few hotel workers I interviewed in both Seattle and Vancouver reported temporarily receiving public assistance or social welfare benefits in the past. Elizabeth Hubar, a room attendant at the Hotel Deluxe Vancouver (whose unemployment experiences are discussed earlier in this chapter), arrived in Canada as a refugee. While waiting eight months after making her claim for a work permit, she survived because of "welfare and then I worked in the kitchen, in the kitchen [off the books]." She reported earning a "couple of hundred dollars a month [from welfare for] about five or seven months." Elizabeth Hubar said it was difficult to get welfare, "Yeah, you have to sign it every time and then they ask a lot of questions. Then once I get my permit, I got a job, exactly that time I got my job and then my husband got his job. . . . now it's okay." But living on welfare was very difficult, even earning some money on the side as a kitchen employee, especially because, "at that time, when I came here, you have to buy a lot of like [things], I didn't bring my furniture, so, [we had] nothing. . . . [It was] very hard."

Ivana Markov, a forty-three-year-old room attendant at the Hotel Deluxe Vancouver, was one of the few nonrefugee immigrants to temporarily receive social welfare benefits. She arrived from the Ukraine with her daughter two and a half years ago. One of her friends told her to apply for public assistance until she found work. She said she received $680 per month for two months from this program—surviving on her savings from Ukraine—until she found her job at the Hotel Deluxe Vancouver.

In Seattle, the small number of hotel workers who received public assistance in the past received only a small amount per month. Alma Meteko, an eighteen-year-old Somali refugee working full-time as a room attendant at the Globe Hotel Seattle while attending high school full-time, said she received "the welfare, two months only. . . . Yeah, $200 [per month]." Sumar Bonadu, a twenty-seven-year-old banquet houseman at the Globe Hotel Seattle, arrived in the United States with his aunt as a refugee in 1992 following the civil war in Somalia. He received $200 per month government support as public assistance for a couple of months. When I asked how he survived on so little, Sumar Bonadu replied, "We survived by getting together." Pooling resources for survival and to minimize hardship was a common theme among recently arrived ethnic minority refugees working in Seattle's hotel industry. Although Sumar Bonadu had owned a shop in Somalia, his first job in Seattle was as a driver at Sea-Tac Airport for $7 per hour, which he did for two years before starting work at the Globe Hotel Seattle five years ago. He does not earn much more as a base salary at the hotel—only $7.50 per hour and his last raise was only $0.25 two years ago. But the tips are better and work out to an extra $6.50 to $7.50 per hour by his estimate. Still, Sumar Bonadu supplements his Globe Hotel Seattle income by working on-call for twenty hours per week over his full-time job as a part-time banquet service worker at another multinational hotel chain in Seattle.

Other Policies That Matter

The importance of a broader conception of social welfare policies than simply unemployment benefits and public assistance emerged from the interviews. Several other policies in Vancouver act to create financial buffers to material hardship for hotel workers and their families. These include British Columbia labor policy codes mandating vacation pay for all employees, Workers' Compensation benefits (WCB), child tax credits and benefits, subsidized day-care programs, and the government-subsidized retirement savings programs.[20]

Mandatory Paid Vacation   Every employee in Vancouver is entitled to at least two weeks paid vacation after one year of employment under the British Columbia labor code.[21] Many of the hotel workers I interviewed in Vancouver had accumulated four or even five weeks paid vacation per year. Few hotel employees reported vacationing with their families in Hawaii or Disneyland during this period, although a handful have; paid vacation benefits act as a financial reserve that employees draw on, particularly during the hour cuts in the winter slow season.

Julie Lee, a forty-five-year-old laundry attendant at the Globe Hotel Vancouver, was born in Guangdong, China, and immigrated to Vancouver in 1988 with her forty-three-year-old husband Chung Lee and ten-year-old son Ernest Lee. When I asked why she came, she said, "I come, because I like the Canada is the freedom . . . and I think it's for my son in here, the school, they get the better." Her mother joined them in Vancouver in 1990, and she helped out with child care. "She used to watch after him when he was young." In China, Julie Lee was an accountant, but her and her husband's first jobs in Canada were as cloth cutters in a garment factory, earning between $7 and $8 per hour each. "Yeah. First jobs are very difficult. But now it's get the more money, it's okay."

Her husband, Chung Lee, continues to work at the factory and earns $1,500 per month by working lots of overtime. Ernest Lee is a twenty-year-old student majoring in electrical engineering at the University of British Columbia in Vancouver. He tutors relatives, friends, and even other hotel employees to earn some extra income for the household.

Julie Lee began working as a seamstress in the laundry department of the Globe Hotel Vancouver repairing ripped uniforms and other material. She is one of the few remaining staff in the Globe Hotel Vancouver's laundry department; most of the jobs have been outsourced. She began working at the hotel seven years ago, earning $10 per hour. Her hours vary from 20 to 40 hours per week, depending on the season. With regular wage increases, she currently earns $14.84 per hour. She waits to take her paid vacation until the yearly slow season, when it becomes difficult to get shifts. For employees faced with temporary lay-offs, vacation benefits provide a 100 percent replacement income during the mandated waiting period between filing for EI and beginning to receive benefits. Vacation pay also helps mitigate unexpected financial hardships. For example, during the month-long hotel strike in summer 1999, Hassam Mansour, a thirty-year-old immigrant from Cairo, Egypt, who works as a maintenance engineer at the Globe Hotel Vancouver, took his paid vacation in order to continue to receive a full salary during this period rather than just strike pay.

Paid vacation is not mandated by Washington state labor law. Although the hotels in Seattle do provide some paid vacation as part of their benefit packages, paid vacation days accrue more slowly than in Vancouver, even in the same job position for the same company. Generally, employees in Seattle had fewer vacation days than employees in Vancouver; recently hired employees had none. With fewer days, employees in Seattle did not report using paid vacation to make ends meet during difficult economic times.

Workers' Compensation Benefits Hotel work involved strenuous physical labor for many employees. Regular routines for room attendants, houseman, and laundry staff involve repetitive lifting and exposure to potentially dangerous chemicals. As Kendra Smith, a forty-three-year-old African-American laundry attendant at the Globe Hotel Seattle said, "So I don't want to be at the hotel for the next five years. It's not good for the body, standing on concrete all day. And I'm constantly hurting. You get tendonitis, you get carpel tunnel, bad back. So I don't want to do that. I'm too young to have a torn up body."

Injuries happen. Tara Wang, a forty-year-old immigrant from Guangdong, China, works as a room attendant at the Globe Hotel Vancouver. As a result of the repetitive physical strain making beds and cleaning rooms, she developed serious shoulder pain that made it very difficult to continue working. While she received rehabilitative physical therapy, the British Columbia Workers' Compensation Board program provided her with about $5,000 to compensate for lost wages over the six months her injuries limited her to working part-time. Several hotel employees reported experiencing on-the-job injuries—particularly to wrists and backs—in both Seattle and Vancouver.

Tara Wang was one of several hotel workers in Vancouver who described relying on WCB to prevent material hardship when injured on the job. Every employer in Vancouver contributes to a Workers' Compensation Board fund to ensure workers full salary protection in the event of an injury on the job. Julio Oracia, a fifty-four-year-old immigrant from the Philippines, works as a maintenance engineer at the Hotel Deluxe Vancouver. He received 100 percent of his income for six months while recovering from injuries sustained on the job.

George Chan, a houseman at the Globe Hotel Vancouver (whose experiences with unemployment insurance are discussed earlier in the chapter) has never received WCB. Yet the benefits prevented material hardship for his household when his wife was injured working at her job in a sewing factory. She received $2,000 per month (to make up for lost earnings) for three months while she recovered. George Chan told me that this money had been critical to the family's financial well-being during this time.

In Seattle, no hotel workers I interviewed reported receiving any kind of WCB for time lost due to injury on the job.

Supplemental Income Programs for Low-Income Parents   Parents face greater income needs than childless singles and couples because of the costs of raising children. Hotel employees with children in both Seattle and Vancouver qualified for programs that provide tax breaks and supplemental income for low-income parents.

Both the Canadian federal government and the British Columbia provincial government have several programs to help provide extra income to lower-income families: Canada's Child Tax Credit (CCTC), which provides a tax-free benefit for all families with children (the benefit level paid per child increases for each child under the age of seven); the National Child Benefit Supplement (NCBS) for children in low-income families; and provincial programs that supplement the CCTC program, the British Columbia Family Bonus and the British Columbia Earned Income Benefit. For a family living in British Columbia with two children under seven years of age and a combined pre-tax income of $20,000, the combined federal and provincial child benefits in 2003–2004 provided $563.40 per month, or nearly $7,000 annually—a 34 percent income supplement through the tax system (see table 6.2). Of course, the CCTC is reduced substantially for higher earnings.

For hotel employees with children, these child benefit programs provided a

Table 6.2 Vancouver estimated child tax benefits for two-parent family[a] (CA$)

Benefit program	Monthly amount	Annual total
Basic amount	233.50	2,802.00
National Child Benefit Supplement allowance	226.41	2,716.92
British Columbia Family Bonus amount	19.33	231.96
British Columbia Earned Income Benefit amount	84.16	1,009.92
Total	**563.40**	**6,760.80**

Source: Based on the Canadian federal government's website calculator (http://www.ccra-adrc.gc
.ca/dchmf/icbc-simn/SimnController).
[a]With two children under 7; annual income of $20,000.

major supplement to their annual income. Mark Heung, an ethnic Chinese immigrant from Vietnam, works as a houseman at the Globe Hotel Vancouver. He has two young children and estimated that he received approximately $3,000 back from his taxes the previous year because of these child tax programs. Hassam Mansour, a maintenance engineer at the Globe Hotel Vancouver, also has two children: four-year-old Ahmed and five-year-old Lily. He said that his family received $420 per month through the CCTC programs.

In the United States, Child Tax Benefit program and the Earned Income Tax Credit (EITC) together are analogous to Canada's family tax credit programs. The U.S. Child Tax Benefit provides an annual flat per-child tax credit, currently $600 per child, phased out for single tax filers beginning at $75,000 and for married filers at $110,000. Created in 1998, this program was reformed to make it "partially refundable," meaning that it could provide some supplemental income—beyond taxes paid—for low-income households with earnings over $10,350 in 2002.[22] The U.S. EITC program provides refundable tax credits to lower-income earners who file. Although the program provides some tax relief for single filers who earn less than $11,000 a year, it is designed to provide the majority of benefits to low-income workers with children. Most of the hotel employees with children in Seattle qualified for EITC and received benefits from the program.[23]

Although twelve U.S. states have implemented a supplemental EITC program (similar to the British Columbia supplements to CCTC), Washington state is *not* one of them.[24] In Washington state, a two-parent family with two children under seven years of age and an income of $20,000 would receive a $2,550.71 income supplement from the U.S. EITC program (see table 6.3). The family also would receive a $1,200 tax credit through the U.S. Child Tax Benefit program, so the subsidy could be as much as $3,750.71. As described previously (see table 6.2), the combination of Canadian federal and provincial income support programs in Vancouver equals $6,760.80 per year for a family with the same characteristics—*nearly double.*

Table 6.3 Seattle estimated child tax benefits for two-parent family[a] (US$)

Benefit program	Annual amount
U.S. Earned Income Tax Credit program	2,550.71[b]
U.S. Child Tax Benefit program	1,200.00
Total (annual)	**3,750.71**

[a]With two children under 7; annual income of $20,000.
[b]EITC supplement (based on 2001 data) calculated using a web-based calculator (http://www.connect2jobs.org/connect2cash/#) for a two-parent household with two children and precisely one full-time earner making $9.62 per hour, or $20,009.60 gross (pre-tax) household income.

Whereas most parents in Vancouver reported that they received the Canadian Child Tax Credit—and how much—the case in Seattle with U.S. EITC and Child Tax Benefit was different. Only one employee interviewed in Seattle explicitly reported receiving income from this program. Susanna Frulio, an immigrant from the Philippines who works as a house attendant for the Hotel Deluxe Seattle and has five children (but only three under the age of eighteen), estimated that her family received $3,500 in annual income from the EITC program. Although many hotel workers with children did receive income support from the EITC program, they largely did not know about or acknowledge the help of this program in their interviews.

Because the U.S. EITC program, in particular, targets low-income families, perhaps there is some stigma in the United States associated with its receipt. Or, given the complexity of the U.S. tax system, perhaps many low-income workers simply did not understand why or what program determines the size of their tax refund and hence did not identify the EITC program as a source of income, even though it supplemented their income. The higher levels of subsidy clearly helped hotel workers with children in Vancouver. Supplemental income programs are an extremely economically efficient way for a government to raise the income of the working poor above the poverty line. By putting income into the hands of low-income parents—who need it the most—these programs help counter the impact of the growing number of poverty-wage jobs in the service sector.

Day-Care Subsidies Formal child-care programs are expensive and out of reach for working-poor parents. Most workers relied on family members and other relatives to take care of children. But, for some, government subsidized child-care programs were crucial. Public child-care and early education programs are not very strong in British Columbia or Washington state, particularly when considered in comparison with the $7 per day programs currently

offered by the province of Quebec or the comprehensive early education programs provided universally in many Scandinavian countries. Yet subsidies to
low-income parents for private and nonprofit day-care programs did make a
major difference for some hotel workers. Marianne Lakon, a room attendant at
the Hotel Deluxe Vancouver, described the critical role of government-subsidized day care for her family's well-being:

> You turn to the Yellow Pages and I called daycare, because they [said this] day-
> care is really good. It's a good daycare, and it's convenient and I said, "I can't af-
> ford $650 per month, but I want my child in this daycare, how, what do I do?"
>
> And they said you can apply for daycare subsidy, so they gave me the forms
> and I brought them there. And then they called me and they said, they want to
> show, they want me to show my income, so I put my paycheck. . . . [The] day-
> care is [normally] $650 [per month], but I pay $120 [per month]. . . .
>
> And he [my son] stayed there [at that daycare program] for about three years
> [nearly every day]. . . . Yeah, because I worked seven days a week.

Marcus, her son, continues to go to a babysitter near their house after school,
for only $10 per day, also subsidized by the government. "It's the most we can
afford," Marianne Lakon told me.

Vincente Moreno, an immigrant from the Philippines who works as a maintenance engineer at the Globe Hotel Vancouver, also benefited from the subsidized child-care program. "[My son] used to go to daycare after school. . . .
[The daycare] was very good. Yeah. . . . We paid a small percentage [and the
government paid the rest]." Although most hotel workers with children used
their own personal networks for child care in both Seattle and Vancouver, the
availability of government-subsidized day-care programs in Vancouver proved
essential for some low-wage hotel employees.

Subsidized day care exists in Washington state through both state and city
government programs. Only one hotel employee interviewed in Seattle reported using a subsidized child-care program. Susanna Frulio, a house attendant at the Hotel Deluxe Seattle, reported that her five-year-old daughter Thia
received day care for free. She was also the only Seattle employee interviewed
who reported having his or her child in a formal day-care program at the time
of the interview.

Relying on relatives for child care can have consequences—exchange relations require reciprocation—and the consequences can undermine the long-
term capital accumulation among low-income families, as described by Carol
Stack in *All Our Kin*.[25] Kendra Smith, an African-American woman who works
in the Laundry Department of the Hotel Deluxe Seattle, was fortunate to get
Section 8 housing assistance while she was a lone parent so that she could move
out of a public housing project and into a house. Even with the subsidy, she had

to supplement her income working second jobs and odd jobs through the slow winter season when she was laid off for three months. "I moved into the house, and I was there for thirteen years, and I was on housing, Section 8. It was all Section 8, so the rent wasn't that much, but then in this, when you work for a hotel, wintertime comes and then, I didn't work for three months. Yeah, so slow and I was low seniority, so it was like, you have to have that mind to stash this money, stash that, and then you do odds and ends jobs." Despite having a formal job, she could not afford to pay for day care at the time, so she relied on her sister and watched her sister's children in return.

> If I wasn't working, then my sister was and I'd watch her kids and she'd pay me, so it worked out. And none of our kids have ever been in daycare. It was all family members either watching, and always watching them. You just can't put your kids in daycare. Too expensive! One child was $600 a month. $600 is more than my paycheck. That's [laughs], more than my paycheck, and groceries, and if you made a certain amount of money, then you didn't qualify for food stamps or any of that stuff and I was a single parent. It was hard. But it was a learning experience, and I think it taught my kids a lot too, to become independent. They need to get their education, they need to keep a steady job.

Although relatives and family members provided most of the care for younger children, the universal public education system provided most of the child care for older children in both cities.

Government-Subsidized Retirement Savings Programs   Both the United States and Canada have similar government-subsidized savings programs to provide a tax incentive for workers to save money for their own retirement. The primary program in Canada is the Registered Retirement Savings Plan (RRSP) program; in the United States the analogous program is known as the Individual Retirement Account (IRA) 401k. Although the program rules are quite similar, there are some differences, including a 10 percent penalty on withdrawals from the IRA 401k if the holder is younger than fifty-nine and a half compared to no penalty in Canada for early withdraws from RRSPs (although the money withdrawn is taxed as income for that year). In fact, a special government program, the RRSP Home Buyers Plan, allows single Canadians to withdraw up to $20,000 and common-law or married couples $40,000 *tax-free* from their RRSPs to purchase or build a first home.[26] Overall, more Vancouver hotel employees interviewed reported having retirement savings than Seattle employees (76 percent compared to 52 percent), and those Vancouver employees had had more savings: CA$17,846 compared to US$9,793.

Several hotel employees who had experienced unexpected financial difficulties in Vancouver described cashing out or drawing on their RRSP when they needed to make ends meet. Anjana Shiva, a thirty-six-year-old immigrant from India who is a room attendant at the Hotel Deluxe Vancouver, had used her RRSP savings after she and her husband, Rajiv Shiva, were injured in a car accident. "[My husband] has taken a year training, appliance repair. But he still has his back problems, he can't do this job. . . . Yeah, so he is left with the choice [but to work], with no choice. We have to pay the bills and we have to live somewhere." The lost income and expenses from the injuries sustained in this accident left Anjana Shiva and her husband in a very precarious position: "I did not have any disability [benefits]. I was more on living on my credit card. And all my savings went, you know, all my RRSPs. I had about $15,000 RRSP, but I had to cash it." With that money, they were able to buy food, but they still could not make their monthly house payments.

> No, I was pretty behind in the payments thing. I kept on telling the bank and all that, nothing much I can do. And I kept on giving them doctor's notes and things. I'm not faking it. It's just my health does not allow me to work. It's not that I don't want to work, or I can't find a job. It's just my health is not allowing me. We worked hard on our back. We went to physiotherapy; we went to the Canadian Back [Association]. So, then slowly I started a security job, easy job, and I was getting a lot of hours in security. I was putting about 100 hours, every two weeks.

They also relied on family members for loans: "Yeah, a lot of times. I had to borrow money from my friends, my family. I owe my brother about another $10,000. But it's okay, I mean. I'm paying them off, slowly. . . . Oh it is really difficult." Thus, the family made it through this difficult period by drawing on their RRSP.

For those who do not need to tap their RRSP, the savings act as a pool of funds that can be used to increase financial security through equity. Hotel workers (on occasion) were able to accumulate enough savings in their RRSP accounts to purchase their own home. Marianne Lakon, an immigrant from the Philippines, works as a room attendant at the Hotel Deluxe Vancouver. She worked several jobs simultaneously in order to save most of the money required for a down payment on a home:

> And you know what I did? In the Lexicon Executive hotel we keep our tips, and I had my own [long-term stay suite to clean]. It's a Japanese [man staying there], so in one week, I got $400. You won't believe me, in one day I got more than $30 a day [in tips]. That's a lot of money. That's a lot of money. . . . because in my floor, [the guests are] *very* rich. . . . And you know what I did, I worked two jobs, on my day off, I cleaned houses.

She worked as a room attendant at both the Lexicon Executive hotel and the Hotel Deluxe Vancouver for one year. "But [before] the Hotel Deluxe Vancouver [was built], I work at the Lexicon Executive hotel, and then I work as house cleaning ten hours a day. And I have so many tips. . . . I save money, my one paycheck goes to my, I call it my secret account. Yeah, secret account from expenses account. So that's the way I save. So that's the way I save money for the down payment." When I asked how much she saved this way, Marianne Lakon replied, "Because I put only 5 percent [through the] first homebuyer [program], $14,500, including lawyers and everything. Then [the total was] $17,000. . . . I borrowed a few bucks to my friend and I withdraw my $4,000 of [my] RRSP. . . ." Although it was tough financially at first, they now rent out the apartment in the basement to a family friend, which has made the house easier to afford—a common strategy for homeowners in Vancouver's expensive real estate market.

Survival Strategies

Relying on Personal Resources: Turning to Family and Friends for Help

Hotel workers in Seattle turned to personal and family resources in order to prevent major material hardships much more frequently than in Vancouver. The most common strategies included borrowing money from relatives and friends, living with extended family (especially for immigrants who have arrived recently), and using savings from the country of origin. It is difficult to determine how much the low use of public benefits by hotel workers in Seattle is due to a lack of information about the benefits, restrictions on or the low levels of benefits, or the social stigma of receiving government assistance. Yet the combination of low wages at work and minimal government support pressures these employees and their families to creatively cope to make ends meet, sometimes with deleterious long-term consequences.

Turning to Family in Vancouver   Despite the stronger government safety net in Vancouver, compared to Seattle, hotel workers who fell on hard times economically reported relying on family resources. Hassam Mansour, a maintenance engineer at the Globe Hotel Vancouver described his financial hardship when the hotel employees were on strike during the summer. After using up his vacation pay, he turned to a variety of sources, including borrowing from his wife's family in Egypt to make ends meet. His family's electricity was cut off, "and then I had to go and borrow money and pay it." When I asked where he had gone for money, he told me, "MoneyMart . . . I pay $20 on top of that $300." When their phone service was cut off, he also borrowed money: "Yes. But not from MoneyMart, from friends." They also made several late payments on their credit card and could not afford to pay rent for several months. The apartment building supervisor allowed him to complete pro-bono maintenance jobs for the apartment complex in exchange for not being sanctioned or evicted for deferring several months rent to the following year. He reported that his in-laws provided $5,000 or so in support every few months to help them.

Beth Kay, a fifty-three-year-old room attendant at the Globe Hotel Vancouver, grew up in Honduras. In the past, Beth Kay had to rely on family resources to get through hard times: "In the early [19]90s, when it was the time I separate from my husband. And I don't have enough hours at the hotel. Just made it, but made it. . . . What did I have to do? I just go to the bank and tell them I be late. . . . [It happened] maybe three times." She almost had her electricity cut off: "I received the notice. And then, tried to get money from line of credit and then they pay until you get the paycheck." There were times when Beth Kay could not make the minimum payments on her credit cards and line of credit. "Well, I ask my daughter, to borrow [money] from my daughter. . . . But I paid them back."

Kathy Wan, a forty-six-year-old immigrant from Hong Kong who works as a room attendant at the Globe Hotel Vancouver, reported a frequent consequence of major financial hardship: having to move in with relatives. After the birth of their first child, her husband was unemployed for two years and he received only $400 per month as unemployment benefits. But they did not experience hardship "because I live [with] my mother-in-law, we don't need to pay for rent. Only pay the bills, you know, for telephone, cable, things like that." Kathy Wan's husband began working again, and their mother-in-law currently looks after the children in exchange for living with them and food.

Many immigrants described living with relatives when they first arrived. Julio Oracia, a maintenance engineer at the Hotel Deluxe Vancouver, arrived from the Philippines with his whole family and lived "with a friend, who adopted us." While they lived at that apartment, he worked as a security guard:

> Then my wife worked [as a] nursing temporary while she was taking her review, until she passed the examination for nursing. Then she got a full time job. . . . [I started taking courses] because security is paying only $5.50 per hour. Which is very tough for us. I have two children to raise too. Something to rent, and something to pay for the car loan, so I have to do something you know. To study, try to struggle harder, so we will have a more high paying job.

Alfred Domingo, a twenty-nine-year-old houseman at the Hotel Deluxe Vancouver who emigrated from the Philippines, lived with his father at his sister's townhouse for six years after arriving in Canada. During that time, he managed to save up enough to rent an apartment after his wife joined him in Vancouver.

Despite the stronger safety net and social programs in Vancouver, several hotel employees still had to turn to extended family and even friends for help. Overall, more hotel workers in Vancouver could afford to live in independent households, without relying on extended family.

Turning to Family in Seattle More employees interviewed in Seattle reported borrowing money occasionally from others in their social networks, to pay the rent or outstanding bills in times of crisis. Dan Rogers, a single white man in his early thirties who is a concierge at the Globe Hotel Seattle, described some of his hard financial times:

> The worst thing is not having enough money to eat. The hotel provides [free] meals, so it was like [I would] eat twice before you go home. Have your lunch and then eat again before you leave. That was the worst thing. . . .
>
> I also had someone living [sharing my room] with me at the time. So it helped. So it [the rent] was split into thirds [in a two-bedroom apartment] that way, instead of just in half, so that cut back on it. . . . There were points when I had to borrow a little bit of money to pay rent. And then make it up on the next check when it wasn't the rent check.

During difficult financial times in the past, Dan Rogers borrowed money, "from friends, and from family" to make ends meet and to avoid having his phone service and electricity turned off.

More than twice the percentage of employees interviewed in Seattle lived with their parents or extended family members, compared to those in Vancouver. Some younger single workers in both Seattle and Vancouver lived at home with their parents, but many more in Seattle who were married with children also lived with extended family members to make ends meet—almost 40 percent of the employees at the non-unionized Globe Hotel Seattle, a clear consequence of their low hourly wages.[27]

Many recent immigrants to Seattle reported living with extended family members for several years after they first arrived before they could move out on their own. Two relatively large families reported sharing a house built for one family. Lan Zhang and her sister-in-law Hue Chung arrived in the summer of 2001 from China. They both work as room attendants at the Globe Hotel Seattle. They and their families—their husbands (both food-service employees at the same Chinese restaurant) and three children each—share a house, including the sleeping space. Both Hue Chung and Lan Zhang were interviewed separately on different occasions; both said they wished their family could move out on their own as soon as possible.

Kevin Johnson, a twenty-eight-year-old white man who works as a maintenance engineer at the Globe Hotel Seattle, described how his family moved in with extended family members in times of financial hardship. They rented a house near his wife's sister and closer to Seattle for $1,200 per month. While trying to start her business, his wife earned a little extra money providing child care for her sister's two children. But then the financial strain of the failed small-business venture forced them to move in with his in-laws: "we were in a bind. So that was the crisis that her folks let us, we came in there. Actually we lived with her sister for awhile. . . ." They clean up the house in lieu of paying rent: "Then basically we worked on helping them get everything cleaned up. . . . basically we had to clean out a lot of junk and do all that stuff."

Some younger employees at the hotel who did not live at home with parents also reported sharing housing to make ends meet. For example, Alma Meteko, an eighteen-year-old Somali refugee who is a room attendant at the Globe Hotel Seattle, shares a bedroom in an apartment with her older sister, Sofie Meteko, also a room attendant at the Globe Hotel Seattle. "I don't like get along with my dad [who "cleans toilets" as a janitor at Sea-Tac Airport]. I see him regular[ly], every weekend. . . . [I share a two-bedroom apartment] with my brother and my cousin [who both work as van drivers at Sea-Tac Airport] and my sister also." She goes straight from high school to working a 3 p.m.–11 p.m. shift cleaning rooms at the hotel. When I asked her when she managed to do her homework, she replied, "I skip first period. I finish my homework and then I take fifth period then I came here [to the hotel]."

As a third strategy, recent immigrants often used personal savings from their country of origin when they did not earn enough from their jobs. Jennifer Shih, a room attendant at the Globe Hotel Seattle who emigrated from Taiwan to Seattle with her husband and three children, faces reduced hours in the wintertime. She said she planned to use her savings to cope financially. She is anxious about the upcoming slow season, "[I] would like to find a part-time job. Otherwise [we] might not have money to pay the rent. Yeah, [I] will be worried, if there is no income or no job."

Working More than One Job to Make Ends Meet

Working multiple jobs simultaneously is a strategy used in Seattle and Vancouver to cope with low pay and economic downturns. In both cities, workers who need more income turn to second and odd jobs to make ends meet. More hotel employees interviewed in Seattle reported working more than one job in order to make ends meet than in Vancouver.

Hotel employees in both cities reported working either a second formal job or odd jobs: 39 percent in Vancouver and 49 percent in Seattle. Odd jobs included handyman jobs, babysitting, and occasional house cleaning. Most second jobs were formal part-time positions at another hotel; other second jobs included cleaning jobs, newspaper assembly, parking garage attendant, and school cafeteria employee. Seattle employees were more likely to be working a second formal job (44 percent, compared to only 21 percent of employees in Vancouver), whereas Vancouver employees were more likely to be working odd jobs. However, half of the non-union Globe Hotel Seattle employees interviewed worked at least one second formal job.

One indicator that the hotel employees in Vancouver endured less material hardship than in Seattle is that they reported somewhat higher personal annual income from all sources.[28] The difference is magnified in the employees' average reported household income from all sources: CA$46,555 in Vancouver compared to US$35,800 in Seattle.

Hotel employees in Vancouver were better protected from material hardship during difficult economic times by social welfare policy than were their counterparts in Seattle. Vancouver residents had easier access to more generous employment benefits. For hotel industry employees, public-assistance programs mattered much less than unemployment benefits for preventing hardship during economic downturns. The differences in strategies used by hotel employees to cope with economic downturns reveal the important role of easily accessible and generous government programs to protect working-poor families.

In Vancouver, many immigrants benefited from a government program that paid tuition and expenses for them to attend hospitality-industry training programs while receiving unemployment benefits. These programs provided a hand up for many recently arrived immigrants. Subsidized day care also helped some employees successfully combine work and family responsibility. Other government programs and the Canadian and British Columbia labor codes indirectly helped buffer hotel employees in Vancouver against the material hardship by encouraging savings through tax-subsidized RRSPs, mandating paid vacation, and maternity leave. The universal child tax benefit and low-income supplements from the Canadian and British Columbia governments also provided critical income for working parents with children.

Hotel employees in Seattle largely did not access government support or programs during tough times, even when comparable programs existed; they relied almost exclusively on other kinds of strategies to cope. These strategies included sharing housing with extended family and borrowing money from relatives and friends. More employees in Seattle than Vancouver also reported working at multiple jobs simultaneously in order to make ends meet, although this was a necessity for many in both cities. Overall, government social welfare programs provided a stronger social safety net for the working poor and their families in Vancouver than in Seattle, protecting them from some of the deleterious consequences of material hardship and economic downturns.

As advanced industrialized countries have experienced macro-level economic and social transformations, including the shift toward service-sector-dominated economies, changes to social welfare policies have mitigated and/or exacerbated the impact of these transitions on poverty, inequality, and the lived experiences of low-income workers and their families. For example, expansions in the United States and Canada of programs and policies supplementing the income of working-poor parents have helped prevent hardship. The next chapter discusses broader policies, such as public infrastructure investments, that can also help stem the deleterious consequences of growing income inequality.

CHAPTER 7

Public Investment and City-Level Differences

Social policy is not just about wages, job protection, health care, and social welfare benefits. It is also about public investment in quality of life. The previous chapters explore how policy differences directly impact individuals and their families. In this chapter, I explain how higher levels of public investment in high-quality public transit, parks and community recreation, urban redevelopment, and neighborhood institutions improve the quality of life of hotel employees in Vancouver compared to Seattle. These differences are maximized for the ethnic minority immigrant hotel employees with children who live in ethnically diverse neighborhoods close to downtown business districts.

Policy Differences and Quality of Life

Employees in Vancouver were, in general, more positive about their neighborhoods than were employees in Seattle. The higher hourly wages paid to hotel employees in Vancouver allow them to live in relatively better neighborhoods than do similar employees in Seattle. Yet the difference also has to do with the greater government support for the institutions and infrastructure in the neighborhoods where the ethnic minority, immigrant, working poor live in Vancouver. These neighborhoods often more closely resembled middle-class neighborhoods in terms of quality of life and density of community institutions than did those in Seattle.

Sociologists have begun to rediscover the importance of community institutions, public infrastructure, and neighborhood quality. In *When Work Disappears*,[1] William Julius Wilson describes the devastating impact of the lack of community institutions and infrastructure on high-poverty urban neighborhoods. Elijah Anderson's *Streetwise*[2] also describes the dynamics of street life created by urban infrastructure abandonment and racial segregation. In the United States, federal government cuts, combined with the flight of jobs and tax-paying families to the suburbs, dramatically reduced the financial resources of cities, whose urban public infrastructure began a long and steady decline.[3]

Cities had to fund public education and essential city services for a higher needs population with lower per-capita resources. Maintaining the crumbling schools and roads consumed an ever-increasing portion of city coffers and little was left for large public projects unless they were funded by state or federal governments.

There has also been increasing concern in the sociological literature about segmented assimilation, as described in Alejandro Portes and Rubén G. Rumbaut in *Immigrant America* and *Legacies*.[4] Evidence from the literature suggests that some of this concern about the eventual structural assimilation of recently arrived immigrant groups in the United States is warranted. The interactive effect of cumulative disadvantages, due to changes in the labor market and social welfare institutions, may create barriers for recently arrived minority immigrant groups with low skill levels that prevent them from structurally assimilating into the U.S. middle class over the next few generations.[5] Downward structural assimilation could potentially have serious consequences for the patterns and process of incorporation of these groups as well as for the health of U.S. cities and democracy.

Comparing the cases of Seattle and Vancouver from the perspective of hotel employees, we can see the role of public investment differences in shaping the city, community, and neighborhood milieu. A greater inequality exists between the services and programs offered in lower-income neighborhoods and wealthier areas in Seattle than in Vancouver, affecting neighborhood quality, an issue that has, thus far, been largely absent from our discussion. City-level public investment differences include the quality of pubic transit and free or low-cost recreational opportunities (such as parks). National-level investment differences include urban redevelopment.

The Public Transit Difference

The benefits of high-quality public transit are social as well as environmental. Public transit matters particularly for the working poor because of the high cost of owning an automobile and using it for commuting. For those who cannot afford the high cost of a car or are unable to drive, public transportation reduces geographic isolation and the sense of exclusion, as well as facilitating job hunting.[6] Approximately 50 percent of the employees I interviewed in both Seattle and Vancouver commuted primarily by public transportation—approximately 15 percent rode a bike or walked to work. High-quality public transit into the inner-ring suburbs and beyond can shape regional development to reduce sprawl by creating new transit hubs rather than isolated single-family-home bedroom communities. With an extensive regional public transit system, lower-income workers can afford to live in a greater variety of neighborhoods in and around the city.

High-quality public transit also reduces concentrations of poverty and increases housing options for working-poor families. It also allows a greater diversity of people, including young people and seniors, to travel to and from downtown—increasing the vitality of the downtown core even during the evenings and weekends. At the same time, public transit reduces pollution, greenhouse gas emissions, and the deleterious impact of urban development on the environment.

Seattle, it must be noted, is among the better cities in the United States in terms of public transit. An extensive bus system connects people to downtown from the suburbs all around the city, earning Washington Metropolitan Transit System one of the Outstanding Public Transit System Awards from the American Public Transit Association in 1987 and 1997 (British Columbia Transit was one of the recipients in 1995).[7] The free-ride zone in the downtown Seattle Core Business District (CBD) encourages tourists, business people, and residents to leave their car parked and take the bus through the downtown core. Express buses quickly connect downtown to the University District and other major neighborhoods and other centers around downtown.

Despite its earlier start with a monorail system, Seattle failed to create a viable public rail-based transit system. Public transit use declined in Seattle after World War II, from 130 million passengers in the mid-1940s to 30 million in the mid-1960s.[8] In 1962, Seattle built an elevated Alweg monorail train for the 1962 Expo/Seattle World's Fair, Century 21 Exposition, and the famous Seattle Space Needle. "The Monorail was supposed to be the beginning of a new transit system focused on downtown and capable of bringing workers and shoppers to the CBD more easily. But the Monorail was not expanded beyond the original one-mile stretch. Today it strikes one more as a quaint relic from an earlier time than as the basis for tomorrow's mass-transit system."[9] Monorail expansion plans were rejected in a city referendum in 1970.[10] The Alweg Monorail continues its 1.2 mile (almost 2 kilometer) one-stop journey through downtown, connecting people from the Westlake Center mall to the Space Needle and Seattle Center as others walk below it.

Although Vancouver experienced a similar post–World War II decline in transit use, the government chose a different path in the 1970s, and construction began on a urban rail-based public transit system, technically termed an Advanced Light Rapid Transit (ALRT), in 1981.[11] Opening with the 1986 Expo, A World in Motion, A World in Touch, the SkyTrain connected the Canada Pavilion (now Canada Place) to the Expo Center (now Science World) in the International Fair/Yaletown District and continued on to the edge city of New Westminster. Although the SkyTrain is not technically a monorail because it runs on two tracks, it shares the look and feel of a monorail and gains power from a third rail down the middle of its tracks.[12]

The SkyTrain runs underground between its four stops in the downtown core and continues above ground, southeast along the corridor where many ethnic minority immigrants live for the rest of the fourteen-mile (twenty-eight-kilometer) trip into the suburbs, with over twenty additional stops. It is fully integrated into the regional bus systems, allowing for free transfers within a 1.5-hour time period, in any direction.[13] At the last stop in downtown, Waterfront Station, SkyTrain passengers can switch over to the Seabus, which crosses over to the Lonsdale Quay on the North Shore and links to the North and West Vancouver bus systems. From the Waterfront Station, commuters can take the West Coast Express commuter train during rush hour to Port Moody and other suburban cities in the Fraser Valley east of Vancouver. In the 1990s, the SkyTrain was extended again, eastward, into a new set of suburbs, with the goal of shaping suburban growth into limited areas clustered around the stations.[14] In 2002, a new line opened—effectively shaping part of the current line into a large loop—and future growth is planned, including a Richmond-Airport-Vancouver (RAV) line connecting the airport to downtown for the 2010 Olympics. Currently, service runs every three to five minutes. Although constructing the SkyTrain in Vancouver required massive public investment, many middle-class commuters who would not take a bus would commute by rail-based transit—subway, streetcar, ALRT, light rail, or commuter train (especially when they look out the window at the rush-hour gridlock below). Approximately 50 percent of the Vancouver hotel employees interviewed who commuted using public transportation reported riding the SkyTrain to and from work.

Highway Systems

Vancouver is one of the few large North American urban centers *without* a large highway slicing through the center of the city. Plans for a major highway through the heart of Vancouver in the 1950s were scuttled only as a result of the political organizing and action on the part of a large group of activists, including many of the Chinese residents of the Strathcona community.[15]

Seattle, on the other hand, has a major interstate highway dividing the city and isolating its residential communities from one another and from the downtown core. A second smaller elevated highway slices between the downtown core and the wonderful waterfront piers with ferry terminals, aquarium, shops, and boats. The noise and pollution of this second highway takes away from the serenity of what could be one of the most beautiful public areas in Seattle.[16] It also creates large underbridge areas, abandoned urban spaces generally used for parked cars and marked with disrepair and strewn trash.

These two highways through downtown directly and indirectly reduce the quality of residential life for many living in Seattle. The emissions and noise pollution impact many who live near a highway. At the same time, the highways cut off and isolate the various neighborhoods. The area southeast of the downtown core, where many of the employees I interviewed live, is physically isolated and cut off from the districts of west Seattle, the International District, Central District and the Southern Industrial District by the Interstate 5 (I-5) and I-90 highways, which in some cases are more than a city block wide.

The differences due to the highway systems also have implications for the health and vitality of the downtown core as well as the city tax base. The large highway through Seattle has accelerated suburban sprawl and contributes to the abandonment of the downtown core after dark.

Public Parks and Community Recreation Differences

Both Seattle and Vancouver have public parks, community centers, and public swimming pools. Yet significant differences exist in the quality of these public institutions, and these differences impact the quality of life for hotel employees. The working poor are often excluded by the high cost of privately owned recreation opportunities. For example, in 2000, a new 140,000-square foot Frank Gehry–designed Experience Music Project (EMP) museum opened at Seattle Center, largely with the support of Paul G. Allan (of Microsoft fortune) and his sister. Because one-day admission tickets cost $19.95 for adults and $14.95 for children over six years old, the museum is a prohibitively expensive experience for many low-income families. In a *Seattle Post-Intelligencer* article, reporter D. Parvaz estimates it would cost $218.68 for a family of four to visit the EMP museum for one day.[17] Even going to the movies was considered to be prohibitively expensive by many of the hotel employees with children. The quality and accessibility of free or low-cost public recreational opportunities matters more for low-income families than wealthier families.

As public policy, the city of Vancouver has focused on building and maintaining high-quality waterfront public promenades and parks. Vancouver is unique in North America in this way—the city explicitly protects public access to the waterfront as a matter of public policy. In contrast, although Seattle has substantial urban park space compared to many other U.S. cities, Seattle's parks are often very difficult to access, especially by public transportation. Seattle's parks also do not have family-friendly public amenities as the parks in Vancouver do.

These public infrastructure investments require sustained commitment and government spending. The first act of Vancouver's City Council in 1888 was to open the 1,000-acre Stanley Park immediately adjacent to the downtown core:

What the City of Vancouver has done with Stanley Park demonstrates the critical role of investment into infrastructure to maximize enjoyment of public resources. While it took nearly fifty years to complete in 1970, a 5.5 miles (8.55 km) public seawall was constructed all the way around the park (to prevent erosion) and allows for pedestrian, bicycle and rollerblading use around the circumference of the park.[18]

The seawall has public restrooms and small concession stands located throughout. Well-maintained natural trails cross the mostly undisturbed forest at the heart of this park. Stanley Park also has a golf course, lawn bowling, rose garden, children's farmyard, tennis courts, aquarium, children's train ride, and several restaurants. In total, the City of Vancouver's public policy of waterfront property acquisition has resulted in the city owning over half (58 percent) of the waterfront, with much of the space dedicated to public walks and parks.[19] Vancouver has developed a total of eleven miles (eighteen kilometers) of beaches around downtown. A person can walk for miles along waterfront paths, beginning in the downtown core, without crossing a street. Many of these parks have free tennis courts, beach volleyball courts, and modern playground equipment. They also have clean family changing and washroom facilities.

Seattle's major parks, such as Discovery Park, are located relatively far from downtown Seattle. Although it has some trails and playing fields, Discovery Park does not have many public facilities. The U.S. military maintains housing and occupies a major part of the 534-acre park.[20] A huge water-treatment plant blights the waterfront sections, as well. Overall, the majority of Seattle's parks are less than one acre. In many neighborhoods, the parks are simply empty lot-size squares with one or two benches.[21] It is important to note that visits to the park were rarely mentioned by hotel employees with children interviewed in Seattle, in sharp contrast to Vancouver. Indeed one Seattle hotel worker, Kendra Smith, talked about how she and her son enjoyed visiting Vancouver, where he could bike around Stanley Park.

In terms of public recreation amenities, Vancouver's city government also has an extensive network of extremely well-maintained public swimming pools, including nine indoor pools and six outdoor pools, many in beautiful waterfront locations. At Second Beach in Stanley Park, the large heated pool fills with families and children from all over the city at subsidized rates of $4 per visit for adults and less for children (there are cheaper rates for passes that can be used at any pool in the city). The public pool at Kitsilano (Kits) Beach is nearly three times the size of an Olympic-size swimming pool and overlooks the beach, waterfront, and mountains. For the colder months, Vancouver's downtown public Aquatic Center has an Olympic-size indoor swimming pool, whirlpools, sauna, and modern fitness room that cost less than $4 a visit. Some high schools also act as community centers open to the public with indoor swimming pools, tennis, and other recreational programming. Vancouver's

Parks and Recreation is also responsible for 150 playgrounds, 200 public tennis courts, 24 water/spray parks, and almost 400 sports fields. These public facilities are heavily used by all members of the public. "In 2004, more than 5 million visits were made to the Park Board's 23 community centres; swimming pool and ice rink admissions topped 2.3 million; nearly 4 million visits to the beaches were recorded; and nearly 350,000 rounds of golf and pitch & putt were played."[22] In addition, the Parks Board recorded 800,000 visits to the ice rink.

Vancouver's city government runs an extensive system of high-quality community centers. Whereas thousands of community centers have closed in U.S. cities, Vancouver continues to build, expand, and improve on their neighborhood community centers. As a universal program, they exist in both the wealthier and lower-income neighborhoods of the city, and most employees interviewed in Vancouver described having at least one center near their homes. These centers offer extensive recreational and educational programming as well as community meeting space and extensive recreational facilities. Most have a fitness center, with modern weights. Some have indoor ice rinks, and others feature indoor swimming pools. There are also Neighbourhood Houses, which provide a range of services, including day care and courses.

Seattle also offers quite a number of neighborhood services and public institutions. For example, Seattle has eight indoor pools and two outdoor public pools and as well as numerous spray areas for small children to play. Seattle also has a total of twenty-five community centers, located throughout the city.[23] Although these centers provide vital community services, there were fewer institutions in the neighborhoods where Seattle hotel employees with children lived compared to Vancouver. Whereas employees in Vancouver frequently mentioned using the resources of their nearby community centers, most employees in Seattle did not discuss them at all.

Urban Redevelopment Difference

In terms of public policy, Vancouver has put more effort into urban neighborhood redevelopment than Seattle during the past forty years. The federal, provincial, and city government have prioritized the redevelopment of declining industrial areas in and around the downtown core into dynamic residential communities. These redevelopment projects have focused on rebuilding vibrant, high-density mixed-use communities, with significant public institutions and dispersed subsidized housing units throughout.[24]

In Vancouver, Canadian federal government investment and planning helped create in 1970s Granville Island, a public marketplace with a food market, artisan shops, restaurants, art schools, studios, parks, a community center, day-care facilities, and a hotel. The declining industrial area around False Creek of Vancouver near Granville Island used to share many similarities to Lake

Union in Seattle. In the 1960s, "Both areas were about 2 square miles around, ringed by housing, boat yards, machine shops, and storage depots."[25] Despite major redevelopment plans, Seattle converted only a decrepit gas plant in the midst of this area into a small Gas Works public park; False Creek, in contrast, has been completely transformed into a well-planned, dense, urban community with housing, shops, marina, parks, waterfront promenade, community center, and public schools for 5,000 people.[26]

Vancouver's urban redevelopment projects also reduce sprawl and economic segregation. The policy of requiring affordable housing units in these redevelopment areas allow some of the working poor as well as public-assistance recipients to choose to live in Yaletown and False Creek. Mandating the inclusion of subsidized units throughout more upscale condominium developments reduces the concentration of poverty and number of low-income neighborhoods in Vancouver. These redevelopment projects also keep many middle- and upper-middle-class families living in the city rather than self-segregating into exclusive suburban bedroom communities.

The Neighborhood Institution Difference

The hotel employees with children who I interviewed, particularly the ethnic minority immigrants, generally live in and around two comparable neighborhoods in Seattle and Vancouver. Interviewing in people's homes and participant-observation research in these neighborhoods allowed me to get a sense of the impact of public investment differences on the communities in which the children of these employees will grow up. The comparison of these two neighborhoods is useful for understanding the concerns about incorporation and segmented assimilation as well as some of the pathways that limit today's immigrant youth's opportunities for advancement.

Vancouver Neighborhoods

In general, the majority of neighborhoods in Vancouver feature a surprisingly similar urban design. Outside the downtown core, most consist of a mostly single-family homes built densely on a grid. Multifamily units are interspersed throughout and tend to be located closer to major thoroughfares. Every neighborhood has some park areas, elementary and secondary schools, and a community center. The main thoroughfares feature one- or two-story commercial units, with many small retail shops and some larger grocery food chains. Some of these commercial buildings have residential apartments above shops. All neighborhoods are serviced by bus lines and a limited, but increasing, number by the SkyTrain.

As in many other North American cities, Vancouver has an east-west wealth divide, with the west-side neighborhoods being wealthier. Although these distinctions exist, differences between neighborhoods are not nearly as large as in most U.S. cities. The similarities across these neighborhoods shape the conditions and standard of living for the vast majority of the Greater Vancouver–area residents. The city has twenty-three official neighborhoods, including Kitsilano, the West End, Shaughnessy, Kerrisdale, Yaletown, Mount Pleasant, Kensington-Cedar Cottage, and Strathcona (see fig. 7.1). Some ethnic minority immigrants interviewed live in suburban municipalities, including Burnaby, Port Moody, Coquitlam, New Westminster, Richmond, Surrey, North Vancouver, and West Vancouver. All of these suburbs are part of the Greater Vancouver Regional District (GVRD)—a regional governance structure with metropolitan-wide responsibility for planning and some other public services, notably transit.[27]

In Vancouver, approximately 15 percent of respondents live in the downtown core, 10 percent live east of downtown, 20 percent live in inner-ring suburbs, and less than 10 percent live in more distant suburbs. Over 35 percent of employees interviewed live in neighborhoods located southeast of the downtown core, including most of the ethnic minority immigrants with children.

At the heart of this area is the east Vancouver neighborhood of Kensington-Cedar Cottage. It has a remarkably similar development pattern to the wealthier neighborhoods to the west and north, although the area is clearly poorer. According to Statistics Canada, 27.5 percent of the population of Kensington-Cedar Cottage lives in low-income households.[28] The main thoroughfares, especially Kingsway, are somewhat unkempt with graffiti, traffic, and trash on the streets. The street has fast-food and ethnic-food restaurants, grocery stores, hotels, gas stations, independent used-car dealerships, travel agencies, antique stores, and other small shops.

Street homeless and other impoverished people occasionally walk through the alleys with shopping carts picking through the trash to collect cans and bottles to claim the return refund—something that happens in most Vancouver neighborhoods. Yet, for the most part, the people out and about in this neighborhood are immigrant ethnic minorities—Chinese, East Indian, Filipino, and Vietnamese—or low-income white Canadians. In 2001, according to Statistics Canada Census data, more people in this neighborhood listed Chinese (37.8 percent) as their mother tongue than English (32.8 percent); other first-languages reported included Vietnamese (5.5 percent), Tagalog (5.0 percent), and Punjabi (3.9 percent).[29] There are several churches and parks as well as several ethnic community organizations, including the Portuguese community center and Gandhi Banquet Hall.

Once you turn off the busy thoroughfares that run through Kensington-Cedar Cottage—Kingsway, Victoria, and Nanaimo—the majority of the neighborhood consists of single-family homes on small lots. In 2001, 47 percent of the dwellings in this neighborhood were single-detached homes.[30] Although

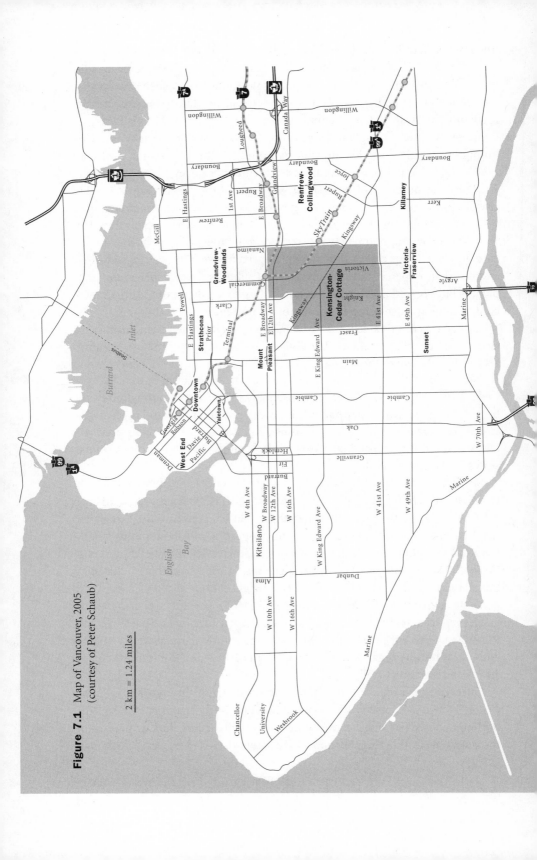

Figure 7.1 Map of Vancouver, 2005 (courtesy of Peter Schaub)

2 km = 1.24 miles

the homes in this area are definitely smaller than those on the west side of the city, the neighborhood also has several large homes and feels almost as peaceful and clean as wealthier neighborhoods in Vancouver. There are a few small developments with condominiums or townhomes, but they are seamlessly integrated into the single-family-home neighborhoods. It also has nonmarket housing—for low-income seniors, families, and the disabled—dispersed throughout. Many of the single-family homes in this neighborhood have one- or two-bedroom basement apartments as rental units. Kerry Wong, a single, childless, 47-year-old Chinese immigrant who is a room attendant, rents one such small basement apartment for $260 per month. Other hotel employees I interviewed own single-family homes in this neighborhood.

In the midst of these residences are several parks with playground equipment and the Creekside Secondary School complex. As modern and nice from the outside as most large suburban schools in the United States, the Creekside Secondary School appears to have very good facilities—it has many large windows and sports fields. The students attending the school are an ethnically diverse group; many are children of immigrants from China, India, and the Philippines. Several of the hotel employees interviewed have children attending Creekside.

In Canada, public schools are largely funded by provincial governments. Unlike the case in Washington state (and most U.S. states), per-pupil funding in a school district is completely detached from the value of the local property tax base. Because the British Columbia government does provide extra per-pupil funding for special-needs students, city schools can have more public funding per pupil than suburban schools, to educate a higher-needs population of students. According to the principal of Creekside Secondary, the school does receive some extra per-pupil funding for ESL students and to cover the cost of free or subsidized lunches for low-income children.

At the same time, Creekside does not qualify for extra resources provided by the inner-city school program, which provides additional resources to several public schools in and around the downtown eastside. Yet many of Creekside's students come from low-income families. The parents are not able to donate as many goods and services to their children's public school as the parents in wealthy West Vancouver, whose donations and fund-raisers have funded film-production studios; nevertheless, the parents are involved despite the constraints. For example, Creekside's parents' group helped the school apply and receive $60,000 in casino funding from the provincial government to buy computers. According to the principal, what the parents lack in financial resources, they make up for in heart—each year they are one of the top schools in terms of donations to the annual citywide food-drive competition.

The centralized system of funding reduces the inequality between urban and suburban schools in Vancouver. Not only does the school funding system help provide a greater equality of opportunity, between urban and suburban school children, but it also reduces the incentive for parents with children to move out of the city into suburban neighborhoods.

The Vancouver school district also has multicultural school liaison workers for different language groups. Multicultural liaison officers are based out of the District Placement Reception Center, which receives incoming students, and is the first line of contact between families and the school system. They arrange school placement and help with the transition of new students studying in Canada. A Chinese liaison worker is based at the Creekside school. Vietnamese, Punjabi, Hindi, Spanish, Korean, and Cambodian liaison workers have also helped students. As the principal expressed it, "Multi-cultural workers are very very important for cultural mediation and interpreting the system to the newly arrived families." The school also has extensive programming to celebrate ethnic diversity and cultural heritages and traditions.

As I toured the school site with the student government president, he proudly exclaimed that Creekside is the "most diverse school in all of Vancouver." He told me that he felt "people consider the eastside schools to be poorer and have 'one ply toilet paper,'" but said that even though they might not have the financial support of west side schools that they had a lot of spirit. The classrooms I looked in on appeared neat and orderly, and the students seemed attentive. The top floor has the math and business classrooms. I noted that several of the rooms have large computer labs, with many students sitting at terminals. Most of the classrooms also have large windows, some with a view of the mountains in the distance; they are nice, clean, and colorful. I observed a drama class and visited the arts and music facilities. The science labs appear to be well-equipped with Bunsen burners and lab stations. Walking down the halls, I got the impression that, although the building is old, it is also pretty well maintained. The paint is chipped in places, but there certainly are no holes in the walls or ceilings; nor are there major leaks.

There are pictures of every graduating class since the early 1960s, which reveals the dramatic transformation that has taken place in the neighborhoods surrounding Creekside. In the photos from the 1960s, the vast majority of the students appeared to be white. But by the 1980s, the ethnic makeup of the school has become progressively more Asian and Southeast Asian, and now it is a majority minority school. My overall impression was that, although Creekside does not have the super-campuses of some secondary schools located in the wealthy suburbs of Chicago, as described by Jonathan Kozol in *Savage Inequalities*,[31] it is not at all underfunded or as run-down as many of the urban secondary schools in many U.S. cities.

Extensive investment in bread and butter public infrastructure has improved the quality of life for residents of the Kensington-Cedar Cottage neighborhood. Just like all neighborhoods in Vancouver, Kensington-Cedar Cottage has its own Neighborhood Integrated Service Team (NIST), which includes police, planning, and library services. The NISTs bring together staff of all city departments responsible for a particular neighborhood and address resident concerns. The United Nations recently awarded Vancouver an Innovation in Public Service Award for the successful implementation of the NIST program.[32]

There are two community centers in Kensington-Cedar Cottage: Trout Lake Community Centre and the Kensington Community Centre. Trout Lake Community Centre is located adjacent to the John Hendry Park, a seventy-acre (27.40-hectare) park in the neighborhood, and Trout Lake. The center has an indoor ice rink, fitness center, preschool, youth center, tennis courts, racquetball courts, pottery studio, games room, and playground. It also hosts a First Nation's powwow, an active seniors' group, and a summer/fall east Vancouver farmers' market, as well as many recreation programs. Kensington Community Center is also located next to a second fifteen-acre (6.39-hectare) park. It has a "fitness centre, pre-school, pottery studio, gymnasium, dance studio, meeting rooms, and a leisure swimming pool," as well as a seniors' lounge, racquetball courts, playing fields, and playground.[33]

Mark Heung, a thirty-two-year-old immigrant from Vietnam who works as a houseman at the Globe Hotel Vancouver, lives in the Kensington-Cedar Cottage neighborhood. He described the neighborhood as having "Yeah, community centers, like they have lots of programs for kids and even adults. It ranges from even cooking, dancing, you know, social events. Even like day camp for the kids. . . . I usually go for swimming, working out."

The Kensington-Cedar Cottage neighborhood has two community health centers: the Midtown Community Health Centre and the Evergreen Community Health Centre. It also has one of Vancouver's twenty-one public libraries, the Kensington Public Library, and one of Vancouver's twenty-one storefront Community Policing Offices, the Cedar Cottage Neighborhood Safety Office/Community Policing Office. Kensington-Cedar Cottage also features institutional services available to support working parents, including several child-care centers, for which low-income families can get a significant government subsidy.[34] Community institutions promote social capital between neighbors.

A diverse array of family-focused community institutions contribute to greater feelings of public safety and security. George Chan, a fifty-year-old houseman at the Globe Hotel Vancouver, lives just on the border of Kensington-Cedar Cottage and Renfew-Collingwood to the east. He said, "The neighborhood is good. All the people are familiar in the neighborhood and we greet, when we met, we greet. When you have a function, what have you, they know you live here and they [are] there. If you have any trouble and you have any questions you can ask. Yeah, it's very good."

Many hotel workers also lived in the eastside communities bordering Kensington-Cedar Cottage. Stacy Tsai, a forty-three-year-old immigrant from Shanghai, China, works in Banquet Services at the Globe Hotel Vancouver and lives just south of Kensington-Cedar Cottage in the neighborhood of Victoria-Fraserview. She described her neighborhood as "Really nice people and nice street, it's quiet and then, it's so handy. About five minutes and I go the main street and then I got all the shopping and the grocery and there are Chinese food. It's really handy place. . . . Multi-cultural . . . Some of them German, like my neighbor, and some of them Vietnam and then some of them Chinese and some of them India." Stacy said it is easy to shop for the things they need. "Yes, it's easy. It's really convenient place." When I asked if she would recommend the neighborhood to a friend with school-age children, she replied, "Oh yeah, I would real, I would do that, yeah. I like it." She reported that there were no problems with crime in her neighborhood, but that "At night, we are not going out." But she feels it is safe for her children, and no one has been a victim of crime. Kathleen Leun, a forty-nine-year-old immigrant from Guandong, China, also works as a room attendant at the Globe Hotel Vancouver and lives in Victoria-Fraserview. She shares Stacy Tsai's positive assessment. She thinks it is a "good neighborhood. . . . I like it. They [neighbors] always, even you just, when you walk on, everybody say 'Hello.' Say 'Hi.' Very nice families. Smiling. Oh, comfortable. Yeah, wonderful."

The Mount Pleasant neighborhood borders Kensington-Cedar Cottage on the northwest. Maria Artemis, a forty-seven-year-old immigrant from La Union, Philippines, works as a room attendant at the Globe Hotel Vancouver. She described Mount Pleasant as, "The surroundings? I think they good. Comfortable. Everything is close, actually is very safe place." Michael Anthony McDonald, a doorman at the Globe Hotel Vancouver, also lives in Mount Pleasant. He said, "We've got the Mount Pleasant Community Centre and that's where most of the east side people meet, you know, like go there." Although he was never afraid to walk around alone, day or night, Michael Anthony McDonald hoped for more community policing: "Well, I would say to be more visible and like have more cops on the beat. So they can get to know the people in the area, instead of being in a car and being kind of isolated. But get to know the community more, you know? More, have more beat police." Because the interview was held during a long bus strike in Vancouver, he was less sanguine about public transit: "At the moment it [the public transit] is non-existent. It's terrible. Usually we have buses, you know, it's pretty good otherwise. You know, usually, when the strike isn't on."

Residents of different eastside Vancouver neighborhoods were also positive about their neighborhood. Tse Leung, a fifty-four-year-old room attendant at the Globe Hotel Vancouver, lives in the Killarney neighborhood southeast of Kensington-Cedar Cottage; she said, "I like this area. Because the climate is good." There are many shops and a large grocery chain is located in walking distance on Kingsway. They have a, "Community [center], is close. Down the street . . . swimming pool and exercises and things like that. And [for] the older people in the morning, they have a lot of activities." When I asked if she goes to the community center, Tse Leung said, "I go there, it's a free because I have a low income. I can go swimming, I go exercises." Her children go with her, as well. She feels that it is safe on the streets during the day and night, for her children too, and no one in her family has ever been a victim of crime.

Although hotel employees living in the downtown core reported more problems with petty crime, they also were very positive about where they live. Hassam Mansour, an Egyptian immigrant with two young children, described his Yaletown neighborhood, "It's a really good place to meet people. It's very safe place to put the kids in. It's very nice neighborhood." Some of the younger hotel employees live on their own or with roommates in high-density neighborhoods in the downtown core, such as the West End. These neighborhoods had problems with homelessness. Jen Havel, a twenty-two-year-old born in Winnipeg, works as a room attendant at the Hotel Deluxe Vancouver and lives in a condominium apartment with a view of English Bay in the West End.

Actually, I don't know what the crime rates are like. I know there's so many homeless people, our dumpster is right here, I watch the homeless people there sleeping and stuff, I guess from the management there's been problems in our Parkade, but I don't think it's because of the homeless people, the homeless people are generally, I'm not afraid of them. Because they're not out to hurt you and stuff. So it's not bad.

There were a few exceptions in Vancouver who were not happy with their current neighborhoods, especially those living near the downtown eastside. Gee Yong Chow, a fifty-one-year-old maintenance engineer at the Globe Hotel Vancouver, lives in Grandview-Woodlands neighborhood bordering the downtown eastside on the east: "I wouldn't say [the neighborhood is] very good. Because around there, we have problems with the prostitution, and then that area is light industry there. And it's, we are quite close to the dock, so we have these problems. So we are thinking of moving out from there. . . . The people are not bad. Mostly working class. . . ." He was one of the few hotel workers who would not recommend his neighborhood to friends with children and hoped to move.

Employees also thought positively about the quality of life in Vancouver's inner-ring suburbs. The wife of Hernando Reys, a houseman at the Hotel Deluxe Vancouver, described their inner-ring suburban neighborhood in Port

Moody, "And the park there, it's beautiful and then our, across there is the main street of Port Moody and we are located in a condominium. . . . and you can see the mountain with the sea. So, and it's quiet. And we are near a schools, the three schools are there. And church and transportation and quiet neighborhood." They live in the center of Port Moody so it is easy to shop for the things they need. Ethnically, she described their neighborhood as quite mixed: "Yeah, mostly white Canadians. In that building where we live, we're the only Filipinos. But there are different nationalities there. There would be like from East India, that would be one. . . . There would be Europeans, all different. But they are all home-owners there." She would highly recommend the area to friend with school-age children. "We don't have crime there. . . . And the police in Port Moody is the best. They're very vigilant."

When I asked Sven Johannsen, a server and a union shop steward at the Globe Hotel Vancouver, who lives in Burnaby, if he had ever been a victim of crime, he replied, "Years ago, in Seattle. I got mugged in Seattle. . . . That has to be the early [19]70s."

In general, nearly every employee interviewed in Vancouver described his or her neighborhood as "nice," whether they lived in or near downtown or in an inner-ring suburb.[35] Many described their neighbors as a diverse group, immigrant and nonimmigrant, white and ethnic minority. Most had a community center with a pool and community programs located near by. Most hotel workers also reported high levels of personal safety—they felt safe in their neighborhood and on the street both during the day and night.

Seattle Neighborhoods

Seattle has a wide variety of neighborhoods, located in and around the city. Seattle's urban design is like a wheel, with the downtown core connecting to many separate and somewhat isolated hub communities. In between these areas, large industrial areas, highways, dead zones, and natural barriers isolate each area, contributing to their unique characteristics. Younger and single hotel employees tended to live in Seattle's various downtown neighborhoods such as Belltown and Capitol Hill, which are caught between gentrification and a mini-recession caused by the collapse of the dot-com boom. Employees living in these areas also must contend with a significant number of homeless people and with petty crime (similar to Vancouver).

As in Vancouver, Seattle hotel employees live in a variety of neighborhoods. Approximately 10 percent live in the downtown core; 20 percent live in the (wealthier) neighborhoods north, northwest, and northeast of downtown; and 30 percent live in the suburbs. Approximately 40 percent of the employees interviewed live in the neighborhoods southeast of downtown.

The flow of ethnic minority immigrants in Seattle is almost parallel to that found in Vancouver. Many recently arrived immigrants initially live in the dense, higher-crime areas of the International District just south of the central business district; as they become more settled, they move out of downtown, settling in communities to the southeast of downtown along Rainier Avenue, concentrating in the Rainier Valley and Beacon Hill communities. (Recall that in Vancouver, many ethnic minority immigrants move up and out of Chinatown along Kingsway also to the southeast.) The urban poor tend to live just to the north of this area, in somewhat neglected (non-high-rise) public-housing projects of the Central District just east of downtown and up the steep Yesler Way. The southeast area of Seattle can be divided into several neighborhoods: Beacon Hill, Columbia City, Georgetown, Holly Park, Jefferson Park, Mt. Baker, Rainier Beach, Rainier Valley, and Seward Park (see fig. 7.2). Although some southeast areas such as Columbia City are gentrifying as young white middle-class couples buy and fix up homes, the areas closer to downtown have serious problems with crime, gangs, and drugs.

The Seattle employees I interviewed expressed more varied views of their neighborhoods than did those in Vancouver, with more negative assessments.[36] Crime is a problem for low-wage workers. The quality of institutions is weaker. Neighborhoods are more isolated and lack amenities such as community centers and stores. The proximity to the airports and flight patterns means many residents have to deal with the loud noise of jet planes landing both at nearby Boeing field and Sea-Tac International Airport. At the same time, most Seattle employees joined their Vancouver counterparts in praising their access to public transit, with bus routes extending far into the suburbs. Although Seattle is more generous in providing amenities than many other U.S. cities, the hotel employees interviewed did not report using or benefiting from most of these services.

The largest concentration of Seattle hotel employees I interviewed lived in or near the urban hub village of North Rainier Valley, especially those who are ethnic minority immigrants with children. A comparison of this neighborhood to the Kensington-Cedar Cottage neighborhood in Vancouver is useful for understanding concerns about segmented assimilation and some of the obstacles that limit the opportunities of ethnic minority immigrant youth. Both of these neighborhoods are populated heavily with ethnic minority immigrants, with the largest groups from China and the Philippines. North Rainier Valley is located southeast of the downtown core and is somewhat isolated. On the west, I-5 divides this area from the massive industrial area that runs for miles and miles immediately south of downtown Seattle. A highway provides access over the industrial area to the middle-class neighborhoods of west Seattle. I-90 cuts across the North Rainier Valley neighborhood and over the lake to the east, crossing over the extremely wealthy Mercer Island.

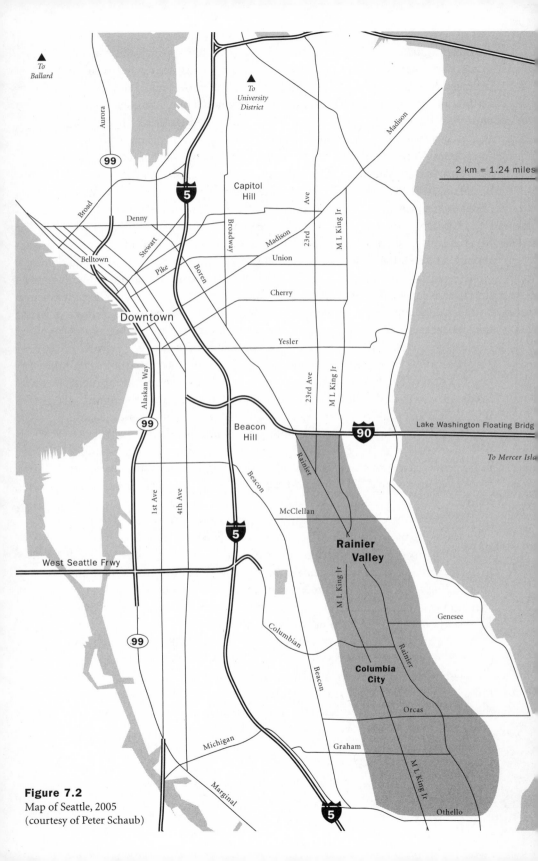

Figure 7.2
Map of Seattle, 2005
(courtesy of Peter Schaub)

Stories about crime and fears for their personal safety were much more prevalent for residents of North Rainier Valley in Seattle than for those living in and around Kensington-Cedar Cottage in Vancouver. While waiting for a ride outside her home just before 4 a.m. to go to work as a coffee service attendant at the Globe Hotel Seattle five years ago, Kay Chiang was robbed. "In the morning, when [I am] ready to come to work with the co-worker they basically just rob [me]. Kind of grab [my purse] and run away."[37] As discussed in Chapter 1, Sujita Hassam, who works as a room attendant at the Globe Hotel Seattle, described being afraid in her home sometimes because of the neighborhood criminal activity.

Even in parts of the neighborhood where the crime situation is somewhat better, it remains a defining issue. Lucy Cho, a thirty-seven-year-old Vietnamese immigrant who works in the laundry at the Globe Hotel Seattle, lives seven blocks southwest of Rainier Avenue, north of Beacon Hill and south of I-90. She said of her neighborhood: "It's a small area. It's not really bad, it's good." Her neighbors are mostly families, including ethnic Chinese, Japanese, and whites. She does not think crime is much of a problem because the residents watch out for one another: "Yeah, watch out for the neighbor all together. Yeah, they keep like make sure somebody is like, if people don't live here, sometimes you saw people and you need to make sure, who are." It is also well lit: "Yeah, it's good at night because we have on the street we have lighting. And then you can see people who is running, going yeah, they have many dog in front the house." The police also have a presence in the neighborhood: "because we have police always like hang around. Drive around. They make sure it's safe for people, they will check. They will stop and ask you who you looking for." There are no community centers or churches around, but "I [would] love that but I don't have time." She does not really know much about the public transit because she does not use it.

Problems of crime and insecurity are also prevalent in nearby downtown neighborhoods. As a single parent, Kendra Smith, an African-American laundry attendant, received social welfare benefits and Section 8 housing benefits for many years. As her children grew older, she earned an occasional $3.50 per hour doing maintenance work for the building she lived in at the time:

> And it [the apartment building] was roach infested, so you go in with head gear and everything and you go in and you pull an appliance off the wall and the roaches all come at you, and it's like, 'oh my god,' the way people would live. And then you look at the apartment conditions, people that the apartments go down and the management wouldn't do anything about it, and I'd be like, 'How can people live like that?' So, that was one of the reasons I had to move out of there, because I kept my apartment up, but anytime you have somebody next door to

you having their kids outside playing and they drop a toy and the roaches run out, you know it's time to go . . . .

The neighborhood Kendra Smith moved to as a single parent was tough. Many of the ethnic minority immigrant employees with children lived near the area she described: "Oh, in my last neighborhood, drive by shootings. It was in South End, Rainier Valley Area. . . . That was just crazy. You can just sit out on your front porch and watch everything, you don't even have to go to the movies. You can see them shooting up, you can see them tricking, you can see them shooting, you can see the house getting broke in. Wow, 'I didn't know they were moving?' 'Why is that U-Haul parked right there?'" The associated problems of concentrated poverty reduced her quality of life. When I asked if it was difficult to raise children in that environment, she replied:

> It was. It's really hard to, when you are single and you are working, and the kids get out of school, the time until you get home from work. To keep them straight, you are always on the ball calling to make sure they are home. "If you are going to leave, call me and let me know where you are going." You got to make sure you know who their friends and their parents are. And if their parents are kind of shaky, then you have to be like, "Hmmm, I don't want you over there." But then, the more you say no, no, no, the more they want to go, go, go. And so you just keep pushing and pulling; yeah, it was hard to try to keep them even . . . .
>
> It's bad, every time you take your kids trick or treating and your son says, "Don't go to that house, mom that's a crack house. Mom, that's a crack house." Well how do you know these are crack houses? "Well, I just know these things." And then you're wondering, OK, why does he know these things? He's working, what is he knowing about this stuff about a crack house. And then I [decided] had to switch my hours, and switch my days, yeah.

Kendra Smith's neighborhood description shows that the neighborhoods that some Seattle hotel workers could afford to live in or near were worse in terms of crime and less safe than those of their Vancouver counterparts.

Part of the reason for this is that Vancouver hotel employees earn somewhat more income and can therefore afford to live in better neighborhoods. But the difference is also related to the more extensive and higher-quality community and public institutions, both in low-income neighborhoods and the city, in general. Vancouver has managed to avoid the expansion of high-poverty and extremely high-poverty neighborhoods, and so far it has avoided many of the deleterious consequences of concentrated poverty—with the notable exception of the downtown eastside. Because there are few neighborhoods with high concentrated poverty in Vancouver, almost all the hotel employees interviewed were able to avoid living in high-poverty neighborhoods. In contrast, in Seattle many hotel employees lived in or near high-poverty neighborhoods. The high crime rates in these neighborhoods reduce the quality of life for people living in neighboring areas, as well.

After Kendra Smith married her long-time beau, a firefighter with a relatively high income—boosted with lots of overtime pay—they moved in together into a largely white neighborhood in Seattle. This neighborhood should be considered an improvement over where she used to live. When I asked about this new neighborhood, she said, "There is an awful lot of [crime], well not on our little block, we don't have very much crime. But about two blocks over, there is a lot of car theft. We are two blocks from Des Moines, Memorial Drive, Pacific Highway, a lot of prostitution. But right in our little, like a little city enclave. Right in our enclave, it's calm. You have a golf course, so you're fine." The trade-off for safety is isolation; when I asked if she felt safe on the streets during the day, Kendra Smith said, "Yeah. We live on this hill and there are no buses. So you have to get to, get dropped off at the Park and Ride, and then you take the bus there, and you got to go and you get dropped off at the Park and Ride and then they come and get you. So it's kind, if someone wants to get to our house, then they are really trying to get there."

Other areas in Seattle suffer some of the same problems. For example, Lee Wang, a mini-bar stocker at the Globe Hotel Seattle, lives north of the University District, northeast of the downtown core. She said, "I don't know, I think that America, Seattle, everywhere is very beautiful. I don't know, I think my part, not so beautiful." She thinks her neighborhood is safe, "Things are OK. Quiet. In the last year, someone stole my car, I don't know why, my car is so old. I call the police and they come here."

There are some very nice neighborhoods in Seattle with many community institutions. Generally, only the childless hotel employees can afford to live in these areas, often renting an apartment with a partner or roommate. For example, Herbert Michaels, a forty-five-year-old single white man who works as an on-call banquet server at the Globe Hotel Seattle, loved his neighborhood:

> Yeah, they have, well they have Green Lake, which is only about a mile away, so I love living there. And it's you know, lake, and it's got a rollerblading, walking path around there. . . . And I rollerblade a lot, so that's good exercise. And they've got a swimming pool there that's run by the city. . . . That's only a couple of blocks to swim, that's really great. . . . Yeah, that's the community center. . . . I used to swim fairly often there, like four to five times a week and then now that I rollerblade, I just wait for the sun to come out, I go do that.

At the same time, there were more reports of problems with being victimized by crime in these Seattle neighborhoods, compared to Vancouver. Dan Rogers, a thirty-six-year-old concierge at the Globe Hotel Seattle, lives in Capitol Hill and had his car stolen:

My car got stolen last year, but other than that. . . . It was recovered. It has been stolen and broken into, you know, in the last few years. But, it was recovered just down the road, and nothing was missing, but the second time they got everything out of it. . . . It got broken into the second time. The first time, they took it on a joyride and parked it. The second time, they smashed, no they didn't smash the window out, they slim-jimmed it and stole everything from the [secure] parking garage.

Peter Keyes, a thirty-eight-year-old single white man, works as a doorman at the Globe Hotel Seattle and lives in the neighborhood of Ballard with a roommate. He described it as "I'd say it's great. It's a quiet neighborhood." But when I asked about crime, he said, "Uh, in southern Ballard, it is a lot of problems." When I asked what kind, he replied, "Oh, vandalism. Theft. Vandalism and theft."

Employees who live in the suburbs of Seattle were also generally positive about their neighborhoods. Yet they still described problems with crime, auto theft, and vandalism much more frequently than Vancouver employees, even those living in lower-income neighborhoods. Joey Harrison, a thirty-seven-year-old maintenance engineer at the Hotel Deluxe Seattle, described his suburban neighborhood in Bothell, Washington: "It's very quiet. People keep to themselves. I really don't know anybody. We know [some of] them just because we do a lot of fundraisers for Scouts. . . . They are older Americans. . . . Some are retired, some are in their 70s and working. . . . Some of them were laid off from Boeing. And they are not working and they are doing their welfare deal, or unemployment and some are on welfare and some are working." When I asked Joey Harrison about crime in the area, he said:

I'm finding out that there is crime . . . theft, break-ins, stabbings. Yeah, there was that terrorist living, you know, they caught someone that was five blocks away, he lived there at one point in time. Kind of scary stuff. We know from the bulletin, that there are those people that look at kids, or pedophiles that have gotten out of jail and they are living, on the list, in the neighborhood. Convicted but living a few blocks away. We know that there is a few of those around. I mean, you know, its kind of hard, there is a web page you can look up and find out all, where all these people live in your neighborhood, where they are. But what can you do, you just know, and that's worse.

When I asked if he felt safe on the streets, he said:

I have a different sense. I feel like if something happens to me then that's just too bad it happens. My wife on the other hand, she freaks out when she goes out at night. . . .

She doesn't feel safe here in downtown Seattle [too]. She doesn't understand how I can just walk around in the dark and walk down alleys and not have a fear. I figure if someone pulls a gun on me, I'll give him what I got.

But as for his son, "We still are very, keeping an eye on him, I don't want him to go out on the street by himself." When I asked if anyone in his household had been a victim of crime, Joey said, "Just theft. Not from our house. We did have all our window screens taken off at one time, like they were trying to get in, find out if there is an unlocked window. That was a little weird. But we've just been victims of theft, breaking our car windows and taking stuff out of our cars."

Perhaps part of these differences relate to the myths of a crime epidemics perpetuated by the media in the United States, as described by Barry Glassner in *The Culture of Fear*.[38] But it also reflects the greater insecurity and exposure to crime that negatively affects the quality of life for all residents—not just poor ones—of Seattle as compared to Vancouver.

Improving the Quality of Life

Differences in public maintenance and bread and butter infrastructure investment contribute to a higher quality of life for the residents of Vancouver than for those of Seattle. These differences also help explain why Vancouver consistently has been ranked as one of the best cities in the world in terms of quality of life, according to Mercer Human Resources Consulting. In the latest 2004 ranking,[39] Vancouver slipped from second to third place in the rankings of cities in the world for quality of life, tied with Vienna, Austria, and scoring slightly lower than Zurich and Geneva, Switzerland. In the same 2004 ranking, Seattle dropped from thirty-sixth to forty-fourth place, tied with Lexington, Kentucky; Pittsburgh, Pennsylvania; Osaka, Japan; and Barcelona, Spain.

The higher-quality bread and butter infrastructure in Vancouver improved the quality of life of hotel employees there compared to Seattle. Today, a much-celebrated revival of some U.S. central-city downtown cores is occurring. Yet it is largely limited to the large inflow of young, single, childless people back into the urban centers. As young urban professionals move in, some of these neighborhoods improve dramatically, as shops, restaurants, and other high-end stores move in to service their needs. At the same time, many of these neighborhoods become unaffordable for many working-poor families. Sometimes the very same young urban professionals leave one gentrified urban neighborhood and move into the next new trendy neighborhood, taking advantage of initially cheaper rents.

Many city governments in the United States have completed large public infrastructure projects in partnership with other levels of government and corporations. At substantial public expense, new stadiums have been built to lure suburban families back into the urban core for a night on the town.[40] The new stadiums create some (low-wage and inconsistent) employment during games, both in the stadiums themselves and in the restaurant and parking sectors. But the high cost of tickets to many public events, such as football games and concerts, exclude many people with low incomes, especially working-poor families with children. Downtown shopping centers, convention centers, and shiny office towers, similarly, are built with the promise of expanding the city revenue base for public services, but they do not benefit all city residents equally.

What is missing is a massive public investment in the bread and butter infrastructure that will dramatically improve the quality of life for families raising children in U.S. cities. This kind of public infrastructure investment, in contrast to the corporate public infrastructure projects just discussed, acts as a countervailing force to the growing income inequality created by the marketplace. Bread and butter infrastructure projects include high-quality public transit, primary and secondary schools and other educational institutions promoting life-long learning and retraining, community centers, child-care facilities, public recreational facilities, medical facilities, and well-maintained parks. Tragically, in many U.S. cities these are the exact domains of urban public infrastructure that have been neglected and that lack sustained investment.

A day at the park is largely free, and if the park is well-maintained, safe, and attractive, people of all economic means can enjoy it. Where high-quality public facilities do not exist, the financially better-off rely exclusively on their own private recreation, such as yacht clubs, private gyms, and private pools. Any remaining public facilities, available to all, begin to decline in quality—exacerbating the flight from these programs and facilities by those who can afford to. This vicious downward spiral cripples public institutions and isolates lower-income families.

Seattle is a liberal city that has extensive public investment compared to most U.S. cities. It is also a university town with extensive academic and cultural resources. As a result, it is more similar to Vancouver in some areas (such as parks) than other U.S. cities. Many other U.S. cities are far behind Seattle in terms of these kinds of public infrastructure investments. Finally, after forty years, concrete plans have approved by Seattle voters for the construction of a $1.75 billion fourteen-mile Green Line elevated monorail train that will connect many Seattle neighborhoods. The existing 1.2-mile 1962 monorail will be torn down, and construction on the new system is due to begin in 2005, with the completion of the full line scheduled for 2009. A second monorail line and complementary light rail system has been proposed to connect the airport and other suburbs to some downtown communities.[41] Although Seattle's transit plans are clearly on the right track, the long delay in developing the system contrasts sharply with Vancouver's public infrastructure investment in urban rail transit.

In both Seattle and Vancouver, ethnic minority employees with children tend to live in neighborhoods southeast of downtown. Extensive investment in neighborhood institutions such as community centers, neighborhood service teams, parks, community policing, and public education in Vancouver has improved the lives of working-poor families. Hotel workers in Vancouver were more positive about their neighborhoods than were workers in Seattle. Fewer reported problems with crime and violence. Vancouver neighborhoods are also more institution-rich and do not vary as much in terms of quality compared to in Seattle. The disparity between the neighborhoods in southeast Seattle, with their lack of social institutions, high level of isolation, and lower levels of public infrastructure investment, and the institution-rich, wealthier city and suburban neighborhoods in Vancouver support theories of segmented assimilation in the United States.

Policy differences as they relate to neighborhood quality and public infrastructure affected the quality of life of hotel employees. High-quality public transit, parks, schools, educational opportunities, roads, and recreational programming counteract the growing levels of market-generated inequality in a service-sector-based economy. Vancouver's public investment in high-quality, low- or no-cost recreational and public programming has improved the quality of life of all its residents. Like other universal government programs in health care and education, greater investment in public amenities allow the hotel workers in Vancouver to enjoy a higher standard of living. Public investment policy differences shape the lives of the employees outside the workplace and thus contribute to their perceptions of their place in society and the future outlook for them and their children; these issues are discussed in the next chapter.

CHAPTER 8

Subjective Perceptions and Future Outlook

What are the cumulative impacts of the interactions between the economy and government policy that shape the quality of life of low-wage workers? Subjective perceptions of place can be even more illustrative than concrete measures of material well-being. In this chapter, I discuss how employees saw themselves and their families. Where did they see themselves compared to others? How did hotel workers, working at the bottom rungs of the service sector, perceive their future? What did they think their children's future would be like? Hotel workers had a wide variety of views about where they stood in society and what the future had in store for them. Certain patterns emerged from the interview data that suggest the policy regime in Vancouver provides a foundation for somewhat more optimism than in Seattle.

Closer to the Middle Class

How do we understand where people see themselves in society? How can we compare these responses cross-nationally? In order to get a measure of perceived place, I asked the employees I interviewed (as the final, "sigh-of-relief," interview question) to place an X on a drawing (see fig. 8.1) to indicate where they saw themselves and their family on a imagined socio-economic ladder. I explained the question to all workers similarly in each city. I pointed to the top rung and said it represented those who are the best off in society, those with the most money, or the "Bill Gates" line. I pointed to the bottom rung and said it represented those who are materially worst off, such as the homeless. Then I pointed to the middle line and said, "This represents the middle of American/ Canadian (depending where I was) society. Where would you place you and your family?"

In their answer to this question, fewer of the employees in Vancouver ranked themselves and their families as well-below the middle of the socioeconomic hierarchy. In Seattle, 23 percent (8 out of 39) placed themselves far below the middle—below halfway between the second and third rungs of the ladder— but in Vancouver only 8 percent (3 out of 38) did. This is a fairly major cross-national difference for employees in the same jobs working for the same com-

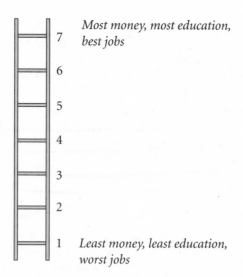

Figure 8.1 The ladder question. Think of this ladder as representing where people stand in Canadian/U.S. society. At the top of the ladder are the people who are best off—those who have the most money, most education, and best jobs. At the bottom are the people who are the worst off—who have the least money, least education, and the worst jobs or no job. The higher up you are, the closer you are to the people at the top; the lower you are, the closer you are to the people at the very bottom. Where would you place yourself on this ladder?

panies.[1] In contrast, the same percentage of employees ranked themselves and their families well above the middle rung (value 5 and above) in each city: 15.8 percent in Vancouver and 15.4 percent in Seattle.

These placements were based largely on perceptions of material well-being and wealth. When I asked her to explain why she placed herself just below the middle rung on the ladder, Beth Kay, a fifty-three-year-old room attendant at the Globe Hotel Vancouver said, "I consider I am here, because first for me is good health, and second I have a work and my family is very important to me. They are okay. They are doing well and I almost paid my home." Work equals pride. In both cities, workers identified working in a paid job, as opposed to being on public assistance or unemployment, as an explanation for why they placed themselves above the bottom rungs of the ladder. For example, Elizabeth Hubar, a thirty-seven-year-old room attendant at the Hotel Deluxe Vancouver and refugee claimant from Sri Lanka, said, "Yeah, I'm earning and all that. I think I'm there [just above the middle rung], some people are still on welfare, they're not being productive. We are proud. So far, I make it."

In Seattle, hotel employees who placed themselves far below the middle rung generally explained their position in terms of a lack of middle-class material possessions, such as not owning a car or their own home. Some focused more on their low income, dead-end career path, or level of education. Jennifer Shih, a forty-six-year-old immigrant from Taiwan who works as a room attendant at the Globe Hotel Seattle, explained why she placed her and her family on the second rung from the bottom: "[I] thinks [I] is better than them [the bottom rung]. Better than the homeless. [We] don't have a lot of money and [we are] renting. [We] pay $600 something and other people pay $1,000 something, so [we are] less than them."[2] Jennifer Shih's income limits her choice of housing to areas with low-rent apartments. The dramatic difference in quality of life between these neighborhoods and middle-class neighborhoods in Seattle caused her to feel that she and her family were socially excluded from mainstream U.S. society.

Other hotel employees in Seattle who ranked themselves well below the middle focused more heavily on income, education, and material possessions. Lan Zhang, a forty-year-old room attendant at the Globe Hotel Seattle who recently emigrated from Taishan, a city in Guangdong, China, placed her family below middle. She explained that "[We] think they need more education and more income." Lee Wang, a fifty-one-year-old immigrant from Taiwan who works as a mini-bar attendant at the Globe Hotel Seattle, explained that she placed herself below the middle because "my car is very old."

Employees who ranked themselves above the middle in Seattle also did so, generally, because they had achieved certain landmarks or middle-class symbols such as home ownership or a university degree. David Hopkins, a forty-eight-year-old who was born in Seattle and works as a supervisory bellman (earning $7.80 per hour plus tips) at the Hotel Deluxe Seattle, explained:

> Well, this is real tough. I like to try not to compare myself to other people. You set yourself up for disappointment. I'm certainly not homeless and I'm certainly not Bill Gates. Gosh, anywhere in the middle there. I own my own home, and a lot of people don't even have a house, so I have to put myself up above in here somewhere. You know, I don't make $100,000 a year though, so I'd say this [up at the top of the ladder] is like the $100,000 a year bracket. So I'd put myself right in here. . . . One rung above [the middle]. . . .
>
> I own my own home, and I like I said, we're pretty fortunate to do that, a lot of people don't. So I'd have to put myself there somewhere.

Owning a home and car emerged as symbols of middle-class success. Lacking these symbols in Seattle—renting an apartment or shared house in a low-income neighborhood and relying on public transit—was associated with a self-assessment far below the middle rung in Seattle. The high degree of institutional/structural similarity between the neighborhoods where hotel employees in Vancouver lived and wealthier neighborhoods probably helps explain why these hotel workers largely described themselves as feeling like they were not far below the middle class in Canada.

A More Positive Outlook for the Future: Vancouver Workers

I asked the hotel workers that I interviewed how they imagined their life in five years and ten years time? From the responses, hotel employees in Vancouver can be divided into two related groups when it came to future outlook: the strivers and the satisfied. Strivers had concrete action plans to advance in their career, either within or outside of the hotel. In contrast, the satisfied expressed a strong desire to stay in their current job position for the foreseeable future or even until retirement. These satisfied employees defined their aspirations in terms of achievements or benchmarks outside the workplace: amassing certain middle-class symbols such as home ownership or funding children through university.

Hassam Mansour, an Egyptian immigrant, is definitely a striver. A maintenance engineer at the Globe Hotel Vancouver, he hoped to be chief engineer at the hotel in five years time and director of engineering in ten years. When asked about his current job, Hassam Mansour said, "I love it. I just love my job." He believed that a stable unionized hotel job provided potential opportunities for advancement and a lifetime career in his new country. After many years working in a hotel, other employees in Vancouver looked forward to a comfortable and financially secure retirement.

The theme of taking advantages of opportunities for self-improvement and achieving a measure of financial stability and success were common in Vancouver, particularly among immigrant men in their thirties or early forties. Gee Yong Chow, also a maintenance engineer at the Globe Hotel Vancouver, hoped to strike it rich through real estate investing and product sales: "Yes, I'm trying to make a change, to get out of this, what they call the forty-five-year plan. Go to work, come back, go to work, come back—and you retire. Same thing every year, you've gone nowhere." When I asked Gee Yong Chow how he felt about his job at the Globe Hotel Vancouver, he said, "Yeah, I'm very happy with my job. I enjoy it a lot." He said he would not like to switch jobs right now and that he felt the job made use of his skills and experience. But when I asked him about his dream job, like many hotel workers (and the rest of us) he said that he wished he could "Be my own boss." He is also taking real estate investment courses. Through this program, Gee Yong Chow has invested some of his savings in real estate.

Mark Heung, an immigrant from Vietnam who works as a houseman at the Globe Hotel Vancouver, also believes that "Ten years from now. Hopefully [life] will be better than five years from now. But seriously I'm very optimistic about my future. And I look forward to it." As a striver, Mark Heung hoped to become an accountant and to remarry. He planned to "Buy a house, car, vacation, the whole package of what living is about. Successful as a person foremost. Seeing my kids going to university." As for working at the hotel:

> I see it as just a dead-end job. . . . I would love to switch. And I'm working on that. After ten years of it, I guess I don't see myself working at this career in the hotel industry in the grunt work atmosphere. No. Maybe in more of a managerial, administration, but I'm leaning towards finance and taxing, an accounting type. . . .
>
> I feel that I am more capable than what I'm doing. At the same time, I don't know why I'm hanging on to this. Perhaps it's simply security and what I'm used to and I know that I'm capable of more. And I'm working slowly towards, I guess, realizing that.

Striver employees in Vancouver tended to have concrete plans about how they were going to achieve their future career ascendancy.

Vancouver workers discussed specific requirements, tuition amounts, courses, and qualifications. (Seattle workers, in contrast, were more vague about the path from here to the future dream job.) Mark Heung, knew for example, that he would have to spend $10,000 and take courses part-time for six years to become a Certified General Accountant (CGA). "And I would love to go full-time, but economically it's just impossible and I don't want to go into debt doing that, right? It would be fine if I was just single and no responsibilities. I can definitely find other means, and go full-time, but as it stands, part time is my only option. Not until I hit the 649 [the British Columbia lottery]. . . . That's the universal dream." Last year he tried to get a government job in the corrections system, but was rejected: "perhaps it's due to a combination of a lack of education, lack of volunteer, in that particular field, corrections."

Many of the younger hotel employees, particularly in Guest Services, looked forward to no longer working in the hotel industry and advancing their life career goals. For example, John Richards, a twenty-two-year-old bellman at the Hotel Deluxe Vancouver, said, "I hope to have got my ass in gear and gone back to like University and got my teaching degree. That's my goal. I really got to sort of go after." For these striver employees, working in a hotel is a temporary job, suitable for helping them pay for university or enjoy a time-out on their way to achieving more middle-class careers.

I was initially surprised at how many satisfied hotel workers I met in Vancouver; a new rung on the service-industry labor-market ladder, with decent wages and job security, afforded them the opportunity to live a decent life. Kathleen Leun typifies what I what I call a satisfied employee. A forty-nine-year-old immigrant from Guangdong, China, she works as a room attendant at the

Globe Hotel Vancouver. In answer to my question about the future, Kathleen Leun said that she hoped that they will have sold their house and bought a nice retirement apartment. "And my husband say when we have the money, buy the [Mercedes] Benz." Kerry Wong, a forty-seven-year-old immigrant from Shanghai, China, and also a room attendant at the Globe Hotel Vancouver, and also a satisfied employee, was optimistic about her future. In five years, she said, "I like to win the 649 [British Columbia Lottery]! [Laughter] If no win the 649, I think I like to the more [hours on the] job for me. . . . And find a good boyfriend, eh? Good boyfriend." In ten years, she said, "Oh maybe retire! I just like the health be good, no more sick. Also can make money. I'll buy a new car. Buy the new car. Make money, buy the new car." For these employees, working at the hotel in their current position made them happy.

After working in poor conditions in low-wage and unstable work in restaurant kitchens and garment factories, many ethnic minority immigrants were pleased to be working in a major downtown hotel in Vancouver where greater stability and higher wages prevail. They recognized that their lack of English language fluency greatly limited their job options and thus were quite content to look forward to rewards extrinsic to the workplace. Their wages afforded them a quality of life closer to the middle class, compared to those in Seattle, and they lived in neighborhoods with a relatively good quality of life, vibrancy, and accessible and family-friendly public institutions such as parks and community centers. The lower barriers to participation in public education and public institutions in Vancouver, as well as the high quality of the public institutions, act to counterbalance the impact of income inequality.

Hoping for a Better Deal: Seattle Workers

In Seattle, hotel workers were more somber about their future outlook compared to those in Vancouver. Some employees expressed hopes of acquiring material goods, similar to Vancouver. At the same time, many more employees in Seattle hoped to move to better neighborhoods. The same division between striver and satisfied employees existed in Seattle, but there were fewer satisfied workers, particularly at the non-unionized Globe Hotel Seattle. The combination of poor pay at work and difficult neighborhood circumstances circumscribed the hopeful, optimistically forward outlook that defines most immigrants. Kay Chiang, an immigrant from China who works as a coffee service attendant at the Globe Hotel Seattle, said that in five years, "[I] want to buy a car. [I] would like to have a new house if [I] can afford. Middle school, better middle school [for my children]." Whereas some focused on a desire to escape poor-quality public institutions, such as inner-city schools, other workers hoped to work for a different employer, in a better job. Sujita Hassam, a room attendant at the Globe Hotel Seattle (whose story I share in Chapter 1) said, "In five years, I just like to buy the house, I want to have a good job, and I was thinking for working in the hospital." The answers to the questions on future outlook revealed that many Seattle employees felt they did not have a "good job." For many, like Sujita Hassam, even a lateral switch to a similar cleaning job in a different sector, such as health care, would be a step up. Sujita Hassam believed there would be more opportunities for advancement in health care than in the hotel industry. Her co-worker Juan Martinez, a thirty-four-year-old immigrant from Mexico, works as a coffee service attendant at the Globe Hotel Seattle and also as a houseman at a nearby office tower, agreed. In the future, he wanted to "Have another nice job. . . . I continues in service, but better job."[3]

Fewer employees expressed hope that their own personal material, financial, or work situation would improve as dramatically in Seattle than in Vancouver. Some aspired to return to their country of origin; Charles Duado, a seventy-year-old houseman at the Globe Hotel Seattle, hoped that "If God will, I'll retire and my two children will get their visa to come here [to the United States]. Maybe that's it, I will go back to the Philippines." Trapped at the bottom of the increasingly hourglass-shaped economy, many hotel employees in Seattle were less positive about their future than similar employees in Vancouver.

A Bright Outlook for Their Children's Future

Although most of the parents I interviewed were very optimistic about their children's future, in general the Vancouver parents expressed brighter hopes, with less trepidation than the Seattle parents. As uncovered in Richard Sennett and Jonathan Cobb's seminal work *The Hidden Injuries of Class*[4] on working-class British men in the late 1960s, many hotel employees interviewed hoped that their children would have a better work and class situation than theirs.

Vancouver

Mainstream middle-class themes of academic achievement, marriage, good jobs, and bright futures dominated Vancouver hotel employees' expectations for their children's futures. Optimistic sentiments were expressed repeatedly by most employee parents in Vancouver. For example, Beth Kay, an ethnic Chinese immigrant from Honduras and room attendant at the Globe Hotel Vancouver, felt that her three children have a "Oh, good future. It will be a good future for them." Stacy Tsai, a banquet services employee at the Globe Hotel Vancouver, has three children: a twenty-two-year-old, a nineteen-year-old, and a thirteen-year-old. What will their lives be like?

> It will be nice. Like after five years later then, my two girls, I don't know, they're married or whatever. They will all very much very good job. Right and then my younger girl she will be graduating already. After five years she will be job and every body to college or university, is more better for me. . . .

I hope they can find a good job and they can take care of their selves, that's only I wish on them. Take care of themselves, I hope their life like me is good too. I don't want they have any problems, I don't want anything happen to them also, I want they are people, safety and they are happy forever.

Many other Vancouver employees had specific ambitious career aspirations for their children. Hassam Mansour, an Egyptian immigrant and maintenance engineer at the Globe Hotel Vancouver, had high hopes for his two children, five-year-old Ahmed and four-year-old Lily: "I hope they will become something more like doctors or lawyers, something more. I want them to finish complete education and get into university."

In Vancouver, most parents expressed hopes that their children would complete university education and get "good jobs." Tse Leung, a room attendant at the Globe Hotel Vancouver, has two adult children: a twenty-four-year-old and a twenty-two-year-old. She believed that: "I think it's a better future for them in Canada. That's why I come to Canada. More freedom, have more future for the kids. They can more opportunities for the job, that's why, if they want, they try, right. So they need to spend time for their life. They should study hard." Tse Leung was also hopeful about her family's future: "In five years I hope my son can get a job again, right? Maybe go to the university, get high level and I hope my daughter can finish school and training, look for job something she like. And my husband in retired in five years. I will retire too. . . . I come here, I just want my son get a job, he likes. So if my son, my daughter, they can get good job then I can retire."

At the same time, Vancouver employees' responses to questions about their children's futures were less likely to involve "protecting" children as much as "guiding" them in their decisions. For example, Tse Leung said, "We try do everything we can, make my life good for my family to work hard right, make people happy right. Let them [our children] grow by self." Vancouver employee parents were more likely to express the idea that children need independence and that they were responsible for their own decisions and future than were Seattle parents. Perhaps part of the reason for this is that Vancouver employees felt that their children were more assured of success than did similar Seattle employees. George Chan, a houseman at the Globe Hotel Vancouver, also expressed bright hopes for his seventeen-year-old daughter Alice:

She has bright future. . . . Yeah, certainly. Because certainly her English is better than mine. Children, very easy study language. When she going for university, I think her English is better than the local people, including the local accent. . . . She will have the English diploma and, is very very, it's great here for her. . . . She also can work what she want. What she can choice. . . . She has a bright future.

Julie Lee, a forty-five-year-old immigrant from Guangdong, China, who works as a laundry attendant at the Globe Hotel Vancouver, also sees a bright future for her son, a twenty-year-old studying computer science at the University of British Columbia (UBC) in Vancouver: "I don't know. Maybe he get two more years and finish UBC then go upper level [graduate school]. . . . Maybe he like to after UBC go to the work and working and studying together. . . . Cause work in computer is very good. Very important."

How realistic are these proud parents? Tuition rates averaged CA$2,181 for an undergraduate arts and science student during the 2001–2002 school year at the University of British Columbia. A ban on tuition increases by the provincial government created some of the lowest tuition rates in Canada.[5] In contrast, at the University of Washington, in-state tuition and fees for arts and science undergraduates were US$3,983 for the 2001–2002 school year.[6] Other non-university-level postsecondary education is also available to Vancouver residents at very low cost. For example, adult basic education courses at Vancouver Community College are free.

Also, employees suggested that the cost of not completing a university degree is not as high in Vancouver as in Seattle. Marianne Lakon, an immigrant from the Philippines and room attendant at the Hotel Deluxe Vancouver, has three children, ages twenty-three, twenty-one, and eight years old. She has bright hopes for her youngest son, Marcus. When I asked her what she thought about his future, she answered, "Oh it's very ambitious. He wants to be a Chief of Police and go to Hollywood. Oh my goodness, and he will buy me a house in British Properties [the most expensive property development in the region, up the mountainside in West Vancouver]." She expressed less optimism about her adult children: "Oh my daughter, she is very ambitious. But she's still doing good. She's very nice, not just because she's my daughter. She's very hard working. She got a job at Tim Hortons [a Canadian donut chain], and she just got a job there and she's very hard working. She looks after the baby at night. She goes to job early, she's very patient. Very patient. . . ." And about her older son, Marianne said, "I don't know, he loves his money. He's working full time as security guard, making more than $11/hour. . . . Because sometimes he works too hard." While service-industry jobs do not pay very high wages, they still allow these young people to make ends meet. Perhaps parents are less apprehensive in Vancouver because there are many publicly funded low-cost opportunities to gain further work-related skills and move up the career ladder. Perhaps with their greater feelings of personal safety, parents are less concerned their children will be victims of violent crime or get caught up in gangs, thieving, hard-drug addiction, and other social problems that can ruin a young life. Because the quality of life is better for low-wage workers in Vancouver, they also have fewer obstacles to face in terms of helping and ensuring their children access the resources necessary to join mainstream Canadian society.

Seattle

Although most Seattle employee parents I interviewed also expressed positive hopes for their children's futures, they were more cautious in their predictions than Vancouver parents. Many Seattle employee parents also expressed hope that their children would have better jobs than their own.

Several employee parents in Seattle were cautiously optimistic about their future. Jane Donaldson, a fifty-nine-year-old immigrant from South Korea and Housekeeping supervisor at the Hotel Deluxe Seattle, has two adult children: "Well, I hope them, I hope they better than us and things working a lot better than what we did." She hoped that her children would not have to repeat her challenging experiences as a new immigrant in Seattle:

> But I can't say I [had] the best life either. Because I was six or seven, have Korean War. We went through that. After the war, years and years so poor, can't recover from the war quick enough. And there everybody is so poor, and [there is] not enough to go around. This is not us, this is the whole country, the whole country was so poor. And just as it start to getting better, I come here.
>
> And now is Korea is just, real good living, real good country, and so I didn't see that, because just starting to get a little bit better and I come here. When I come here, in the late [19]70s and early [19]80s, the economy is so bad in America. . . . Us lower average American people, we work hard.

Jane Donaldson's experiences in Seattle, where her children grew up, has tempered her optimism about their future. Their family has faced major challenges. They lived in an old downtown hotel rent-free in exchange for cleaning services for many years after arriving to Seattle. Now, they are having difficulty accessing disability benefits for her very ill husband.

Recently arrived immigrants often expressed cautious optimism, in part because they are still learning about the U.S. system. From their vantage point, there are both significant opportunities and challenges. Jennifer Shih, a forty-six-year-old Taiwanese room attendant at the Globe Hotel Seattle has three children: a twenty-three-year-old, a twenty-one-year-old, and a seventeen-year-old. She responded to the question about whether she thinks her children's future will be bright: "Depends on the economy. [I] think that here should be better than Taiwan, because they are working and they have some experience and they can used to another society." Whereas some thought that the economy was important for their children's future, like Jennifer Shih, other immigrant parents with younger children discussed the critical role of a university education to material success in U.S. society.

Several Seattle employees discussed anxiety about the cost of postsecondary education for their children. Lan Zhang, a recently arrived Chinese immigrant who works as a room attendant at the Globe Hotel Seattle, has three children, ages seventeen, fifteen, and twelve years old. She said about her children's future, "[I] think better. Their future will be better than in China. . . . Yes, if [I] can afford [to send them to college], [I] will send them." Although they understood the role of a university degree in ensuring successful careers for their children, they were apprehensive about whether they could finance their children's education. In contrast, recall that, because all the postsecondary programs in Vancouver are public, they generally are more accessible to working-poor families. Even if generous financial aid exists for private U.S. programs, the higher tuition figures caused much more concern for the working poor in Seattle. Thomas Kane, an economist, for example, shows how increases in public education tuition decreased the likelihood that children from lower-middle-class and working-class families would attend university.[7] At the time of the interviews, annual in-state tuition and fees at the University of Washington in Seattle were almost twice as much as the University of British Columbia in Vancouver. Lan Zhang's sister-in-law, Hue Chung, also a room attendant at the Globe Hotel Seattle, has three children, ages sixteen, fourteen, and twelve years old. She said, "[We] want education for [our] kids' future. It's better for them. The education and working environment is better. . . . For the work, for the education, the pressure is a lot. . . . The [primary] school is free. [We] don't have to pay for it. But [we] still have a lot of financial pressure for education." Hue Chung also thinks that the future is bright for her children in the United States, "[I] think they will have a much better life. The better is they go to university and then [I] will be very happy."

In Seattle, hotel employees who were financially better off were more confident about their children's futures. For example, Tung Sing Chang, a club lounge attendant, coffee service attendant, and mini-bar attendant at the Globe Hotel Seattle, recently emigrated from Taiwan to Seattle with significant savings from his professional career. After living with relatives in the suburbs, he purchased an expensive home in a suburb north of Seattle. Despite working in a job below his skills and experience, he said his experience in Seattle so far was "Very good. What's good about it? The life is very stable. Everybody is healthy, health is good. [We] own a house. [We] have place to live, car to drive. [We] are saving. So [I am] very satisfied." He believed that his children, "They have to study hard. It's better for them [here]. So in the future they will have a better opportunity here." When I asked what career they would pursue, he said, "Daughter should be staying in Accounting field. The boys will probably be related to computers."[8]

Native-born white hotel employees with young children living in the sub-urbs were also positive about their children's futures. For example, Joey Harrison, a long-time maintenance engineer at the Hotel Deluxe Seattle, has two children, seven-year-old Danny and eight-month-old Helen, and lives in the Seattle suburb of Bothell. He said, "I love the future for my children because my boy can really do anything he wants and I'll be happy." With decent neighborhoods and resources, these parents believed that the future for the next generation is bright. Hotel employees who owned homes, lived in the suburbs, or had more resources were more optimistic about their children's futures in Seattle. In contrast, recall that in Vancouver, a household's wealth or neighborhood was not as related to parent's views on their children's futures.

More parents in Seattle talked about the vital role they themselves will play in shaping the future of their children than did parents in Vancouver. Instilling the confidence to succeed in their children was a more common theme among Seattle employees than Vancouver employees. Perhaps this is because of the greater emphasis on individualism and family responsibility for mobility in the United States. Several parents in Seattle also explicitly expressed concern about shielding their children from negative elements in their environment. Former public-assistance recipient Kendra Smith, a laundry department employee at the Hotel Deluxe Seattle, recalled:

> I remember getting, going to school in Montana, we would have to fight to get on the school bus. Like, fight to go to church. My mom would put quarters in socks and wrap them around our heads and we would have to go out and defend ourselves. And we had book bags with rocks and books in it, and we just had to fight. And I mean these were like lumberjack kids, these kids were huge. Yeah, I remember being spit on and called all kinds of wild names. That's been an experience; because it's an experience I can tell my children about.

Such experiences of racism while she was young has made Kendra Smith more aware of the need to teach her own children and grandchildren skills to grow up in a multiracial community where not everyone is tolerant.

> And my grandson is Laos and black, so he's going to have to go through some things because he looks more Asian than black, and he's going to have to go through some things. And this is a learning experience I taught my son, I told my son. And he can tell him, that he is just going to have to stand tall and be proud of both. They are going to teach him his mother's language and teach him his mother's heritage and he is going to learn our heritage also. I think bi-racial children need to know both sides, because if they don't, I think they will confuse which ways they want to go.

Lower levels of public safety and weaker community institutions in Seattle's low-income neighborhoods contributed to more cautious subjective assessments of their children's future by parents.

Previous chapters described some of the specific effects of U.S.-Canadian policy differences in labor, health, and social welfare policy on hotel workers. This chapter considers these differences from a different—"softer"—perspective. How do the cumulative impacts of the interactions of differences impact the subjective perceptions of hotel workers about their place in society? Do these differences matter for the workers' outlook for the future? Comparing employee responses to these questions reveal part of the reason fewer employees in Vancouver than in Seattle perceived themselves to be well below the middle class. Beginning from the same occupational starting point, we see some notable differences in outlook in hotel employees' futures, including their perceived trajectories. In addition, hotel employees in Vancouver with children expressed fewer concerns and were more hopeful about what the future had in store for their children than those in Seattle. In the next chapter, I discuss some of the policy implications of these findings.

CHAPTER 9

Improving the Lives of the Working Poor

So far, we have discussed some of the hardships experienced by working-poor families in Seattle and Vancouver and some of the strategies they use to cope with difficult financial times. What kinds of policy would improve the lives of Sujita Hassam, Lan Zhang, Alfred Jones, and Elizabeth Hubar? In this chapter, I outline policy recommendations based on the findings of the Global Hotel study. I begin by describing some of the reasons we need to think creatively to come up with concrete and viable policy solutions to help the working poor and end the growing crisis of working poverty in the United States and Canada; in part, we need to emphasize building the capacity and power of those fighting for the interests of working-poor families. Although reforming union-organizing rules in the United States might not seem as exciting as ending child hunger, such a reform could lead to the kind of rebalancing in U.S. political life that results in just these kinds of bold outcomes. I also make some specific recommendations that will improve the lives of workers like the ones I interviewed in Seattle, and Vancouver.

Some argue that it is politically unrealistic to think that new government policies and programs can be implemented in a conservative political climate dominated by issues of war, terrorism, and moral panic. But this pessimism belies the historical experience of the United States, Canada, and other countries in which policy development is often uneven and unexpected. This chapter heeds William Julius Wilson's recommendation to scholars in *When Work Disappears*: "Progressives who are concerned about the current social conditions of the have-nots and the future generation of have-nots not only have to fight against the current public policy strategies; they are morally obligated to offer alternative strategies designed to alleviate, not exacerbate, the plight of the poor, the jobless, and other disadvantaged citizens of America."[1] As Wilson urges, the policy reforms I discuss are not "constrained by an awareness of the current political climate in the United States. The dramatic retreat from using public policy as a means to fight social inequality has effectively discouraged calls for bold new social programs."[2] Yet they are tempered by the knowledge that, ultimately, these policy reforms will not be implemented on their own. It will take the continued struggle of activists, organizers, and coalitions as well as political leadership (and bravery) at all levels of government—from local school boards to national representatives—to create the kind of change that will improve the lives of those left in an increasingly vulnerable position by the global marketplace. In moments of pessimism and doubt, we should remember, as Studs Terkel describes in the introduction to his latest book *Hope Dies Last*: "Activists have always battled the odds. But it's not a matter of Sisyphus rolling that stone up the hill. . . . It's more like a legion of Davids, with all sorts of slingshots. It's not one slingshot that will do it. Nor will it happen at once. It's a long haul. It's step by step."[3]

Make Work Pay

The crisis of working poverty is a serious and growing one in North America; the middle class in the United States is shrinking due to growing inequality and the worsening of extreme poverty. The problems of urban poverty will not be solved without improving the lives of the working poor, as Katherine Newman in *No Shame in My Game* argues, "For there is little we can do to solve the conundrums of the inner-city unless we fix the labor market problems of the working poor."[4] The problem of working poverty extends well beyond urban poor neighborhoods. According to Elizabeth Warren and Amelia Warren Tyagi in *The Two Income Trap,* this year "Americans will file more petitions for bankruptcy than for divorce. Heart attacks. Cancer. College graduations. Divorce. These are markers in the lives of nearly every American family. And yet, we will soon have more friends and co-workers who have gone though bankruptcy than any one of these other life events."[5] They point out that in the past decade, the United States has "bankruptcy filings that have quintupled, mortgage foreclosures that have tripled, car repossessions that have doubled."[6]

The answer is not simply more jobs at any cost, as all too many state and local governments have discovered in their race to the bottom—offering tax incentives as well as anti-union and other policies to lure corporations to relocate to their municipality. Solving the employment problem will not necessarily solve the poverty problem. As Kathryn Edin and Laura Lein succinctly put it in *Making Ends Meet*: "Not only does low-wage work pay as badly as welfare without much opportunity for advancement, it is much less reliable."[7]

Gains for working people have only come through organizing, political action, and activism. No public-private venture, inspiring individual political leader, or charity-only organization—although by no means do I want to discourage the support of these well-intentioned and worthy causes—will lead to the structural transformation that will reduce inequality and poverty in the United States and Canada. Lasting social change comes through organizing and political activism, bringing together coalitions and fighting for change through creative campaigns at the local, state/provincial, national, and international levels. In the United States and Canada, some of these organizations include the Association of Community Organizations for Reform Now (ACORN), Interfaith Alliance, Council of Canadians, Public Citizen, and the Canadian Centre for Policy Alternatives. Others organizations are local. Internationally, Oxfam combines both aid and activism. As Wilson proposes, organizations need to build bridges across issue divides:

> The foundation of this vision emphasizes issues and programs that concern the families of all racial and ethnic groups so that individuals in these groups will come to see their mutual interests and join in a multiracial coalition to move America forward; it promotes the idea that Americans have common interests and concerns that cross racial and class boundaries—such as unemployment and job security, declining real wages, escalating medical and housing costs, the scarcity of quality child care programs, the sharp decline in the quality of public education, and the toll of crime and drug trafficking in all neighborhoods."[8]

The goal is for unions, churches, environmentalists, transportation advocates, minority-rights groups, academics to work together on causes that unite and do not divide them, acting on local, state, national, and, increasingly, international levels.

The right wing has learned this lesson well, organizing unlikely allies from chambers of commerce to advocate for corporate interests, armies of political lobbyists, and grassroots movements in communities. As Joel Bakan in *The Corporation* asks, "Yet where are the desperately needed countervailing lobbies to represent the interests of the average citizen? Where are the millions of dollars to act in *their* interests. Alas they are notably absent."[9] In his explanation for wage stagnation in *The New Dollars and Dreams*, Frank Levy, an economist, concludes, "The final factor is the shift in power away and toward a firm's shareholder. Deregulation, globalization, and technology have reduced the typical employee's bargaining power, and no countervailing institution has arisen to exert an opposing force."[10] One answer is unions, acting in coalition with other progressive organizations.

Despite its current governance, the United States is one of the most progressive countries in the world. It is the birthplace of the labor union and the first country to create a public education system. It is not unbridled capitalism that created the great U.S. middle class; rather, it is public investments in schools, universities, roads, infrastructure, and cities that built the American dream. The United States has a long and celebrated people's history in which insurmountable odds have been overcome to extend equal rights to women and ethnic minorities. For every celebrated hero and leader—Martin Luther King Jr., Jane Addams, Mother Jones, Cesar Chavez—there were thousands of people working tirelessly on the ground, fighting to change policy. Canada too has had its share of heroes—Pierre Trudeau and Tommy Douglas—but it is the political coalitions and activism of ordinary citizens (beyond the Royal Commissions) that explains the enactment and expansion of Canada's social safety net.

Nonviolent democratic political organizing in the United States has been a model for movements around the world and for the growing global social movement against poverty. As Charles Derber urges, "The great abolitionist campaign of the coming century is ending global poverty . . . and the new civil rights struggle of the twenty-first century: to secure the rights of workers everywhere to organize for dignity and a living wage. Unions, labor rights and organizing are all going global."[11] It is an exciting time to be a progressive.

Looking to Canada provides a helpful model for those in the United States who are fighting for progressive policies. Yes, there are long-standing differences between the United States and Canada related to their unique histories and geographies (as Seymour Martin Lipset describes in *Continental Divide*[12]). Yet, in the past thirty years, in terms of social, health, and labor policy, Canada has implemented what the people in the United States tell pollsters they want from government: universal health insurance, somewhat greater income and wealth equality, more union representation of the labor force, lower levels of poverty, and less hardship. These goals have been achieved from—in terms of social policy—a similar starting point to the United States.

Specific Policy Recommendations

Progressive policy reform in the United States would improve the level of well-being and quality of life of service-industry workers and their families, with positive benefits for business and the health and vibrancy of democratic society.[13] In Seattle, policy reform should include the expansion of health insurance coverage for the presently uninsured and the implementation of an effective state supplemental Earned Income Tax Credit (EITC) program to lift the incomes of working-poor families above the poverty line. Labor policy reform to improve workers' access to union representation would also be extremely effective in improving the lives of the working poor by improving job security, benefits, and wages.

Improving the quality of life and reducing material hardships of working-poor families in Vancouver requires maintaining existing social supports, such as accessible employment insurance benefits and training programs, while increasing the minimum wage and child tax benefits to reverse the growing tide of poverty among families.

Improving the Lives of Hotel Employees
and Their Families in Seattle

The findings of this book suggest the need for Washington state and U.S. policy makers to take action to improve the lives of low-income workers. The following policy recommendations would improve the quality of life and reduce the levels of material hardship experienced by the urban working poor in Seattle:

- Reform health-care policies in Washington state to create the conditions for the gradual realization of universal health insurance coverage.
- Reform union-organizing policies at the Washington state and federal levels to bring them in line with existing Card Check procedures for *all* workplaces and to create a system in which employees who want union representation in the service sector can successfully unionize their workplace.
- Increase the federal Earned Income Tax Credit to lift most working-poor families above the poverty line.
- Create a Washington state supplemental Earned Income Tax Credit program that is fully refundable, following the lead of the eight other U.S. states that have systems with requirements similar to the federal program.
- Increase the minimum wage, and index it to inflation so a full-time worker earns enough to remain above the poverty line. Increase the Unemployment Insurance benefit replacement rate of income to at least 55 percent of income for single employees.
- Create a low-income family supplement for the Unemployment Insurance benefits of workers with children or other qualified dependents at up to an 80 percent income-replacement rate.
- Close loopholes and lift caps to reform the federal and state tax systems to make them truly progressive so that income inequality is *reduced* after taxes, not increased.
- Create a one-year Parental Leave Program using the Canadian system as a model, with benefits paid through the Unemployment Insurance system to provide a 55 percent replacement income (capped at $30,000 per year) so one parent can stay home with an infant during these most critical months of child development.
- Expand the eligibility requirements and number of slots available while publicizing the Washington state, King County, and Seattle subsidized day-care programs to help working parents.
- Encourage, through financial incentives and support, the use of school buildings as community institutions to provide adult education, universal before- and after-school care, and other community programs.

- Create universal early education programs for all two- to four-year-olds.
- Increase levels of investment in urban infrastructure such as parks, public transit, and other civil society institutions, with a focus on high-quality, low-cost, family-friendly institutions.
- Build high-quality community centers with extensive facilities aimed at attracting residents to take advantage of fitness programs, community services, and other facilities.
- Expand rail-based public transit in the Seattle-Tacoma area, including street cars and light rail, following the excellent model provided by Portland, Oregon.
- Reduce tuition and increase financial aid, especially scholarship grant aid, for postsecondary education.
- Enact living-wage ordinances in local municipalities.
- Pass legislation to limit rental security deposits to one-half month's rent in order to improve access to independent stable housing for the working poor.

The following sections provide additional details about some of these policy recommendations.

Health Care

Washington state must dramatically reduce the proportion of residents who lack health insurance coverage. A plan should be voted on and implemented to create universal health insurance coverage within the state as quickly as feasible in the next several years. Whereas the Canadian health system efficiently provides health-care coverage to all through a single-payer system, the implementation of such a system in Washington state remains politically unfeasible. Yet the method employed to achieve universal health insurance coverage matters less than the outcome. In *Rethinking Social Policy*,[14] Christopher Jencks recommends that the working poor be allowed to purchase health insurance coverage through the existing Medicaid program, the cost based on a percentage of their income. Extending the availability of Medicaid benefits—currently available to a fraction of the poor—to working-poor families and shoring up the portability of health insurance coverage between jobs would help cover many of the working poor through an existing program. Fewer and fewer employers are providing health benefits to employees in the United States. According to Katherine Newman, "In 1994, more than two-thirds of the working-poor children who had some form of medical coverage received it through Medicaid. We must do the same for their parents."[15]

The U.S. government already provides health insurance benefits to Americans over sixty-five years of age through the Medicare program. Reforming policies to allow a Medicaid buy-in by the working poor and other workers who face challenges getting private coverage, such as employees working for small businesses and the self-employed, would be the foundation for the growth of a universal health insurance system in the United States gradually, from the ground up. As a first step, Washington state should lower the cost, increase the eligibility, and better publicize its Basic Health Program. Other U.S. states should come up with their own programs or policy reforms to meet the goal of access to affordable health insurance for everyone.[16]

Unemployment Reforms and Training to Help the Working Poor

Washington state should eliminate the punitive and complicated benefit calculation formula for Unemployment Insurance benefits (discussed in chap. 6). Replacement income should be set at 55 percent for childless workers. A low-income family supplement is *critical* to making the unemployment system work for low-income parents. A supplement to the standard unemployment benefits should increase benefits to 80 percent of income for low-income families with children. Unemployment Insurance benefit recipients should also have the option of completing government-funded job-training and education programs to help them move into long-term, living-wage, sustainable employment.[17]

Labor Policy Reform for a Global Era

Washington state and the U.S. federal government should reformulate the onerous union-organizing rules (discussed in chap. 4) to bring them in line with the new reality of a predominantly service-sector economy. The current procedures are rigged heavily against the unionization of workplaces, even where a large majority of employees want to be unionized. That is a sign of a system that is not functioning or democratic.

According to a study by Kate Brofenbrenner, in the United States, when employees want to unionize:

> 92 percent of private employers force workers to attend closed-door meetings to hear anti-union propaganda; 80 percent require supervisors to attend training sessions on attacking unions; 78 percent require that supervisors deliver anti-union messages to workers they oversee; and 75 percent hire outside consultants to run anti-union campaigns. . . .
>
> One simple way to give workers more meaningful organizing rights would be to establish the right of workers to start a union through the Card Check process. If a majority of workers sign a form authorizing union representation, the company would have to recognize the union. Under current law, companies can ignore the workers' wishes and demand an NLRB election, which gives managers the opportunity to engage in these coercive anti-union activities and create an atmosphere of fear.[18]

The U.S. congress is considering changing some labor laws: "Legislation introduced in Congress last month [November 2003], called the 'Employee Free Choice Act,' would give workers the right to unionize through Card Check, as well as provide mediation and arbitration for first contract disputes, and establish stronger penalties for violation of employee rights during organizing drives and first contract negotiations."[19] If passed, this legislation would make it easier for employees to unionize in all industries when a majority of employees want to be in a union.

A new rung in the service sector needs to be constructed—the secure living-wage unionized job. Labor union representation in the service sector increases the wages of workers in the entire sector. The collapse of union coverage of the labor force over the past thirty years is one of the major causes of increased working poverty and income inequality in the United States.

Although there certainly are challenges to organizing service-sector workers, these obstacles—which are no greater than the private militias, police, and other powerful forces physically overcome in the previous era of unionizing factories—can be overcome. Labor unions can also help spark this process by organizing workers as members even if they have not (yet) successfully unionized their workplace, as suggested by Richard Freeman.[20]

The right to organize is enshrined in the Universal Declaration of Human Rights. It is critical that unions continue their recent focus on organizing the new vulnerable workers in the twenty-first-century global economy—the service-sector employees. Their toil and needs are not altogether different than Firestone plant workers at the beginning of the last century. Unions represent a critical countervailing force to the increased power of multinational corporations over the governments of all countries and multinational trade institutions.

Reforming the Tax System to Make the United States More Equal

The current U.S. tax system creates, instead of reduces, inequality.[21] The reductions in inequality created by the nominally progressive income tax system are wiped out by regressive taxes[22] and extensive loopholes and tax exemptions for wealthy households, including the mortgage interest tax deduction for homeowners. Reforms to reconstruct a system of progressive taxation would provide more resources for social programs and much needed infrastructure improvement for all levels of government. Small policy changes, such as lowering the ceiling allowed for the mortgage interest tax reduction, would generate more income tax revenue from high-income households.[23] Increasing the income cap on social security contributions would force the wealthy to pay their fair share and reduce the pressure for further increases for lower-income workers. Small tax increases on the extremely wealthy, coupled with increased refundable tax credits for lower-income earners, would create a truly progressive tax system.

The U.S. EITC is one of the most successful anti-poverty programs ever implemented, and it is a model internationally. According to Newman, "The Urban Institute has determined that about 4.5 million Americans are lifted above the poverty line through the tax credit."[24] It is incredibly economically efficient, putting money directly into the hands of working-poor parents who need it the most. It also does *not* stigmatize those who benefit because it is processed through the tax system.

The EITC program should be expanded and further improved at the federal and state levels. U.S. states—such as Washington state—should implement supplemental EITC programs. The key dimension to the success of these credit programs is that they do not just reduce the taxes paid by the working poor, but also provide refundable tax credits—supplemental income—above and beyond the income generated from poorly paying service-sector jobs. Families should have the opportunity to receive these credits as a monthly check to supplement their incomes. Some might consider these refundable tax credits as indirectly subsidizing the bottom lines of wealthy corporations who take advantage of poverty wages. I argue that, on the contrary, it represents a critical, efficient, direct, and nonstigmatizing approach to the growing presence of market-generated incomes that are not high enough for working Americans to raise their families and make ends meet.

Build Community Institutions for the Global Era

The public institutions of U.S. communities have failed to catch up with the dramatic transformation of the socioeconomic landscape. Children still attend school from 8 a.m. to early afternoon with long summer breaks, as if we were still in the agricultural age. Mothers have rapidly entered the labor market; however, full-time work is still defined as forty hours per week, and part-time work is treated only as supplemental work worthy of poverty wages. Although the reliance on these second, third, or even fourth incomes has dramatically increased, the minimum wage has stagnated in real value over the same period. Worse, although children are sent home from school in the early afternoon, mothers and fathers have to work late, often until six or seven in the evening. The highest levels of juvenile crime and injuries occur between these weekday hours.[25] At the same time, in the United States "the working poor are the least likely of all income groups to receive assistance with child care costs."[26] During the summer, lower-income children fall behind their more advantaged peers.[27] Subsidized day care, year-round school, and free before- and after-school care are cost-effective ways to improve the quality of life for lower-income working families. According to Warren and Tyagi, "the annual cost for a four-year-old to attend a child care center in an urban area is more than double the price of college tuition in fifteen states."[28]

Universal preschool programs beginning at age three—employing trained and certified early childhood educators—is one of the best investments that could be implemented. Every dollar spent on early childhood education is an estimated $8.00 savings in government expenditures in the future.[29] Schools represent the most vibrant public institution in most U.S. neighborhoods.

Although more affordable day-care spots are always desirable, the best solution for child care is universal early childhood education—particularly the full funding of and enrolling of all eligible children in Head Start programs.[30] The Scandinavian countries and France provide excellent models for this, worthy of emulation. According to Wilson, "In France, children are supported by three interrelated government programs—child care, income support and medical care. The child care program includes the establishments for infant care, high quality nursery schools (*écoles maternelles*), and paid leave for parents of newborns."[31] Enrolling all eligible children in Head Start programs would be a big first step in the right direction.

The U.S. urban infrastructure has been particularly hard hit by the disinvestments that have been partially caused by economic and social trends of the past twenty years—including suburbanization, the collapse of manufacturing, and the rise of the service sector. Many public schools in U.S. cities are run-down and underfunded, and Seattle is no exception. Massive investment in public primary, secondary, and postsecondary education would improve the opportunities for people to build their skills and find satisfying and rewarding work matched to their strengths. Using schools and community centers as centers of lifelong learning and high-quality recreational services would improve the quality of life of all urban residents. Reducing tuition for postsecondary education would help lower-income people get the education they need to secure stable, secure jobs.

The shame and stigma associated with poverty helps mask its presence in most U.S. communities—particularly among families with children. In *Unequal Childhoods*, an in-depth study of twelve families in New Jersey (out of a larger study of eighty-eight children), Annette Lareau found that "children's activities were expensive. A $25 enrollment fee, which middle-class families dismissed as 'insignificant,' 'modest,' or 'negligible,' was a formidable expense for all poor families and many in the working class."[32] The dynamics of poverty in the United States means that low-income and vulnerable children are in every community;[33] programs to help should also be universal.

Fundamentally, school reforms require more money for education, particularly in urban school systems. As pointed out by Jennifer Johnson,

School is the workplace of childhood. Success in school means learning facts, skills, and techniques but also learning that learning is possible, rewarding and worthwhile. . . . Because school funding is based on local property taxes, there is a direct relationship between the size of parents' bank balances and the quality of their children's education; as a consequence, the children who need the most generous school resources have the least access to them.[34]

State and federal policies that supplement the per-pupil funding for urban schools are more than a worthwhile investment to create an educated and skilled workforce (and an engaged democratic citizenry); they are also a way to help working-poor families realize the American dream of equal opportunity.

The stable living-wage full-time job for life has all but disappeared, yet government institutions have not been reshaped to accommodate the needs of working people, many of whom find themselves temporarily unemployed. A system of low-cost subsidized lifetime learning and education does not exist in the United States. With several years of free higher-level English language courses, many of the hotel employees interviewed in Seattle (and Vancouver), who in their countries of origin were accountants or small-business owners, would not be cleaning hotel rooms. Their talents are an untapped resource for both the United States and Canada.

This book shows that social policies have a significant impact on the quality of life and material hardships experienced by the working poor. Adopting these recommended policy reforms to lift families out of poverty, provide universal health insurance coverage, and make it easier for Americans to combine formal employment with raising the next generation would improve the quality of life for millions of Americans.

Improving the Lives of Hotel Employees and Their Families in Vancouver

In the past five years, the trend in Canadian social policy—with some notable exceptions such as child-care and early childhood education programs—is to move toward convergence with the United States. Many of the policies that made a positive difference for the employees I interviewed—for example, the Human Resources and Development Canada (HRDC) programs that provide subsidized training for individuals on unemployment—have been cut back or eliminated by the Canadian government. These cutbacks have multiplicative consequences —some unforeseen and many devastating for those barely making ends meet. Undermining families' economic security hurts more than just the immediate families; it also affects communities and, collectively, the country.

The following policy recommendations would help Canada stem the trend of increasing poverty and hardships among low-income workers and their families. They would reverse the tide and improve the lives of millions of Canadians who are at greater risk of hardship because of the recent policy cutbacks:

- End child poverty in Canada, as legislated unanimously by the federal Parliament in 2000, by raising the minimum wage and increasing refundable tax credits to low-income households to enact a minimum income system that brings the income of all Canadian households above the low-income cut-off (LICO) poverty line.
- Re-reform the Employment Insurance system to cover a higher percentage of the unemployed and provide paid tuition for job training programs for those with difficulty finding sustainable work.
- Extend the public Universal Health Care system to include dental and vision coverage, home care, and alternative therapies.
- Expand the number of subsidized day-care spaces to help families of young children.
- Implement a universal early childhood education programs for two- to four-year-olds. Maintain high levels of investment in urban infrastructure: parks, public transit, public education, community centers, and other civil society institutions.
- Use training, job placement, and child-care support to help people move from public assistance to secure, living-wage jobs; do not rely on punitive measures that harm poor children, who are among the most vulnerable members of society.
- Increase the minimum wage, and index it to inflation. Increase the Child Tax Benefit to lift working-poor families out of poverty.
- Reverse the recent across-the-board tax cuts in British Columbia, and use the additional revenue to pay for social programs to eliminate poverty and hardship and for refundable tax credits to lift all children out of poverty.
- Reduce tuition at public universities, and expand student loan programs to make postsecondary education and training a part of lifelong learning options for all people living in Canada.

The following section provides additional detail on some of these recommendations to improve the quality of life for Vancouver's working poor.

Maintaining Progressive Policies That Matter

The findings of the book confirm the critical importance of maintaining, at all levels of government, the progressive policy regime in place for residents of Vancouver. As a result of these policies, hotel employees and their children suffered less hardship than in Seattle and, combined with the larger public investment in health care and public education, these policies opened up opportunities and prevented financial vulnerability. Although some may argue that these policies cause an unhealthy economic rigidity in Vancouver, there are positive benefits for corporations, including a more stable workforce with higher skills—for example, unionized hotels in both Seattle and Vancouver save money in training, inspection, and security costs. Universal health care means employees have the flexibility to change jobs if they are unhappy. A commitment to progressive taxation to fund social programs should be maintained to continue to reduce market-generated income inequalities among Canadians.[35]

Canada should commit to achieving the goal—unanimously passed in Canada's federal Parliament in 1998—to completely eliminate child poverty in Canada.[36] The increasing effectiveness of the Guaranteed Income Supplement benefit in reducing poverty among elderly households from the late 1960s to the early 1990s suggests that similar subsidies aimed at reducing poverty among families with children could also be effective and politically feasible to implement.[37] Federal and provincial governments should expand the low-income family tax credit programs to lift many more working-poor households with children above the poverty line. Provinces should also consider raising the minimum wage to a living wage for an individual worker. Indexing the minimum wage to inflation would ensure that it increases with prices and keep workers out of poverty. Canada could implement a system in which a full-time minimum-wage worker would earn enough to be above the poverty line and the income tax system would supplement earnings for families with children to eliminate poverty among children.

Higher wages and benefits are associated with less need for network support and greater resource accumulation to purchase a home or provide a household safety net for hard economic times. Most Canadians are vulnerable in the event of economic downturns or corporate restructuring. Recent reforms to the Employment Insurance system should be revisited, including tougher restrictions on benefit eligibility. Canadian government cut-backs to the Employment Insurance program during the 1990s, including the raising of the requirements for the number of hours worked and the stricter eligibility rules, have reduced the percentage of unemployed workers receiving benefits from 80 percent in 1993 to less than 50 percent in 2005. Although this reduction has helped balance the federal budget, it has also no doubt increased the amount of material hardship suffered by Canadians who are now excluded from receiving benefits during periods of unemployment.[38]

Funding for job training or educational programs for the unemployed should also be reinstated. The Global Hotel study provides additional evidence that these programs work—particularly for the recent ethnic minority immigrants in the study, who used them to move from poverty wage jobs to secure living-wage jobs.

Instead of following the "low road" route of punishing those suffering from the impact of economic downturns by making public-assistance cutbacks,[39] policies should be reformed to prevent poverty among working parents with children, no matter what their job is. The effects of welfare time limits in the United States suggest that the proposed public-assistance benefit time limits would increase the poverty and suffering of the worst off, especially families with children. Welfare reform focused on helping public assistance recipients using public policy "carrots," including incentives and support, will be both more effective and sustainable (with higher upfront costs but lower social costs overall). Supports include providing training and job placement programs, subsidized day care, and social services to help the worst off. One-size-fits-all public-assistance reform hurts the neediest the most. Providing caseworkers with discretion, training, and resources to help public-assistance recipients get secure and sustainable jobs, without increasing desperate poverty among poor families with children, helps. Punitive measures, such as time limits, may reduce the number of people on welfare, but they will also have severe long-term consequences on the society as a whole: crime, school dropouts, poverty, hunger, and major hardship.

Income inequality in the past decade has been growing in Canada, with disproportionate income gains going to the wealthiest 10 percent of households. The consequences can be seen clearly in the explosion of food banks across the country. The tax and transfer system in Canada should be reformed to further reduce the increasing income inequality by providing additional financial and program support to low-income families with children. Beyond the fiscal redistribution policy, a continued commitment to urban public investment to maintain and improve universal high-quality public schools, transit, parks, community centers, clean and safe streets also counteracts growing market-generated inequality. Policies and programs that improve the quality of life for all urban residents also limit suburban sprawl by keeping middle-class families living in cities, which is critical to the future vibrancy of Canadian cities. Most Canadians live in metropolitan areas and, because the health of the central cities is vital to regional economic growth, these issues are linked to the Canadian dream of a just society.

The middle class—the foundation of democracy—is shrinking in North America. While some individuals are getting wealthier, many more Americans and Canadians are feeling the squeeze financially and are becoming worse off. In the United States, more of the poor are living on less than half of the meager U.S. poverty line. But many many more are also living on the edge of poverty—on a stressful precipice, possibly one or two bad days away from potentially serious material hardship. Poverty is not equally distributed across demographics. Although elderly poverty has been reduced—more so in Canada than the United States because of Canada's Guaranteed Income Supplement for seniors (not to mention lower medical costs)—it is children that are bearing the brunt, growing up in poor households marked by financial insecurity, want, and stress. Poverty is not increasing because people's values have changed. The economy has rapidly shifted away from manufacturing and agriculture to the service sector, where many jobs are not providing enough income for households, even with people working a total of two, three, or four jobs to make ends meet.

In the United States, health insurance coverage is a major cause of stress for many, including employers facing spiraling costs. In Washington state, unemployment benefits do not provide enough replacement income to act as an effective safety net for working-poor parents. Other than the federal EITC, programs that help low-income working families are few and far between; in the meantime, these families are being squeezed financially more than ever for decent housing, day care, food, clothing, health care, and college tuition. More and more of these families are forced to depend on the generosity of extended family and friends to make ends meet.

In Canada, government institutions and policies have helped soften the impact of these macroeconomic changes for vulnerable families. These policies guarantee health insurance coverage; unemployment benefits to provide a temporary cushion for laid-off workers, including extra help for parents with children; and maternity programs that allow a parent to take a one-year leave from work—with 55 percent pay—to look after a newborn infant. The British Columbia labor code creates conditions in which service-sector workers can easily unionize—to demand a fair shake from employers and improve job security —and the labor code extends real job protections and mandatory benefits to all workers. At the same time, a low minimum wage hurts many service-sector workers. In addition, many of the successful policies have already been cut back and others are constantly under attack in both British Columbia and Canada in general; it truly is a constant struggle.

In both the United States and Canada, social policies and institutions affect workers. Implementing the policy proposals recommended in this chapter will not be easy, but the quality of the life for millions of North Americans depends on it.

CHAPTER 10

Conclusion

In this book, I describe the ways in which social policy differences affect the lives of hotel employees at four international hotels, two in Seattle and two in Vancouver. The findings of the Global Hotel study contribute to our sociological understanding of urban poverty and social stratification. Whereas early sociological research on urban poverty focused on the individual behaviors and the culture of the urban poor, more recent research has pointed to the central role of macro-level contexts, such as deindustrialization and the disappearance of secure well-paid jobs for low-skilled workers.[1] The focus on structural factors helps explain the dismal plight of the increasing number of people trapped in poverty in the United States, despite political advances in civil rights and equal rights for women. At the same time, these structural theories fail to explain why cities in other similar countries such as Canada, despite being subject to similar global economic forces and trends, have not experienced similar increases in urban poverty and country-level inequality.

Explaining Increasing Urban Poverty and Inequality

What the structural theories fail to note is the central role of government social policy in constructing the social order. By sidelining social policy into the realm of *applied* sociology, sociologists miss how central it is for understanding the most basic aspects of inequality. Social policy is especially important for understanding the experiences of the working poor. The Global Hotel study shows that there is practically no aspect of life—employment conditions, wages, housing, health, or child care—that remains untouched by the way social policies structure opportunities, barriers, and resources.

Much of the early sociological research in the United States on the urban poor and immigrants focused intensely on the cultural traits of the poor. From Robert Park and Ernest Burgess of the Chicago School, sociologists have been intensely interested in the study of immigrant fortunes.[2] There has also been an intense interest in the experiences of African Americans in low-income urban neighborhoods.[3] Through ethnographic and quantitative research, sociologists have sought to explain differences among immigrant groups and the differences between people living in urban poverty and the rest of society. Classic examples of this kind of research include William Foote Whyte's *Street Corner Society*, Oscar Lewis's *La Vida: A Puerto Rican Family in the Culture of Poverty*, and *The Moynihan Report*.[4] Although these studies certainly did not ignore structural factors, their emphasis on the different values and culture of the urban poor fed a public dialogue that increasingly blamed the poor for their own circumstances.

The Focus on (the Wrong) Policy

Much sociological research has focused on public-assistance benefits and their recipients. However according to Katherine Newman, "there are millions more working-poor families in the United States than there are people on welfare or workfare."[5] And the findings of the Global Hotel study show that the quality of their lives and their material hardships are closely connected to a broad range of social policies. In the early 1980s, the United States (and the United Kingdom) implemented a conservative agenda at the federal level as described by Paul Pierson in *Dismantling the Welfare State?*[6] Tax cuts, mostly for the wealthy, and cuts to social programs became the order of the day. The mass lay-off of striking air-traffic controllers in the early 1980s represented a watershed moment in U.S. labor history—striking a sharp blow to workers' labor power. Canada did not experience a similar blow to labor power and continues to have a rate of unionization of the labor force similar to the mid-1970s. Although Pierson points out that some programs were more resilient, serious federal budget cuts were made to U.S. cities and to many social welfare policies from the 1980s to the present. During the same period, many of these same programs in Canada were supplemented and expanded.

The Focus on Macro-Level Economic Change

The United States went from a postwar boom—in which rising economic tides lifted all ships and the poorest the fastest—to a quick race to the bottom in terms of social protections. In the late 1980s, William Julius Wilson, in *The Truly Disadvantaged*, shifted scholarly focus to broader macro-level economic factors such as the dramatic shift in the economy from a Fordist manufacturing-based economy to a post-Fordist service-sector-based economy. He connects John Kasarda's arguments about deindustrialization and spatial mismatch theory to the fates of those trapped in U.S. urban ghettos. Wilson explains, "Urban minorities have been particularly vulnerable to the structural economic changes of the past two decades: the shift from goods-producing to service-producing industries, the increasing polarization of the labor market into low-wage and high-wage sectors, innovation in technology, and the relocation of manufacturing industries out of the central cities."[7] These macroeconomic changes interacted with the historical legacy of segregation and race prejudice, as described by Douglas Massey and Nancy Denton in *American Apartheid*,[8] and resulted in the physical expansion of the urban concentrations of poverty in many U.S. cities. At the same time, the forces of globalization and computer technology increased the transfer of manufacturing jobs away from highly unionized urban centers to lower-cost locations—not only abroad but also to the U.S. southwest and even to suburbs.

The decline of manufacturing has concurred with the rise of the service sector. This is clearly an important, but incomplete, part of the explanation of the worsening of urban poverty in many U.S. cities since the mid-1970s. Yet many U.S. scholars erroneously discuss the micro-level social impact of these macro-level changes in the economy with an aura of inevitability, assuming that the service sector must *necessarily* generate more inequality than manufacturing. Thus, the new global city—which Saskia Sassen characterizes in *The Global City* as a center of global finance—must be populated, on the one hand, by well-paid bankers, lawyers, and business executives, who Robert Reich calls "symbolic analysts" in *The Work of Nations*, and, on the other, by masses of poorly paid immigrant cleaners and other service workers.[9] An examination of cities in other countries similar to the United States—such as Canada—challenges the explanatory power of technological and economic changes as determinant factors in the rise of poverty.

No Jobs versus Bad Jobs versus Good Jobs

In the United States, putting the urban poor to work in formal employment has become the solution to the social ills of concentrated poverty offered by both sides of the political spectrum. In *When Work Disappears*,[10] Wilson argues that many of the social ills in urban poor neighborhood result from the devastating impact of joblessness on individuals, families, and communities. He points to a classic study of long-term unemployment in Marienthal, Austria, in the 1930s conducted after the only major factory in town closed in 1929.[11] Researchers found that the unemployed men experienced declining mental health as well as increasing isolation. The researchers attributed these affects to the loss of formal employment as a guiding structure in the men's lives. Yet there could be a different explanatory factor: the loss of their sense of security about the future. Economic research has clearly demonstrated the existence of risk adversity and people's preference for stability and security. Retirement, for example, does not cause the negative consequences observed in Marienthal.

In the Global Hotel study, temporary unemployment for workers in Vancouver did not cause serious stress if they knew they would receive replacement income from unemployment programs and would be returning to work after a few months. These findings point to the central role of future security; the ability of workers to know they will be in a financially secure position six months or one year in the future is critical.

It is not the disappearance of all formal employment but the disappearance of secure well-paid jobs that is responsible for the plight of the U.S. urban and nonurban poor. An insecure low-paying service-sector job creates a great deal of stress, as we have seen for the hotel workers and their families. It does not allow for workers to save, plan for the future, or experience many of the positive benefits of formal employment, but it requires them to spend more on clothes, child care, transportation, and other work-related expenses than a public-assistance recipient.[12] The findings of the Global Hotel study demonstrate that unionization provides greater job security for hotel workers. The study also shows that country-level policies can support the financial stability of low-income service-sector workers. Some of these policies are supplemental income tax credits, unemployment programs that provide an effective safety net even for working-poor parents, and a strong labor policy that protects and extends basic job benefits and protections from unjust dismissal to all workers (see chap. 3). In these ways, national policy can cause the very same low-level service-sector jobs for the same multinational corporations to have a different effect on employees, their families, and communities. Instead of a race to the bottom to attract any employer, governments should be encouraging companies that pay living wages, not poverty wages, and those that extend workers' job security, not insecurity. The findings of the Global Hotel study show that providing training opportunities is a better way to ensure long-term secure employment for unemployed workers than threatening to cut off their benefits (see chap. 6).

Initially, manufacturing did not provide secure living-wage job positions for low-skilled workers. Massive unionization created the secure living-wage manufacturing rung in the labor market. But now this segment of the labor market has declined sharply in both the United States and Canada, as corporations use advances in technology to globalize production, with devastating consequences for low-skilled workers, particularly in the United States. In Canada, the higher rates of unionization have helped protect some low-skilled Canadian workers by creating secure living-wage jobs in the service sector. The Global Hotel study findings show that workers at unionized hotels were more confident and did not fear management in the way they did in non-unionized workplaces (see chap. 4). The resulting "professionalization" of these service-sector jobs reduces employer training costs, inspection, and even the need for extensive security systems. In addition, the union coverage in the Vancouver hotel sector is large enough to create a union wage effect, lifting the hourly wages for employees working at all downtown hotels. Indirectly, political institutional power of the labor unions, as an advocate for lower-income workers, helps shape a stricter labor code and implement more progressive policies at all levels of government in Canada; the same cannot be said of the United States.

The Central Role of Social Policy

The Global Hotel Study demonstrates that, although the ranks of the working poor are growing in both the United States and Canada, the dynamics of urban poverty are different. This points to the critical intervening role of policy and institutional differences. Although most scholarly books on urban poverty now contain a policy chapter at the end, which provides prescriptions for a better world based on the findings of the study, few bring the role of government policy to the center of the analysis; doing so, my findings suggest, is critical.

Cultural studies of urban poverty and working poverty continue to ignore the central role of social policy. Although studies of urban street life in the ghetto abound—such as Elijah Anderson's *Streetwise* and *Code of the Street* and Sudhir Venkatesh's *American Project*—much of this important research on the urban poor focuses only on the worst off and emphasizes cultural factors.[13] Labor-market research on the low-income service sector has largely focused on tertiary industries such as domestic work, garment factories, and fast-food restaurants. The Global Hotel study findings suggest that the scope of research should be expanded to other service-sector occupations in the hospitality, retail, and restaurant industries. It also highlights the importance of studying the less sensational but larger, and largely invisible, group of lower-level service-sector workers in order to understand the new economy and current social stratification.

Social Policy Is More than Public Assistance

Social welfare policy differences affect the material hardships experienced by the hotel employees and their families. The most important differences are not in public assistance but, rather, in the terms and conditions of unemployment compensation policy and other social policies. Whereas the unemployment benefits for hotel employees in Seattle were generally too low to be useful, Vancouver hotel workers received higher benefits, especially the low-income families with children. Government programs in Vancouver also provided funding for unemployed workers to obtain professional skills training. Many recently arrived ethnic minority immigrants who I interviewed took advantage of this job training to ascend from poverty-wage jobs to secure living-wage employment in the hotel industry.[14]

Other government policy differences are also important. The combined Canadian federal and provincial Child Tax Credit benefits provided more of an income supplement for Vancouver hotel workers than the equivalent U.S. federal Child Tax Credit and Earned Income Tax Credit did for Seattle hotel workers. The Canadian government Registered Retirement Savings Plan program helped Vancouver employees save equity that acted to protect against material hardships during periods of unemployment and lay-offs. More employees in Vancouver reported having retirement savings, and those with such savings had, on average, more money saved than did employees in Seattle. Labor policies in Vancouver requiring paid vacation, Workers' Compensation protection, and a one-year paid maternity leave (through the Employment Insurance system) also reduced material hardship during periods of low employment income. Working-poor households in Vancouver generally had more income relative to their expenses than did those in Seattle.

Poverty Does Not Stop at the Poverty Line

This study also challenges the limited way poverty is discussed in most academic studies. With increasing numbers of people (particularly children) living in households earning less than the U.S. poverty line, it is important to have a consistent indictor across time to measure progress (or lack of progress) in reducing poverty. But this study shows that poverty is also multidimensional —involving more than just income—and that the deleterious consequences of poverty—material deprivation, hardship, and future insecurity—can impact individuals and families earning incomes of up to twice the official U.S. poverty line and beyond. Family level resources (including wealth, network resources, and future opportunities) and society level resources (including government programs, neighborhood institutions, and training opportunities) mediate the relationship between income and outcomes for low-wage workers and their families. For example, the current U.S. health care system condemns all but the wealthiest Americans to the fear that they might one day—in an instant—be bankrupted by major medical expenses.

The diversity of experiences among hotel workers interviewed in Seattle and Vancouver demonstrate the non-linear, interactional pathways that can lead to hardship among the "near poor" and working poor. It also shows that as labor markets create more and more insecure jobs in the service sector, specific government policies can help increase security, particularly for working parents with children, and thus reduce experiences of material hardship.

Inequality Is More than Just Income

The findings of the Global Hotel study also demonstrate the inadequacy of the way inequality has traditionally been measured—almost exclusively as income inequality. Melvin L. Oliver and Thomas M. Shapiro in *Black Wealth/White Wealth*[15] show that inequality between blacks and whites in the United States is much more severe if examined from the perspective of differences in wealth and not just income; they also make the critical point that wealth inequality is different than income inequality in its consequences for racial inequality. My research adds a new dimension to inequality research—public resources. The analysis of public investment and amenities (see chap. 7) shows that even in countries that have experienced very similar increases in market-generated income inequality, the way this income inequality translates into the lived experiences of families varies tremendously based on the quality of public amenities such as transportation, schools, and parks. In Vancouver, the greater public investment in high-quality, accessible, and low-cost public transit; public education; waterfront parks; public swimming pools; and community centers create institution-rich communities in both lower- and higher-income neighborhoods. These institutions improved the quality of people's lives, promoted social connectedness, and also counteracted market-generated inequality. In Seattle, without these investments, many hotel workers lived in more socially isolated neighborhoods and in greater fear of being victims of crime.

The relationship between inequality and health has also been increasingly recognized in sociological and public health research, much of the evidence pointing to correlations between levels of inequality and health outcomes. The Global Hotel study adds to this literature by suggesting some of the pathways by which inequality and, especially, poverty in the U.S. context worsen health outcomes. The Canadian universal system of health insurance reduced health-related hardships and financial stress for Vancouver employees compared to Seattle employees (see chap. 5). Despite the provision of health insurance benefits by the Seattle hotels, employees still reported serious problems with the health-care system. More than 25 percent interviewed at both Seattle hotels lacked health insurance because they were still in the probation period before benefits began. Employees who had health insurance coverage found that their insurance could be inadequate to protect them financially in the event of a serious health emergency. These situations caused stress for many Seattle hotel workers and their families. In contrast, Vancouver hotel workers reported not worrying about accessing health care, and their concerns about seeking preventative and emergency care were completely decoupled from financial considerations, even though some workers lost their extended health benefits during lay-offs in the slow winter season.

Bringing Social Policy into the Segmented Assimilation Debate

Because many of the hotel workers were immigrants, my research also contributes to the debates about segmented assimilation and patterns of incorporation of immigrant groups. Debates about the fate of ethnic minorities in

North American cities have intensified over the past thirty years.[16] In the United States, the second, third, and fourth generations of certain groups of immigrants appear to be doing worse economically than the previous generation—trapped in poverty and hardship in the lower rungs of the socioeconomic hierarchy that is growing ever more unequal. Whereas theories of incorporation generally focus on immigrant-related policies, such as refugee settlement policy, human capital, and multicultural policies, as creating the context of reception, this book suggests that broader macro-level social and labor policies are also important in creating this context. In the United States, the current health policy regime acts to socially exclude many working-poor ethnic minority immigrants, with deleterious consequences for individuals, families, and groups.

Many of the most interesting debates about urban poverty are about segmented assimilation (see chapters 2 and 3). By studying immigrant experiences and fortunes, sociologists are highlighting social forces and processes that impact everyone. Thus far, segmented assimilation theory focuses heavily on barriers to inclusion, particularly those disadvantaging specific groups. Much of this research compares the fortunes of different groups of immigrants from different countries of origin, even within one city. This research design tends to highlight group-specific factors, including human capital and other cultural explanations, to explain differences in outcomes. Yet the findings of the Global Hotel study suggest the critical importance of including in the analysis *both* the macro- and micro-level resources available to immigrant groups. They also point to the central role of non-immigrant-specific social policy for determining the opportunities and resources immigrants will have to shape their groups' future destiny. These macro-level resources include government-subsidized savings and equity programs, such as the RRSP savings programs that helped immigrant families in Vancouver build an equity cushion rather than having to rely on extended family to cope during difficult financial times. These programs also enabled workers to accumulate capital for a downpayment on a home, thus gaining the material status that defines mainstream middle-class Canadian society.

In contrast, in Seattle the social welfare policy regime left most hotel employees on their own to cope with the tough financial times that frequently beset low-income workers in the service sector. Working-poor families in Seattle relied on their social networks as a private safety net, borrowing money from family and friends, working more than one job, and living with relatives to make ends meet. In extreme cases, two families would share a housing unit designed for one family. In other words, Seattle employees were generally in a more precarious position in terms of hardship than Vancouver employees, despite working in similar jobs for the same companies. If a worker was laid-off in Vancouver, an accessible Employment Insurance system with a low-income family supplement provided enough income for an employee to survive without having to rely on extended family or other social networks.

The rapidly shifting service-sector-dominated economy in postindustrial North American cities has profound implications for the experiences of all urban dwellers, particularly recently arrived immigrants, struggling to enter the labor force and provide a better life for themselves and their children. The findings of this study are also applicable to the broader theories of social exclusion, segmented labor-market theory, and stratification. Globalization may be creating primary and tertiary labor markets in many countries, but the impact of these macroeconomic changes on workers cannot be understood without studying the policy context that shapes the effects of these changes.

Cross-National Qualitative Employment Research: A New Methodology

This study also adds a methodological contribution to the empirical toolkit of C. Wright Mills' *The Sociological Imagination*.[17] Although in line with Charles Ragin's Qualitative Comparative Analysis,[18] the methodology used in the Global Hotel study goes a step further. Comparing workers in the *same jobs* in two *similar cities* cross-nationally has been demonstrated to be a useful tool for advancing our understanding of the social milieu of disadvantaged groups. The study also provides insights into the potential benefits of using qualitative methods in cross-national comparative research, going beyond simply suggesting causal correlations to explicate the specific pathways connecting policy differences to the subjective experiences of people living, working, and making ends meet in the postindustrial city.

Comparing the lives of hotel industry employees in Vancouver and Seattle demonstrates how differences in health policy, labor policy, unemployment policy, and other social policies affect the quality of life and levels of material hardship experienced by hourly hotel employees and their families. The findings reinforce the importance of understanding the role of government policy in shaping social stratification in advanced industrial nations. The impact of policy differences can be difficult to disentangle because they form an interconnected web that has varying importance for different people at different periods of their lives.

Advancing U.S.-Canadian Comparative Research

The previous U.S.-Canadian comparative literature tends to focus on the impact of policy and institutional differences individually, often constrained by the limited comparative data available at the macro-level. One of this study's findings is that, from the perspective of individuals, it is the *interactions* of different government policies and institutions that matter. This study also shows that the impact of government programs varies greatly over an individual's lifetime, mattering more during a health crisis, unemployment, and the early years of maternity. Together, these two findings point to the critical importance of longitudinal and life-course research for understanding the impact of policy and institutions.

A Country's Choice: The "High Road" or the "Low Road"

Sociological researchers should to continue to strive to explain the causes and consequences of poverty in the postindustrial city. The interplay between theoretical development and new empirical research is critical. The impact of the institutional and policy differences between the United States and Canada does not look so small in terms of the subjective experience of individuals living and working in Seattle and Vancouver. The "on the ground" perspective both challenges and complements the findings of quantitative cross-national comparative studies. Although my findings do not show that Canada is a social democratic nation, they make clear that a "high road" and "low road" exist within the neoliberal model. There is a political choice made by policy makers who construct the social order. Sweden represents one often-discussed model, but Canada has also responded to international economic changes in a different way than the United States. Although the United States and Canada shared similar social welfare systems (and poverty levels) in the early 1970s, Canada has created universal health insurance, maintained and extended social programs, and heavily invested in urban public infrastructure. The United States has, during the same period, cut back social programs and dramatically reduced union coverage, urban infrastructure and worker protections, with serious consequences for the working poor.

Unemployment, health-care, labor, and other social policies shape the socioeconomic milieu in which future generations grow up. We know some of the devastating consequences of poverty, instability, and hardship on child development. For the working poor, this study shows that policies that help employees create household equity cushions to protect against material hardship during economic downturns can matter a great deal. Health insurance coverage and unemployment insurance policies and benefits play a vital role in sustaining the well-being of working-poor families, and government-funded training programs provide a hand up. Public investment in family-friendly neighborhood institutions and urban quality of life can counteract some of the impact of income inequality. A living wage is also vitally important, as is the ability of service-sector employees who want to unionize to gain collective representation in the workplace.

Differences That Matter points to the vital need for sociologists studying the economy and the family to consider the mediating role of state policies and institutions. Throughout history, technological change has been a constant; it will continue to be so. The sociological understanding of poverty must include a detailed examination of the role of social policy in shaping the socioeconomic hierarchy and the quality of life of low-income workers and their families. Rather than being just an applied topic, it is a key issue for theory and substance. Much of the sociological literature on poverty focuses on family formation, cultural expectations, and labor-market discrimination. Yet the role of the state and public policy is fundamental to the way in which poverty unfolds in every society.

Even before an individual's birth, social policy creates the conditions that either enrich or deteriorate his or her life trajectory. Like the soil in which a seed germinates and grows, a child's development into an adult and senior is shaped by the rules and institutions of the concentric rings of family, neighborhood, community, city, nation, and the world that surround him or her. This ecological model from child development theory enlightens sociological research on poverty, policy, and families.[19] The institutions within each ring of the circle interact with one another and are impacted by government policies such as prenatal care, day care, health care, education, neighborhood institutions, transit, labor policy, tax credits and benefits, and retirement benefits on a local, state, national, and international level. Through these interdependent institutions, the experience of poverty in an advanced industrial nation can be ameliorated by government social policies.

APPENDIX

Methodology and Background
This appendix has four parts: a methodology section, in which I discuss how I recruited hotel workers for interviewing, provide detailed information about the interview protocol used during the employee interviews, and discuss follow-up interviews and other research techniques used to gather supplemental data; an analysis section, in which I describe the process I used to analyze the data; a final section, in which I address some reflections on the research; and a personal background section, in which I describe my background and outline why I decided to study the working poor in the United States and Canada.

Methodology

Selecting and Interviewing Hotel Workers
Recruiting hotel workers to be interviewed was a lesson in the gap between ideal research goals and on-the-ground reality. The initial goal for recruiting hotel employees to interview was to generate perfectly matched samples of hotel workers in Seattle and Vancouver along the following dimensions (listed in declining order of priority): job position, company, gender, age, immigration status, educational attainment, ethnicity, and family structure. In reality, the intensive matching process turned out to be prohibitively difficult. With the limited time and resources I had available, I completed in-depth interviews with almost every employee who volunteered. I made an active effort, however, to recruit hotel workers from similar departments in each hotel.

I had planned to request interviews during my participant-observation research in the hotel workplaces and use the snowball sampling technique—requesting each person interviewed to introduce me to other potential respondents (as employed by Kathyrn Edin and Laura Lein). This method proved partially successful in practice. I occasionally arranged interviews with hotel employees I met during my participant observation at the hotels. After their interview, many workers shared their positive experience with their colleagues and encouraged them to volunteer. At the same time, it was difficult to interview significant numbers of staff members using this method of recruitment exclusively. Hence, with the permission of the management and the union (where applicable), I also posted a sign-up sheet with my contact information in the employee areas of the hotels. Some hotel employees, even those referred to me by co-workers, preferred to sign up for an interview and have me contact them; other employees saw the sign-up sheet and decided that it sounded interesting and contacted me to be interviewed. Each employee interviewed received CA$50 or US$40 as compensation for his or her time (approximately two hours).

The Employee Interview Protocol

I began with a survey of background-information questions and then tape-recorded—with the employee's permission—the second half of the interview, which involved open-ended questions and conversation. Most interviews lasted from one and one-half to two hours.

Part 1: Survey Questions   In creating the interview protocol, I decided against re-inventing the wheel. Many of the questions came from instruments used by other researchers, including Katherine Newman, Kathryn Edin, and Laura Lein. I had used some of these questions as an interviewer before, and others came from appendix sections on methodology such as this one. Many of these questions are tried and tested, and I thought they also would generate data that could later be compared to studies of poverty in other cities.

The first section asks for the respondent's essential personal background information to help me match similar hotel employees in Seattle and Vancouver. These questions include:

What is your name?
Where were you born?
Did you immigrate to the United States/Canada? If so, when?
Where were your parents born?
Where did you spend your teenage years?
How many years of high school have you completed?
Do you have a college or other advanced degree?
Do you have any children?

I also asked questions about the respondent's housing situation:

What is your current address?
When did you move to this residence?
Do you rent or own?
How much is your monthly mortgage payment/rent?
Who lives there besides you?
How many bedrooms do you have?
Do you rent out any rooms to others?

What was the address of the last place you lived before this one?
How long did you live there?

Have any of the following things happened to you in your home at any time in the past five years: A leaky roof, ceiling, toilet, hot-water heater, or other plumbing problems? Rats, mice, roaches, or other insects? Broken windows? Major wind drafts? A poorly functioning heating system? Exposed wires or other electrical problems? Holes in the walls? A stove or refrigerator that didn't work properly? Inadequate garbage pick-up?

I asked questions to get a sense of the hardships that the respondent might have experienced so that I could follow up on these in the open-ended section of the interview. These include:

> Have any of the following things happened to you in the past five years: Electricity service suspended? Heat shut off? Hot water turned off? Phone service cut off? Unable to pay rent on time? Been evicted?
> Do you own or lease a car?
> Was there ever a time in the past 5 years when you were without a home?
> How much credit card debt do you owe?
> What is the credit card debt of everyone in your household?

Afterward, I asked every respondent to estimate his or her average monthly expenditures on: Housing (including Condo Fees)? Transportation? Food/Eating out? Child care? Clothing? Telephone? Utilities? Cable TV? Alcohol? Cigarettes/tobacco products? Going out? Gifts? Life/burial/renter's insurance? Lottery, credit card payments? Illegal substances? Layaway payments? Movies? Relatives outside of the house? Children's school supplies? Bathroom products? Kitchen products? Laundry? Medical care/insurance? Church? Other non-profit/charity? Union dues? School loans?

Next, I asked the respondent to tell me about all the different ways his or her household earns money including: Regular job earnings? Odd jobs (under-the-table work, domestic work, babysitting)? Workers' compensation? Veterans' benefits or armed forces allocations? Illegal activities (hustling, selling drugs, fencing goods)? Alimony or child support? Social Security income or Supplemental Security income (SSI)? Food stamps? Welfare payments? Tax credits (Earned Income Tax Credit, Canada Child Tax Benefit)? Money from partner, family, or friends? Other sources of income?

I also specifically asked the respondent to estimate how much he or she received every month from various sources: From their monthly income from work? From child support/alimony? From informal/second jobs? From government welfare? From sales, like Amway, Avon? From the sale of sex, drugs, and/or stolen goods? From contributions from family and friends? absent father? boyfriend? From any legal settlements? From church/community organizations? From energy assistance? From child-care subsidies?

I asked each hotel worker to estimate his or her own annual income before taxes and his or her household's annual income before taxes. I also asked if the respondent had any savings, retirement savings, and term deposits, stocks, bonds, and investments. I asked if he or she had filed a tax return, how much he or she estimated the paid taxes to be, and if he or she had gotten any money back from taxes in the previous years.

The next two sections provide a comparable picture of how the respondent and his or her family make ends meet. First, I asked him or her how difficult it was to pay the household bills. The next section focused on work. I asked many questions about his or her job:

What is your job position?
How many hours do you work per week?
How difficult was it to get the job?
How long have you worked there?
What was your starting salary?
How much do you currently earn? How much do you estimate that you earn in tips?
When was your last raise? How much was it?
What are your typical hours?
How often do you work weekends?
Have you worked overtime in the past six months? Do you get paid extra?
Is the job unionized?
How do you get to work on a typical day?
How long does it take and how much does it cost?

I also had the respondent tell me about his or her other jobs, the last three jobs he or she had held, and any periods of unemployment during the past five years.

Next is the health section, which asks detailed questions about the respondent's health and his or her household's access and use of health services. I had the respondent rate his or her physical health, mental, or emotional health, and compare his or her health overall to someone of a similar age. I asked if he or she had health insurance, who provided it, if he or she has a regular doctor, where he or she accesses health services, and how far it is from his or her home. In order to get a better sense of the respondent's health, I asked:

When was the last time you saw the doctor? Why.

Does anyone in your household have any major health problems?

Were there any days in the last month you could not work or cut back on
    your work because of health problems?

Have you delayed getting medical care because you thought you could not
    afford it?

When was the last time your children saw the doctor? Where do they go to
    see the doctor?

Have your children had a check-up in the past twelve months?

Have your children visited the dentist the past twelve months?

How many days of school did your children miss last year?

Did you have to miss work because a child was ill (if so, how many days in
    the past year)?

How many hours of sleep do you get per night?

Have you or you children been unable to get, because you could not afford
    it, proper medical care, dental care, needed medications, physical therapy,
    eyeglasses, or mental health care?

The next section asks about the respondent's social network. It asks him or
her to answer a set of questions about his or her spouse/partner and up to five
friends, five relatives, and five current neighbors to assess how often the respondent interacts with other people in his or her networks and if he or she
ever uses them for financial or other assistance. Some questions included:

Who do you work with?

Who can you count on in the event of a major crisis, such as taking care of
    your children if they were hospitalized, allowing you to move in with if
    you are evicted or something serious happens?

Who have you counted on for a major favor or in a crisis in the past year?

Who has steady jobs?

Who has told you about job opportunities in the past?

These data helped me understand how respondents used their extended social
networks during times of crisis.

Part 2: Open-Ended Questions   I next asked for the hotel worker's permission to tape-record the balance of the interview. In the three major open-ended
sections, I focused on the respondent's material hardships, neighborhood perceptions, and future aspirations. Some of this part of the interview was necessarily repetitive because I asked the respondent to expound on issues brought

up during the first part of the interview. I had an extensive list of questions prepared in each section, which I used to guide the conversation.

In the material hardships section, these questions include an opportunity for the respondent to tell detailed stories about his or her households' experiences with a range of hardships, including periods of unemployment, not being able to pay the bills, bankruptcy, evictions, experiencing hunger, crowding, not being able to afford appropriate clothing, homelessness, and being forced to board with a friend or relative. I asked the respondent to tell me about these situations, how he or she managed to resolve them, and what resources were used. Some questions include:

> Has there ever been a time when you needed to buy food for you or your family and could not afford to buy it?
> Have you ever gone without food because you could not afford to buy it?
> In the past five years, have you ever been unable to afford the minimum payments on your credit card debt?
> Have you ever had to visit a hospital emergency room or take your child to the emergency room?
> Did you have to pay a large medical bill?

Not all questions related to major hardships. I also asked, if relevant:

> What do your children do after school?
> Who watches over your children while you are working or out?
> If your children are in a formal day-care program, tell me about the program?
> Are your children involved in any activities during the weekends?
> What do your school-age children do during the summertime?

To finish, I focused on a positive topic:

> Tell me about your last vacation? When was it? Where did you go?
> When do you plan to take your next vacation?

The neighborhood perceptions section collects data about the kinds of neighborhoods the matched workers live in. I began with a hypothetical: Suppose you run into a friend from another part of the city, and they ask you to tell them about your current neighborhood, what would you tell them? I also asked them to describe their neighbors, nearby shops, local schools, community institutions, public transportation. Some questions dealt with personal safety:

How about the crime issue in your neighborhood?

Is it much of a problem? If yes, what kinds of problems? Theft? Drugs? Gangs? Homeless? Violence?

Do you generally feel safe on the streets during the day? What about at night? What about for your kids?

Have you or anyone in your household ever been a victim of crime? If so, when? What happened?

How does this neighborhood compare to the last neighborhood you lived in?

Finally, the future aspirations section solicits information about the respondent's thoughts about his or her future and children's future. They include:

Where do you see yourself in five years and ten years from now?

How do you feel about your job?

What would be your dream job?

What groups are you involved in?

How do you feel about unions?

What do you think the future has in store for your children?

I ended with the ladder question, described in chapter 8.

I had hoped to have each hotel worker interviewed provide the name, address, and telephone number of three people who would know how to get in touch with him or her, in case I wanted to interview him or her again in the future. But in practice this, unfortunately, did not prove feasible. At the end of each interview, both the respondent and I were usually exhausted. I thanked him or her and had him or her complete some paperwork for Harvard relating to compensation.

Post–September 11 Follow-Up Interviews in Vancouver

From October to December 2001, I attempted to contact by telephone as many respondents interviewed in Vancouver as possible to ask them how they were impacted by the immediate economic downturn in the hotel industry. The goal of this follow-up was to explore the strength of the safety net under a sudden shock or economic downturn. Had social policies mitigated material hardship among the respondents in Vancouver? At the same time, as I was planning to interview hotel-industry employees in Seattle beginning in the spring of 2002, I wanted to check and see if the conditions of my original interview respondents had changed dramatically in light of the hotel industry recession.

I completed follow-up interviews with twenty-two out of the thirty-eight employees interviewed. It was difficult to contact everyone in my sample because telephone-contact information had not been collected for every respondent during the initial interviews. With few exceptions, however, most respondents, re-interviewed by phone, reported little or no change in their work situation from the previous years. Several lower-seniority room attendants reported they had been laid off earlier and more suddenly than in the past. Of course, the respondents who I was unable to contact may have been worse off. In addition, the full impact caused by the economic downturn might not have been felt until the early spring, especially if room attendants began to finish up their Employment Insurance benefits eligibility before the economy recovered. The general patterns from the re-interviews reinforced the patterns uncovered during the original interviews in Vancouver—the hardships of respondents who were vulnerable as a result of the downturn in the hotel economy were mitigated by the Employment Insurance system.

Supplemental Data

Open-ended interviews with managers and union representatives provided an important opportunity for managers and union leaders to discuss their perceptions of social policy differences between the United States and Canada and their assessment of whether these differences impact their hotel's personnel policies, hiring, quality of workers, and turnover rates. They also opened the door in terms of providing me permission to access the hotel sites to recruit employees for in-depth interviewing and conduct participant-observation research.

I collected data through participant observation at all four hotel sites, observing workers in the hotels, including room attendants, maintenance engineers, and Guest Service employees. I identified and built trust with potential respondents during these experiences as well as recording details about the workplace. I also used the several occasions when I conducted in-depth employee interviews and open-ended management interviews at each hotel to observe the employees' working life and employee relations.

The participant-observation research at the hotels brought me into the employees' homes and neighborhoods and provided an essential complement to the in-depth interviews.

Analyzing the Data

Altogether, the interviews and participant-observation notes generated thousands of pages of material that I needed to assess to determine how social policy differences impacted the quality of life and levels of material hardship of hotel employees in Seattle and Vancouver. The results of the twenty-page survey question sections of each in-depth employee interview were tallied, and the results were recorded in a large spreadsheet for analysis. Transcriptions of employee interviews—completed with the help of Kate Bush at the University of British Columbia—and notes from open-ended and spontaneous interviews as well as from participant observation in- and outside of the hotels were analyzed with the use of Qualitative Social Research's N6 software. The software helped me to discover major themes and patterns contained in the data. Through the text-search function, every mention of a search phrase could be instantly identified within the thousands of pages of data and collected into a "node." From these nodes, I could jump back and forth to each document to uncover the context of the statement in the original interview transcription or notes. The pattern analysis capability allowed me to test hypotheses based on the collected data.

I decided to focus on differences in labor policy, health care, social welfare policy, and urban public infrastructure investment because these areas emerged as dominant themes. Unfortunately I had to make the decision to leave out in-depth discussions of many other fascinating and unexpected themes in the interviews. These include immigration policies that separate mothers from their children, detailed discussions of job routines and the work life of hotel workers, social network differences, a gendered analysis, and race relations in the workplace.

Final Reflections

One way qualitative methodology differs from quantitative methodology is in the thick description of the process of research found in the appendix. While this description is generally not constructed so that other researchers can actually replicate the exact study, it allows the reader to get a sense of where the findings come from and to make their own independent decisions as to what kinds of biases may be involved. It is also valuable learning material for other researchers interested in using qualitative research methods. Although the goal of being unbiased is impossible to attain, I did try to follow the same procedures in sample selection, participant observation, and the employee interviews in all four hotels so that some of these biases might partially cancel out. In an ideal study, I would have done a follow-up with all the hotel employees and completed a second interview, in order to get a sense of how their lives had changed and the role of policy in shaping their experiences.

But this is a project for the future. I am still learning about Canada's social policy regime. Even after spending several years living in Canada and studying the Canadian system, I am surprised to occasionally learn new lessons and gain new insights about social policy—when filling out a tax return, conversing with my partner and her family, attending a seminar, or looking into buying an apartment. Living in Vancouver during my research and while writing up these findings has proven to be immeasurably valuable. I look forward to the joy of future discoveries.

Personal Reflexivity: What Led Me to a U.S.–Canadian Comparative Study?

I come from a family of immigrants. My father was born in India and migrated to Pakistan at the age of eleven. He became an engineer and then accepted an opportunity to travel across the world to attend graduate school in Stockholm, Sweden, on a scholarship. There he met my mother, and they decided to move to Canada, with an eye toward eventually moving to the United States. After staying with a friend in Montreal and interviewing for jobs across Canada, he accepted an engineering job in the cold flat prairies of Saskatchewan, and they moved to Regina. There, they married, went snowmobiling for their honeymoon, and, after a year, moved to Ottawa. After living in Ottawa for a year and a half, my father was offered his dream job in Washington, D.C. So they headed south, and, after a brief relocation to New York City (where I was born) for another job, they settled in Columbia, Maryland, a suburb between the cities of Baltimore and Washington. My dad's mother and brother and his family also shortly moved from Karachi, Pakistan, to Columbia, Maryland; they live a short ten-minute drive from our house.

Columbia, Maryland, has a unique history. On the land from eight large farms, James Rouse, a developer, planned and built his dream—a bold vision for the early 1960s in the United States—of a mixed-race, mixed-income planned suburban community managed by a nonprofit organization, with excellent neighborhood public schools, parks, pools, community centers, and a local shopping area. I grew up on Happy Heart Lane (all streets in Columbia are named after lines from children's stories), which was filled with families, mostly with young children, with a wide range of ethnic, racial, and religious backgrounds. I had early leanings toward social science research—as a third grader I completed a formal survey of my classmates about their allowances in order to convince my parents that my sisters and I deserved one (and how much it should be). I completed a second survey a few years later about the television viewing habits of my fellow classmates to gauge how many hours, on average, they were allowed to spend watching TV. Articles complete with computer-generated pie charts—not peer-reviewed—describing my findings were published in the local *Columbia Flier,* although these studies did not result in the hoped-for weekly allowance or additional TV time. Growing up in Columbia, it was easy to feel that America was indeed the land of opportunity for all. Although not a panacea—murders in the neighborhood twice temporarily shattered the innocence of our childhood—the fundamentals of good schools, diversity, and the ethos that anyone who works hard can get ahead sold us on the American dream.

My bubble was burst when I moved a thirty-minute drive away to begin university at Johns Hopkins. Located in the heart of Baltimore, the inequities of race and class that seemed so distant and unreal in Columbia were an ever-present part of my everyday experiences. I began my undergraduate studies planning to be a corporate lawyer, but four years later I was engrossed in trying to understand the forces that had devastated the communities, lives, hopes, dreams, and opportunities for so many in Baltimore.

An eight-hour police ride-a-long in the Eastern District of Baltimore—the inspiration for the TV show *Homicide*—provided a stark introduction to America's other side: the boarded-up houses, the pot-holed streets, the crumbling buildings, the men on the corner, the barren playgrounds. We answered forty calls in eight hours, each opening up a tale of hopeless desperation, tragedy, and woe: a man dying from several gunshots at my feet, domestic violence, an addict staggering out of a fast-food washroom with a needle still in his arm, the helplessness of the policeman I rode with. I will never forget his words: "We are basically fighting another Vietnam down here." He felt the problems of the Eastern District of Baltimore were invisible and unnoticed; most of America would rather look away and drive quickly on than visit the devastation of urban centers and confront the question: Why do these problems exist in the urban centers of the richest country in the world?

We raced wildly, siren's blaring, through the devastated urban dystopia of east Baltimore to the busy crime scene, an all too frequent scene and a perversely social one—people poured out of the row houses and gathered around. Some nights are better than others for the police. Sometimes this is related to the weather—tempers flare on hot humid summer nights when those forced to live in crowded non-air-conditioned homes pour out onto the stoops and sidewalks. Before my ride-a-long, a massive sweep—the large-scale imprisonment of many black men—had led to a temporary (two-week) calm in lethal violence. But that night it was shattered by gunshots and murder. Enough gunshots still ring out in Baltimore—which has an annual murder rate of around 350 lives—to take hundreds of lives and injure and traumatize thousands.

Those eight hours changed my life. They created the research questions that are driving my research today. The first is: Why are there so many poor families in such a rich country? The second is: What changes would make a difference and improve the lives of those living at the very bottom of the U.S. socioeconomic hierarchy?

During an internship with a public defender in Baltimore and as a student in the esteemed halls of Oxford and Harvard, I have focused on lessons from a comparative perspective. What can be learned from other countries that share many similarities to the United States but have managed to avoid the inequality and severe poverty that have been growing in the United States over the past four decades?

This study is my first major attempt to add to the debate about urban poverty and the working poor. I started with a new idea. I wanted to compare the fortunes of similar groups under two different social policy regimes. At the end of summer 1999, I went on my first trip to Niagara Falls. The contrast between Niagara Falls, New York—with run-down motels along a highway and the rusted-out shells of now-defunct factories—and Niagara Falls, Ontario, was stark. Crossing over the Rainbow Bridge, the Canadian side featured a public waterfront park along the edge of a casino. Along the promenade, children laughed and ran around while their parents browsed tourist shops and stands, and people took photos of one of nature's greatest wonders. Several restaurants, large hotels, and a casino sat by the edge of the falls. There are several levels of lookouts, and in addition tourists can take a ferry into the center under the Horseshoe Falls—feeling the mighty spray on *The Maid of the Mist* boat— or buy a ticket and climb down the stairs to see what a waterfall looks like from behind the torrent. The Niagara Falls are shaped like a horseshoe—with one half in the United States and the other half in Canada. The difference is not in the geography but in planning and public infrastructure investment. I started thinking that perhaps differences between the two countries may run deeper than simply health-care policy.

Comparing the United States and Canada

My analysis began quantitatively, first with my own attempts to compare U.S. Census and Statistics Canada data. I quickly confronted comparability problems and issues—including differences in ways the two countries measure poverty, not to mention currency conversion—that made it difficult to compare poverty and inequality. Fortunately, I learned of the Luxembourg Income Survey (LIS), which uses a "lissification" process to make country-level census data comparable. After attending a short summer training session in Luxembourg, I was able to compare poverty and inequality rates between the two countries over time. At the same time, I realized some of the limitations of quantitative analysis. Interesting U.S.–Canadian comparisons had already been done using quantitative data, but they tended to focus exclusively on one policy domain: unemployment policy differences, public assistance differences, health-care policy differences, or education policy differences. No one had examined how policy differences mattered to people living and working in the United States and Canada from the standpoint of their lived experiences. Although I was aware of the limitations of qualitative methods, I decided to triangulate my methods of inquiry and to embark on a cross-national comparative qualitative study. The idea seemed straightforward: compare workers in the same job positions in the same companies in two similar U.S. and Canadian cities.

One day I read a travel magazine article about Vancouver and went to look it up on a map. It was right over the border, only 120 miles away, from Seattle. I asked my dad about Vancouver—this city that sounded too good to be true —and sure enough, he said he had been there for a conference when he lived in Canada and had loved it. When I talked about it with a friend who had lived in Seattle, David Pinto-Duschinsky, he quickly convinced me that a Seattle-Vancouver comparison was an excellent idea. I tossed around the idea of a Seattle-Vancouver comparative study with several of the faculty at Harvard, including Katherine Newman, William Julius Wilson, Mary Waters, and Jeffrey Reitz, and got a very positive response. The question then became: What kinds of workers should I compare? What large-scale service industries had similar work sites in both cities? I thought of mall clerks and fast food employees; then, Christopher Jencks suggested hotel workers—which I instantly realized was the right answer.

I checked out the website of the Department of Anthropology and Sociology at the University of British Columbia in Vancouver, found the name of a professor—Neil Guppy—who studies issues of poverty, and sent him an e-mail. I went for a short visit in June 1999—I luckily arrived during a long weekend of beautiful weather—and became intrigued by this seemingly vibrant postindustrial city. I met with Neil Guppy on campus and told him about my research idea—which he agreed was great. He invited me to become a visitor in their department and also supported my fellowship applications. I was fortunate to receive a Fulbright scholarship, a Harvard Knox Memorial fellowship, and a National Science Foundation IGERT traineeship fellowship to support my field research.

It took several months longer than I had hoped to get started. First, I had to figure out my way around a new city. Then I had to decide which hotels to study. As described in chapter 3, I began by interviewing the president of the union that represents most hotel employees in Vancouver. I had heard back from the general manager of my first-choice hotel, the Globe Hotel Vancouver (because it has such a similar branch in Seattle), and I was anxious to get started. As I began interviewing, I realized Christopher Jencks's advice about studying hotels was even better than I had thought—people in the hospitality industry are incredibly *friendly* and open and have a strong desire to help. Given the stories I had heard of the difficulties some researchers have had in gaining access to sites for qualitative research, I was amazed at how easy it was to gain access to the hotels and how helpful everyone was in helping me carry out this study, both in Vancouver and Seattle. This does not mean the study was problem free

—frustrating weeks would pass with no interviews completed—but, in general, I quickly met allies, or "insiders," in each hotel, who shared their stories and went out of their way to help me arrange interviews.

Because I interviewed mostly immigrants, the most difficult issue was language. In Vancouver, I did not feel the need to hire a language translator in most cases, but several interviews would probably have benefited from the assistance of a translator (something I realized during transcription). At the Globe Hotel Seattle, I realized very quickly that I would definitely *not* be able to complete interviews without the help of a language translator, and I met a wonderful "insider" employee at this hotel, who volunteered to help recruit and translate for employee interviews. It was a difficult decision, but expediency won out, and in the end I am glad I selected this employee because she helped arrange interviews with many employees who—because of their lack of fluency in English—would have been reticent to volunteer to be interviewed. In general, employees at the two unionized hotels were, unsurprisingly, more willing to be interviewed and somewhat more open in their criticisms of management.

Although I had several hotels to choose from in Vancouver, I was limited to two specific branches in Seattle, which increased my nervousness during the process of gaining access. But the general managers were both wonderful and were totally open to my hanging out in employee cafeterias and observing and were even helpful in arranging for me to meet with other managers. I did not begin my interviews in Seattle until several months after of the terrorist attacks of September 11, 2001. In the aftermath, I felt that some of the employees in the Seattle hotels were more reticent to participate or volunteer to be interviewed. For example, one Somali refugee, Sumar Banadu working at the Globe Hotel Seattle, did not want me to tape-record the open-ended section of the interview (the only case out of seventy-seven interviews). I understood his reticence because that very morning there had been a cover story in the Seattle newspapers about a Somali refugee who had been picked up by law-enforcement officials while walking down the street (despite his having a wife and children living with him in Seattle, this man was reported to have been quickly deported to downtown Mogadishu, Somalia—the city and country he had fled as a five-year-old—where he was left to fend for himself with nothing but the clothes on his back and twenty dollars).

There were a few other tense and uncomfortable moments in Seattle. One Chinese room attendant brought her boyfriend with her to the interview; he was highly suspicious of my intentions and even interrupted the interview to interrogate me when I got to the section of my interview protocol that asked about savings and retirement savings. In another case, I was stood up for an interview by a room attendant at the Globe Hotel Seattle who then later called and asked to reschedule. On the day of the rescheduled meeting, it was absolutely streaming down rain, and I took an hour-long bus ride far south of downtown to a community college campus, where we had arranged to meet. After I had waited for thirty minutes, the employee ran up and told me she was sorry but she had to cancel and that I better leave quickly. It turned out that she had lied to her husband, who did not want her to be interviewed, and the very angry husband had followed and just confronted her. I did not ask any questions, but quickly headed to the bus stop and back home. When I got home, there was a message from the chief housekeeper at the Hotel Deluxe Seattle, telling me that the irate, controlling, and clearly unstable husband had called her to say he did not want his wife to be interviewed. She recommended that I not contact that employee again. I did not disagree.

Despite these exceptional cases, most interviews went very smoothly. In Seattle I was occasionally frustrated with the quality of public transit service in some areas. More frequently, I experienced anger at some of the injustices experienced by workers I interviewed. When I was told that a family would not be having Christmas this year because of hotel lay-offs or I heard stories of adult trauma resulting from childhood sexual abuse, I felt disturbed for days. I was particularly upset by all too many stories of refugees and immigrants in both cities—mostly mothers—who had to leave their young children behind in the care of others and could not see them for years as they negotiated entry for their family to North America. At times, I was struck with a sense of burning indignation, at other times, with hope. Overall, it was a pleasure to meet and talk to so many nice people about their lives. There were times when I wanted to throw out my detailed interview protocol and just chat, and there were other times when I wanted to throw in the towel on interviewing all together and just write up what data I had already collected. It is because of the support and encouragement of members of the Harvard and UBC faculty, particularly of Katherine Newman, and the support of my partner, Joanna Robinson, that I persevered to carry the fieldwork to its conclusion. I am glad I did!

NOTES

CHAPTER 1. INTRODUCTION

1. All names of hotel workers and hotel chains, as well as of most other corporations and unions, discussed have also been changed to pseudonyms to protect the study respondents' identities.

2. All dollar amounts are listed unadjusted in the currency of the respondent's country of residence without conversion because, to compare wage rates cross-nationally, it is important to consider the difference between the Purchasing Power Parity (PPP) values of the two currencies (approximately CA$1.00 to US$0.80–1.00) as well as their exchange values. For a more detailed discussion, see Chapter 4, n. 11.

3. Banting, Hoberg, and Simeon (1997).

4. Deber (2003).

CHAPTER 2. RESEARCH ISSUES

1. Rank (2004).

2. See Katz (1986); Gans (1995).

3. Charles Murray (1984) provides a classic example of the conflation between blaming poverty on public assistance and a values problem among the poor. If public assistance, in Murray's view, did not reinforce behaviors such as lone-parenting and not working, then the U.S. poverty problem would be solved. Mead (1986, 1992) makes somewhat more nuanced arguments about the deleterious consequences of public assistance by arguing that working (in the formal paid economy) is a critical part of social citizenship in the United States, which the current public-assistance system denies. He does not consider the deleterious consequences of being trapped in low-wage work that does not provide enough income to make ends meet or the time and flexibility to raise children. Bane and Ellwood (1994) recommend reforms to public assistance to promote work, which ultimately resulted in the 1996 Personal Responsibility and Work Reconciliation Act (PWORA) welfare reform. See also Ellwood (1998); Blank (1997); Stier and Tienda (2000).

4. All too often, social phenomena such as rising inequality, urban poverty, and economic hardship are examined without an explicit examination of the government policies that have contributed to their formation or crystallization. For example, many stratification sociologists focus on the impact of educational attainment or family background on social inequality and mobility (e.g., Blau and Duncan 1967). Other sociologists focus on the impact of organizational ascription on inequality (see Kanter 1977; Baron and Newman 1990). Yet these theories miss the embeddedness of social stratification in a nation's policy regime that can have a dramatic impact on both outcomes and opportunity. The dominant explanations of increasing urban problems and rising inequality center on the declining demand for low-skilled workers (Wilson 1987), racial segregation (Massey and Denton 1993), corporate policy (Harrison and Bluestone 1988), and other macro-structural factors (Danziger and Gottschalk 1995, 1997). Although these landmark works generally include policy recommendations to strengthen family supports, es-

pecially for the working poor, sociologists have not empirically estimated the positive and negative benefits of such changes or examined them in detail.

5. Rank (2004, 24).

6. In his foreword to Edin and Lein (1997), Christopher Jencks summarizes the research puzzle that drove their study:

> According to the Census Bureau, for example, 1.5 million single mothers had cash incomes below $5,000 in 1992. These mothers typically had two children. . . .
>
> Taking these women's reported income at face value implies that they paid for their rent, utilities, transportation, clothing, laundry, and other expenses from monthly budgets less than $420. Almost half appeared to be living on less than $200 a month. . . . According to the CES [the U.S. Labor Department's Consumer Expenditure Survey], families with incomes below $5,000 in 1992 took in an average of only $180 per month. Yet these families told the CES that they spent an average of $1,100 a month (in Edin and Lein 1997, x, xi).

7. When Edin and Lein's respondents discussed the issue during interviews, it emerged that many considered *child support* to only mean court-sanctioned government-enforced payments. Under-the-table cash payments or in-kind support such as clothes and diapers were not considered child support (Edin and Lein 1997).

8. Hays (2003).

9. See Coontz (1992) for a debunking of myths around the nuclear family of the 1950s.

10. DeParle (2004); Zucchino (1997). See also Hancock (2002) and Winston et al. (1999).

11. Ehrenreich (2001).

12. For an exposition on the "risk society," see Beck (1992). For an excellent account of the gap between risk perception and reality, see Glassner (1999).

13. The live-in nanny/cleaning literature includes, among many others, Hondagneu-Sotelo (2001) for Los Angeles; Pratt (2004) for Vancouver, Canada; Parrenas (2001) for Rome and Los Angeles; and Ozyegin (2001) for Turkey. Ehrenreich and Hochschild (2002) includes findings from research in several U.S. cities and in Hong Kong, among others.

14. Works on working-class culture include Lamont (2000), Halle (1984), Kefalas (2003), Lareau (2003), Johnson (2002), Leidner (1993), Rieder (1985), Sennett and Cobb (1973), Edin and Kefalas (2005), and Rubin (1976, 1994). Other research on the working poor includes: Munger (2001), Levitan and Shapiro (1987), Schulman (2003), Schwartz and Weigert (1995), Buchanan (2001), Newman (2003) and Waldinger and Lichter (2003). Low-wage labor market research includes: Bernhardt, et. al. (2001), Blau (1999), Card and Blank (2000), Elliott and Freeman (2003), Granovetter (1995), Heymann (2003), Holzer (1995), and Moss and Tilly (2001). Research on immigrants and immigration in Vancouver includes: Beiser (1999), Pratt (2004), Creese and Kambere (2003), and Hutton (1998).

15. Tannock (2001). Another low-wage service industry that has received quite a bit of scholarly attention is the garment industry (see Chin 2005; Collins 2003; and Rosen 2002).

16. Newman (1999).

17. Wilson (1996) analyzes ethnographic data from open-ended interviews with a subsample of the *Urban Poverty and Family Life Study* (UPFLS), open-ended interviews with 179 Chicago employers, and data collected by ten research assistants conducting participant-observation and life-history surveys in a sample of inner-city neighborhoods. Wilson's ethnographic work uncovers the hidden aspects of discrimination as well. Forty percent of the employers interviewed reported that they did not advertise entry-level openings, instead relying on informal job networks that conveniently bypassed residents of high-jobless areas; two-thirds reported ad-

vertising in suburban or ethnic papers instead of or in addition to metropolitan papers more commonly read by urban blacks (Wilson 1996).

18. Adler and Adler (2004). Another recent major hotel study is Sherman (2003). Her research examines the luxury hotel as a site of interaction between the wealthy and nonwealthy in an unequal socioeconomic hierarchy; it is based on ethnographic research at two luxury hotels in the San Francisco Bay area. Through her insider perspective—she worked, interned, and shadowed various job positions at each hotel—Sherman identifies processes and patterns that explain how workers navigate and understand their game-playing role in the production of luxury service for wealthy guests. She also interviews luxury-hotel managers and guests, adding their perspectives on consuming luxury service. Her work adds an important dimension to the sociological understanding of hotels specifically and of service work more generally. Many of the Global Hotel study findings were first presented in Zuberi (2004a).

19. Adler and Adler (2004, 18).

20. Presser (2003). See also Fuchs-Epstein and Kalleberg (2004); Hochschild (1997); and Ciulla (2000).

21. Adler and Adler (2004, 132).

22. Shipler (2004). Eric Schlosser—of *Fast Food Nation* (2002) fame—writes compellingly of the modern feudal sharecropping system that oppresses many migrant strawberry pickers in *Reefer Madness* (2003).

23. Shipler (2004, 282).

24. Shipler (2004, 282).

25. Shipler (2004, 282).

26. See Freeman (1994).

27. Esping-Andersen (1990) provides a convincing argument that a welfare state's degree of worker decommodification, not expenditure levels, should be used to classify welfare states into Social Democratic, Old Corporatist/Conservative, and Neo-Liberal welfare states. Under his Weberian ideal-type typology, both the United States and Canada are considered neoliberal welfare states. Yet this classification system obscures significant differences between the U.S. and Canadian welfare policies. Esping-Andersen misses crucial differences in policy that impact the working poor. Other cross-national comparative research on inequality includes: Devine and Waters (2004), Esping-Andersen (2002), Heymann et. al. (2004), Rainwater (1993), and Reitz (2003).

28. Lipset (1990, xii); note that Lipset leaves Mexico out of North America. See Lipset and Meltz (2004) for an updated analyses of the U.S.-Canadian labor policy divergence.

29. Card and Freeman (1993, 1).

30. Atkinson, Rainwater, and Smeeding (1995).

31. Card and Freeman (1993); Freeman (1994); Reitz (1998).

32. Card and Freeman (1993) focus on differences in labor-market policies and institutions for which comparable large-sample survey data are available. For example, the chapter by economists Rebecca Blank and Maria Hanratly, on the effect of social policy differences between the United States and Canada on poverty excludes an examination of critical differences in healthcare coverage because of a lack of comparable data (Blank and Hanratty 1993).

33. See http://www.lisproject.org/. Income data and demographic variables from national sources, including Canada's Survey of Consumer Finances and the U.S. March Current Population Survey, are harmonized so that they have the same meaning across data sets (Smeeding and Ross 1999, 10–11). National data are put through the "lissification," or harmonization, process once every five years. Especially in the early years, comparable U.S. and Canadian data may be a year apart.

Although this process provides accessible and comparable data, it certainly does not perfectly standardize the data or eliminate all the problems of noise in the original data sets (Smeeding and Ross 1999, 11). Some of these noise problems may have a particularly serious impact on the accuracy of analyses of poverty. Hence, it is important to outline these limitations and potential problems and consider the impact of these drawbacks on any comparative analysis. Although the data sets have been cleaned up as much as possible, both are missing income data, probably biased downward, and have inaccuracies in income reporting that are more dramatic systematically at the top and the bottom of the income distributions. Both of these limitations can weaken the validity of findings from cross-national comparisons, particularly if one variable is systematically biased in one direction. The greatest danger in the United States–Canada comparative case is that low-income families in the United States severely underreport their income from all sources, including transfers, relative to Canadian low-income families. Yet the good must not be the enemy of the perfect, and many powerful research findings on poverty have been drawn from these two data sets, despite these potential limitations. Although they are important to consider, these drawbacks probably do not fundamentally invalidate this discussion of poverty and inequality trends. Because both the Canadian Survey of Consumer Finances and U.S. March Consumer Population Survey share these problems of missing data and underreporting at the top and bottom, the detrimental effects are at least partially cancelled out.

The household poverty rates presented are based on relative, not absolute, measures of poverty. Relative household poverty rates are important because they allow the poverty line to change over time and provide a more consistent standard measure across advanced industrial nations. Hence relative, rather than absolute, poverty rates are the more valid metric for the analysis of poverty trends if the primary concern is the comparative cross-national analysis of how policy affects households. Whereas the relative poverty line is explicitly linked to the income distribution, absolute poverty lines also implicitly rely on income distribution because they are based on the value of a market basket of goods (Osberg 2000, 4). There clearly exists a changing basket of goods necessary for inclusion and full participation in society, one that changes both over time and between countries. So, for comparative analysis, the *relative* poverty rate represents the most conceptually useful and empirically valid measure. The use of relative as opposed absolute poverty measures in this book is supported by its concern with households earning enough income to purchase the basket of goods necessary to prevent social exclusion (see Osberg 2000 for an excellent discussion of moral traditions and the significance of income poverty).

The percentage of households with income below 50 percent of the median is a standard poverty measure. The households are also made comparable through the use of a square-root-of-family-size factor, also a standard method in household poverty measurement. As with relative household poverty measurement, the household-income data are standardized, with households of different sizes made equivalent through the use of a square-root-of-family-size factor.

34. As expected, the U.S. Gini measure of household inequality also increased from 32.3 in 1974 to 37.5 in 1994, whereas the Canadian Gini measure of household inequality also dropped over this period from 32.3 in 1971 to 28.6 in 1994.

A closer examination of changes in the rates of inequality suggests that the divergence in levels of inequality is primarily driven by the improved position of Canadian families at the tenth percentile of the income distribution compared to the median household and the somewhat worse position of U.S. households at the tenth percentile compared to the median household rather than by differences in growing inequality at the top of the household-income distribution.

After taxes and transfers, the ratio of incomes of households at the ninetieth percentile of the income distribution compared to the median household income declined only ever so slightly in Canada from 1.90 in 1971 to 1.85 in 1994, whereas in the United States it increased from 1.90 in 1974 to 2.19 in 1994, a change of +0.29. Yet the ratio of median household income in Canada to the income received by those at the tenth percentile dramatically declined over the same period from 2.63 in 1971 to 2.13 in 1994, or a change of −0.50. In the United States, the ratio of median household income to the income of households at the tenth percentile increased steadily from 2.71 in 1974 to 2.93 in 1994, a change of +0.22.

The majority of the increasing divergence in inequality levels between the United States and Canada over this period is explained by the growing income gap between those households at the bottom, or tenth, percentile and the median household in the United States—compared to a shrinking gap in Canada—and not an increasing inequality between those at the top, or ninetieth, percentile and the median household, which marginally increased in both countries.

See Iceland (2003) for additional evidence about how the level of transfers in the United States has failed to stem rising poverty and inequality in the past thirty years.

35. Blank and Hanratty (1993).

36. Reitz (1998). Other U.S.-Canadian comparative research focuses on differences and trends in public opinions and attitudes between the two countries, typified by Adams (2003) and Reitz and Bretton (1994).

37. Simmel (1972).

38. Similar to W. E. B. DuBois, perhaps sociology's first major qualitative researcher with the publication of *The Philadelphia Negro* in 1899, I use these methods of social inquiry to explain not just structural factors but also how these structures shape the subjective experience—or, in Max Weber's terms, *verstehen*—of people living, working, and making ends meet in the postindustrial metropolis. At the same time, through the use of cross-national methodology, I also heed Emile Durkheim's call for empirical social research, using the scientific principles of control and data analysis to explicate social relations, forces, and structures.

CHAPTER 3. THE STORY AND THE SETTING

1. Sassen (2001).

2. I also hoped my research could contribute to debates about patterns of immigrant incorporation and segmented assimilation theory as "rescued" by Alba and Nee (1997) from its original conception by Gordon (1964) and discussed by Portes and Rumbaut (2001) in their study based on immigrant experiences in San Diego and Miami.

3. Bernhardt, Dresser, and Hatton (2003, 37).

4. Dore (1973). Other classics that inspired my qualitative approach include Liebow (1967), Reisman (1967), Rainwater (1970), Sennett and Cobb (1973), Stack (1974), Rubin (1976), Willis (1977), Wilson (1980), Bellah, et. al. (1985), Sollers (1986), Newman (1989), Rubin (1994), MacLeod (1995), and Whyte (1995). Previous cross-national comparative studies of immigrant groups with a Canadian city case include: Toronto and Boston (Bloemraad 2002) as well as Somalians in Toronto and London (Berns McGowan 1999).

5. Card and Krueger (1995, 66).

6. Lipset (1990).

7. MacDonald (1987). See also Morgan (1982) and Warren (1997) on Seattle; McDonald (1996) on Vancouver.

8. Statistics Canada (1991); U.S. Census Bureau (1990).

9. Edin and Lein (1997).

10. MacDonald (1987).

11. Statistics Canada Highlights (1996); U.S. Census Bureau (1990).

12. Freeman and Needels (2003).

13. Statistics Canada (1991); U.S. Census Bureau (1990).

14. Statistics Canada 1991, 1996).

15. For example, the sample of employees interviewed in Seattle was 56 percent male as compared to 47 percent in Vancouver.

16. Immigrants to Canada, on average, have a higher level of human capital than do immigrants to the United States (Borjas 1993, 2001). Some could argue that this difference in human capital explains why immigrants are doing better in Canada and also why the largely immigrant sample of employees I interviewed in Vancouver is doing better compared to the sample in Seattle. The argument is that because the immigrants are more educated and have higher human capital in Vancouver than Seattle, immigration selection policy differences, and not social policy differences, explain why hotel workers are doing better in Vancouver compared to their counterparts in Seattle. Yet immigrants to Canada actually have *lower* levels of average human capital, as measured by years of education, than do immigrants from the *same* countries of origin entering the United States (Reitz 1998). This is not contradictory. The United States, unlike Canada, shares one of the longest borders in the world with Mexico, and the average immigrant to the United States from Mexico has a very low level of educational attainment. That biases the measure of the overall average years of education for immigrants to the United States from all countries sharply downward. My study supports Reitz's findings; the immigrants to Seattle from China or the Philippines often had more personal and family human capital and resources than immigrants to Vancouver from the same country of origin. Based just on these differences, I expect that immigrants from China or the Philippines would be better off in the United States than in Canada. But, as described in the next four chapters, that is not what I found. This points to the central role of social policy differences.

17. Of the five hotel workers who were currently "divorced with children." Only two of them, one in Seattle and one in Vancouver, were lone parents with primary custody of their children.

18. As research on assortive mating predicts (Gardyn 2002).

19. Two of the spouses were unemployed and looking for work at the time of the interview.

20. Shipler (2004).

21. These letters described the study and asked the general manager to contact me to arrange an interview to discuss the hotel industry in Seattle and Vancouver. I also enclosed a letter of support from Katherine Newman describing my research credentials and the importance of the study. Some general managers responded right away; in other cases, I followed up by phone several weeks after sending the letter.

22. In one case, a general manager arranged for me to meet with the human resources director first, who then brought me up to head office for a quick chat.

23. I believe it is very important to compensate interview respondents financially, despite some legitimate concerns that have been expressed about entering into an economic relationship that could be exploitative for the interview respondent in light of the social-class difference between the researcher and respondent. At the same time, not compensating interview respondents, who spend hours sharing information to help with a study that advances the interviewer's career, can also be exploitative. There is, unfortunately, no easy choice. In my case, I reviewed a consent form with each hotel employee at the beginning of each interview that made clear that participation in the interview was voluntary and could be ended at any time, without loss of benefits. The Global Hotel study methodology passed a strict Human Subjects review by Harvard University.

24. Sociologist Erving Goffman also discusses the "backstage" and "show" dynamics of many service-sector workplaces (Derber [1979] 2000).

25. Taylor (1919).

26. As described by Foucault ([1975] 1995), based on his interpretation of Jeremy Bentham's panopticon.

27. He did not describe what these "diversifying" hiring practices entailed.

28. My fieldwork intentionally excluded front-desk employees because they are considered higher-level Guest Service jobs and were almost exclusively filled by university students working to help pay for school. Although front-desk employees receive higher hourly wages (partly because they do not receive tips), they often quickly leave the hotel industry or move up into more senior management or executive roles.

CHAPTER 4. THE UNION DIFFERENCE

1. Rose and Chaison (2001, 36).

2. Riddell (1993). Riddell also used comparative demand side analysis on unionization trends to demonstrate that only 15 percent of the unionization gap can be explained by economic and labor-force structural differences, including the higher percentage of Canadian workers in the public sector (an argument made by Troy 2000) (Rose and Chaison 2001; Riddell 1993).

3. Taras (1997), in Lipset and Meltz (2004, 172–73).

4. Banting, Hoberg, and Simeon (1997); Rose and Chaison (2001). See also, Lipset and Meltz (2004).

5. Rose and Chaison (2001); Lipset and Meltz (2004).

6. Lipset and Meltz (2004, 172).

7. Riddell (1993). For a discussion of the impact of union divergence on wage inequality, see Lemieux (1993).

8. Vogel (2001).

9. Recall that, as with the other names used in this book, the names of all the unions discussed are pseudonyms. In addition to the SIIU, the primary union representing workers at the hotels, other unions represent small numbers of hotel-industry employees in Seattle and Vancouver, for example, the Technical Industry Union (TIU) and other technical trade unions.

10. SIIU website.

11. Unless otherwise specified, Canadian dollar amounts and U.S. dollar amounts are presented without conversion. In order to compare wage rates cross-nationally, it is important to consider both the difference between the currency exchange values of the Canadian dollar and the U.S. dollar and the difference between the Purchasing Power Parity (PPP) values of the two currencies. Although at the current currency exchange rate, CA$1.00 is technically worth approximately US$0.74, the cost of living and of specific consumer goods is lower in Vancouver than in Seattle. Hence, the PPP exchange value of CA$1.00 is approximately US$0.80–1.00. Calculating this PPP value of currency cross-nationally is difficult because the PPP varies from item to item, especially with consumer electronics, airline tickets, and certain imported items. Yet bread and butter essentials cost basically the same dollar amounts in Vancouver and Seattle, and rents are slightly lower in Vancouver than Seattle for accommodations of the same quality. I priced a basket of identical items of the same size at two Large Foodmart supermarkets, one in the hip, trendy Capitol Hill neighborhood in downtown Seattle and the other in Kitsilano, a similar neighborhood bordering downtown Vancouver. The comparison revealed a PPP of approximately 1: CA$1.00 in Vancouver at this supermarket chain went as far as US$1.00 in Seattle.

12. While the employees interviewed at the unionized Globe Hotel Vancouver had an average of 3.62 weeks vacation compared to 1.38 weeks at the non-unionized Hotel Deluxe Vancouver. The employees interviewed at the unionized Hotel Deluxe Seattle had an average of 2.26 weeks vacation as compared to 1.53 weeks at the non-unionized Globe Hotel Seattle.

13. While the hotel workers interviewed at the unionized Globe Hotel Vancouver and unionized Hotel Deluxe Vancouver had been on the job an average of nine years and three months, the average employee interviewed had only been on the job for three years and six months at the non-unionized Globe Hotel Seattle and one year and six months at the non-unionized Hotel Deluxe Vancouver (but the Hotel Deluxe Vancouver had only been open for two years and six months at the time of my interviews).

14. Front desk workers have a higher turnover because these jobs are frequently filled by college students, who often decide to return to studying full-time, switch hotels, move into more senior positions, or change to new fields.

15. Because this interview was not tape-recorded, this quotation was reconstructed from my detailed interview notes.

16. These findings on the impact of unionization mirror the findings of Adler and Adler (2004) for hotel workers in Hawai'i, where the decision to unionize was department by department:

> For Ali'i workers, the presence of a union in their department or hotel usually resulted in a slight raise in pay, protection from management harassment, a guarantee that the management would adhere to state labor regulations and a place to complain should they have a grievance. For Ali'i management, unions generally meant less navigability in their efforts to maintain a flexible workforce, to control costs, and to control workers. (227)

CHAPTER 5. HEALTH-CARE DIFFERENCES

1. See Manuel and Mao (2002); Hornberger, Redelmeyer, and Petersen (1992).

2. In the thirty comparative scientific studies on medical care quality completed since 1971, Canada's health system has performed as well or better than the U.S. system (Marmor and Sullivan 2000, 15–20). The findings of one comparative health outcome study with a focus on the homeless attributed the longer lives of homeless men in Toronto as compared to Boston, New York City, and Philadelphia to the Canadian universal health care system and its elimination of financial barriers for care. The findings were published by the American Medical Association (see "Homeless in Toronto" 2000, 36).

Public health researchers examined rates of avoidable mortality (a measure created by Rutstein et al. 1976) from disease groups from 1980 to 1996 and found suggestive evidence that rates decreased more quickly in Canada compared to the United States, particularly in areas related to public health care (Manuel and Mao 2002).

> The lowest mortality ratios in Canada were for disease groups in which public health or primary care was expected to play a major role (asthma, cervical cancer, hypertension and cerebrovascular disease, tuberculosis, and maternal mortality), as opposed to those most often treated in a hospital (Hodgkin disease, appendicitis, cholecystitis, abdominal hernia, and peptic ulcer). One of the most frequently cited differences between Canada and United States is the degree to which comprehensive health care is freely available at the point of use (Weale 1998, 410; Manuel and Mao 2002, 1483–84)

These studies provide evidence that the quality of care, even for critical health crises, is as good or better in Canada as in the United States.

3. Marmor and Sullivan (2000, 15–20).

4. Other works include Canada and the United States in a multinational comparative study of health systems (see Kawachi and Kennedy 2002; Graig 1993). Boychuk (1999), Imershein (2001), and Blankenau (2001) contrast the development of the U.S. and Canadian health care systems. Tuohy (1999) contrasts health system development in the United States, Canada, and Britain.

5. See, for example, Deber 2003; Bennett and Adams 1993; "The Grass Really is Greener to the North" (1999).

6. For Canada, see Bolaria and Dickenson (2002); Janigan (2003); Frankel, Speechley, and Wade (1996); McFarlane and Prado (2002); Dunn (2002); Federal, Provincial, and Territorial Advisory Committee on Population Health (1999). For the United States, see Weiss (1992); Millman (1993); Japsen (2003); Oberlander and Marmor (2001); Skocpol (1997); Sered and Fernandopulle (2005).

7. Stern (2003, 78–79).

8. OECD Health Data (2001: A Comparative Analysis of 30 OECD Countries, in Deber 2003, 20–24). See also "Heavy Price Paid for Lack of Coverage" (2003).

9. Newman (1999, 276).

10. Warren and Tyagi (2003, 84).

11. Kawachi and Kennedy (2002, 59).

12. Pear (2004).

13. Bolaria and Dickenson (2002).

14. The Canadian government shares the cost of these programs with the provinces, as long as they live up to the five principles of Medicare: "*universality* of eligibility, *comprehensiveness* of coverage, *portability* between provinces, *accessibility* achieved by prepayment through taxation, and *public administration* on a non-profit basis" (Soderstrom, in Bolaria and Dickenson 2002, 23).

15. Deber (2003).

16. Marmor and Sullivan (2000).

17. Romanow (2002). The full Romanow Report, the unofficial name of the Final Report of the Commission on the Future of Health Care in Canada, titled *Building Our Values: The Future of Health Care in Canada* is available at: http://www.hc-sc.gc.ca/english/care/romanow/hcc0086.html.

18. Janigan (2003, 39).

19. Worth (2000, 27).

20. Worth (2000, 25).

21. There is a three-month waiting period for new provincial residents.

22. Vogel (2001); Lee and Long (2001). According to Vogel, "British Columbia is one of the only two provinces to charge additional premiums for our universal health insurance system. However, as the legality of these premiums is questionable under the Canada Health Act, no citizen of BC can be denied care because they have not paid the premium" (Vogel 2001, 18).

23. Lee and Long (2001, 21).

24. Lee and Long (2001, 17).

25. Vogel (2001).

26. Burbank and Sullivan (2001), cited in Vogel (2001, 17).

27. *Seattle Times,* May 2001, quoted in Vogel (2001, 18).

28. See Manual and Mao (2002); Frankel, Speechley, and Wade (1996); Millman (1993).

29. Hue Chung was interviewed with the assistance of a language translator.

30. Warren and Tyagi (2003, 93).

31. As discussed in chapter 3, all hotel workers interviewed were compensated for their time and participation, CA$50 in Vancouver and US$40 in Seattle.

32. Dement, in Gore and Gore (2002).

33. About one-fifth of the hotel workers interviewed in both cities reported their health as "Much Better" compared to others of a similar age. Yet a higher percentage of Vancouver respondents reported their health to be "Somewhat Better" than did Seattle respondents. Notably, no Vancouver respondents reported their health to be "Somewhat Worse" or "Much Worse" than others of a similar age, but a handful of Seattle respondents did. Seattle respondents were most likely to report that their health was "About the Same" as others of similar age than were Vancouver respondents. Further information collected in the question-and-answer and open-ended sections of the survey provides more evidence that the Vancouver employees' health was better than that of the Seattle employees and that health policy differences may explain part of the difference.

CHAPTER 6. SOCIAL WELFARE POLICY DIFFERENCES

1. Although other scholars have compared social welfare policy differences between Canada and the United States (see Card and Freeman 1993; Lipset 1990; Freeman 1994; Reitz 1998), they have only begun to examine the impact of these differences on low-income families in each nation. For example, most of the academic debate comparing unemployment benefits focuses on whether changes to unemployment policy have increased or decreased the rate of unemployment and not on whether unemployment benefits prevent poverty among the unemployed (see Card and Riddell 1993).

In the U.S.-Canadian comparative literature, the exceptions tend to focus on the macro-level statistics on poverty and inequality. Jeffrey Reitz in *The Warmth of the Welcome* (1998), for example, compares the labor, social, immigration, and educational contexts of Canada and the United States (and Australia) and assesses their impacts on immigrant labor market fortunes. Within each country, there is more literature about the relationship between social welfare policy and quality of life. The majority of this scholarship has a limited focus on public-assistance and welfare recipients, particularly in the United States (see Bane and Ellwood 1994; Mead 1992; Murray 1984; Quadagno 1994; Hays 2003).

2. In 1990, the Canadian government spent 2.2 percent of its Gross Domestic Product (GDP) on need-based transfers through the Canadian Assistance program and programs for the disabled, compared to only 1.3 percent total of GDP spent by the U.S. government in 1989 on Aid to Families with Dependent Children (AFDC), Supplemental Security Income (SSI), food stamps, general assistance, and other Social Security programs, except Medicaid (Card and Freeman 1993, 15). Canada also spent 1.77 percent of its GDP on unemployment insurance in 1990 compared to the United States, which spent only 0.32 percent of its GDP in 1989 (15). Overall, in 1987, the United States spent 13 percent of its total GDP on education, health care, and cash social welfare for the nonelderly; the same year, Canada spent 20 percent of its GDP on these items (Atkinson, Rainwater, and Smeeding 1995, 32).

Some other sources that describe and critique Canadian social welfare policy include: Armitage (1996, 2003), Curtis, Grabb and Guppy (2003), Graham, Swift, and Delaney (2000), Hurtig (1999), Lightman (2003), McMullin (2004), Murphy (1999), Pulkingham and Ternowetsky (1996), and Westheus (2003).

3. Blank and Hanratty (1993).

4. This two-year time limit was not in force at the time of my fieldwork. For an excellent account of the historical development of social policy in the United States, see Skocpol (1992) and Katz (1986).

5. Vogel (2001, 17). The figures presented are in Canadian dollars converted with a cost-of-living Purchasing Parity Price (PPP) equivalency.

6. A single childless person in Vancouver received $6,330 in 1999 from public assistance, whereas a couple with two children received $17,830 (National Council on Welfare, Welfare Incomes 1999, in Lee and Long 2001, 32). Under the new welfare regime in Washington state: "Individuals without children, those who have been convicted of drug-related offences other than simple possession, and all adults who have exceeded the five year maximum [under Temporary Assistance to Needy Families (TANF) term limits] are ineligible for any benefits other than food stamps (valued at approximately US$150 per month)" (Vogel 2001, 17).

Single childless residents are not eligible for public-assistance benefits, except for short-term aid through special programs such as the Refugee Cash Assistance (RCA) program.

7. Vogel (2001). The one-year period can be divided between the mother and the father of the child, as they choose.

8. Vogel (2001).

9. Vogel (2001, 20).

10. The seasonal nature of hotel work is not limited to Vancouver. Adler and Adler, in *Paradise Laborers,* report, "At the hotels we observed, the seasonal factor also worked against employees receiving full pay" (2004, 246).

11. According to Beth Smith, the assistant general manager of the Media Hotel Vancouver (a hotel where I did not conduct employee interviews), approximately 30 percent of the room attendants are laid off during the winter season. Fifty-nine percent of the remaining employees continue to have full-time hours through the winter. Those with seniority ranging from five to thirty years are the ones who keep full-time hours. The part-time workers generally get approximately twenty-four hours per week. Some might have multiple jobs, but it is difficult to get hired during the winter season because the low demand impacts all Vancouver hotels.

12. The turndown service is an evening Housekeeping service, provided between 5:30 p.m and 9:30 p.m. The room attendants turn down the bedspread (removing the cover and turning a corner to make it easier to get into bed), turn up the pillows, close the drapes in the room, turn on the TV and lights, tidy up the room, fill the ice bucket, and provide any required clean towels.

13. For example, if an employee's quarterly earnings in the two highest quarters previous to unemployment averaged US$4,200 or $1,400 per month (this equals approximately $350 per week or $8.75 per hour for a full-time employee—the average wage of a room attendant at the Globe Hotel Seattle), the unemployed or laid-off worker would then receive benefits of only $168 dollars per week in Seattle. If the employee averaged $6,220 for the top two quarters or $2,073 per month (or $518.33 per week and $12.95 per hour for a full-time employee), then he or she would receive $248 per week (Washington Employment website, http://www.wa.gov/ esd/ui/wba.htm). In Vancouver, on the other hand, an employee without children earning CA$1,400 per month would receive somewhat more—$192.50 per week. If the employee has children, he or she could receive up to $280 per week in EI benefits. The average Vancouver hotel employee I interviewed, earning CA$14.84 per hour, received $326.50 per week with no children and up to the maximum $413 per week with children when he or she was laid off.

14. Washington Unemployment Insurance Employment Security program website, http://www.access.wa.gov.

15. Whereas in the past, weekly benefit amounts were calculated on the basis of the two highest quarters of earnings in the qualifying base year of employment, as of 2004 the program determines weekly benefits on the basis of the three highest quarters (reducing the benefit level for most claimants). In early 2005, the unemployment system in Washington state provided benefits at 1 percent of the entire qualifying year earnings. This dramatically lowered the weekly benefit levels of any worker on unemployment who experienced any temporary period of reduced hours or a lay-off during the qualifying base year of employment before applying for benefits.

16. For more scholarly research about the stressful experience of being laid off, even from higher-level corporate jobs, see Newman (1989, 1993).

17. This does not seem to be an isolated phenomenon. "In Shalimar's (1981) study of British hotel workers, he found it was common for groups of workers to leave one hotel and go to another en masse. Usually, this was to follow a manager who had moved" (Adler and Adler 2004, 252).

18. As a low-seniority employee, George Chan often does not get full-time hours. During the winter last year, he had to go on EI again for three months. He earned only $16,000 last year, which, combined with his wife's income, brought their household income up to $36,000.

19. Mark Corbain, union shop steward and doorman, received some retraining when he was laid off as a longshoreman because of the reflagging of international transport ships to third-world countries such as the Liberia and Panama. "I went through the Local State of Washington retraining program, which did help me extensively on buying the books for me to brush up on my Spanish and paid my tuition going back to community college. . . ." He really enjoyed translating work, but found that despite the high rate of hourly pay, $27 per hour, he had to travel extensively in order to get enough hours of work to survive. "You've got to chase the work. You've got to go to Vancouver, British Columbia. You got to go down to Olympia. Which I didn't really mind the traveling too; the thing is the traveling only paid one way." So Mark Corbain decided to switch careers and managed to secure a unionized position as a doorman at the Redwood Hotel, an old independent hotel in downtown Seattle. After being laid off, he saw a posting at the SIIU union hall for a doorman opening at the Hotel Deluxe Seattle and applied.

20. Some families in Vancouver also received a small federal Goods and Services Tax (GST) rebate, paid quarterly, for low-income individuals and families. This partially counters the negative impact of higher consumption/sales taxes in Canada as compared to the United States.

21. Vogel (2001).

22. The Finance Project website, http://www.financeprojectinfo.org/mww/childtaxcredit.asp.

23. According the U.S. federal guidelines, a single parent with one child should qualify with earnings of $29,660 or less and a married couple with one child qualifies with earnings of $30,692 or less. With two children, the limits are increased to $33,692 for single filers and $34,612 for married couples (U.S. Internal Revenue Service website, http://www.irs.gov/individuals/article/0,,id=96406,00.html).

24. Of the twelve states with supplemental EITC programs, eight provide refundable tax credits that supplement the earnings of low-income workers with children beyond the amount these families paid for state taxes (Friedman 2000). Washington state Employment Security does have a successful program to encourage low-income earners with children to file their federal tax forms and apply to receive their federal EITC benefits (http://www.workfirst.wa.gov/eitc/childcredit.htm).

25. Stack (1974).

26. The funds used to purchase or build a first home through this program must be repaid/reinvested in a person's RRSP fund within fifteen years.

27. Twenty-eight percent of hotel employees interviewed in Seattle are living with parents or other relatives to make ends meet compared to 11 percent of hotel employees interviewed in Vancouver.

28. In Vancouver, the average respondent earned CA$28,651 compared to US$24,043 in Seattle in the year prior to the interview. While these differences may not seem large, even for workers in the same jobs for the same companies, the Purchasing Power Parity (PPP) differences of these incomes do clearly result in financial security and quality of life differences. Additionally, the average annual income differences also varied across hotel occupation. The Seattle room attendants earned substantially less per year than Vancouver room attendants, while maintenance engineers earned approximately the same between the two cities.

CHAPTER 7. PUBLIC INVESTMENT AND CITY-LEVEL DIFFERENCES

1. Wilson (1996). For an empirically based critique of theories of concentrated poverty, see Small (2004).

2. Anderson (1990).

3. Reich (1991); Bluestone and Harrison (1982); Wilson (1987). For an excellent empirical analysis of the expansion of urban ghettos in American cities, see Jargowsky (1997).

4. Portes and Rumbaut (1996, 2001). Segmented assimilation theory suggests that the second and third generations of certain ethnic minority immigrant groups are not "incorporating" into mainstream U.S. society but, rather, into the segment of U.S. society suffering from the deleterious consequences of urban poverty (Portes and Rumbaut 2001). When Portes and Rumbaut talk about segmented assimilation, they are referring to culture and values.

5. Portes and Rumbaut (2001); Waters (1999); Reitz (1998).

6. Although the government-run automobile insurance program in the province of British Columbia, Insurance Corporation of British Columbia (ICBC), generally provides lower-cost automobile insurance in Vancouver than the private insurance system in Seattle, gas prices are higher for residents of Vancouver—in large part due to a policy of higher gas taxes.

7. See the American Public Transit Association website, http://www.apta.com/services/awards/documents/awardshist.pdf, for a complete list of the winners.

8. MacDonald (1987, 192).

9. Findley (1998).

10. MacDonald (1987).

11. MacDonald (1987).

12. Cities tend to gravitate to either "light" or "heavy" rail systems. Calgary, Alberta, and Portland, Oregon, for example, use "light" rail, which is closer to a streetcar than a passenger train—it has smaller trains, often at grade, with more frequent stops. On the other hand, Toronto and New York City are classic examples of "heavy rail," with longer, wider, higher-capacity trains running longer distances between stops. Vancouver's Skytrain was one of the first successful hybrids of these two trends, combining frequent stops with grade-separated, driverless service. This combination gave it the name Advanced Light Rapid Transit, also sometimes referred to as Advanced Light Rail. (I thank Peter Schaub for this contribution.)

13. Individual tickets for the Skytrain for adults cost $2 for one zone, $3 for two zones, and $4 for four zones. Bulk ticket discounts and unlimited monthly passes are also available, as well

as reduced fares for seniors and students. For more information see the website, http://www.translink.bc.ca/Service_Info_and_Fares/SkyTrain/default.asp.

14. This development concept—called the Transit Oriented Development—is also nicely demonstrated in the eastern suburbs of Portland, Oregon.

15. See the Discover Vancouver website, http://www.discovervancouver.com/GVB/history-of-vancouver.asp.

16. This elevated highway was damaged in the last major earthquake, and there is a lot of discussion about tearing it down. But traffic experts fear such a change would worsen the major bottleneck on the other interstate through Seattle. For more on the devastation visited upon Los Angeles by freeways and suburban sprawl, see Davis (1992).

17. More information on the EMP museum can be found at http://www.emplive.com/visit/visitor_info/admission.asp/. The Parvaz (2000) article is available at the *Seattle Post-Intelligencer* website, http://seattlepi.nwsource.com/emp/cost24.shtml.

18. Vancouver city website, http://www.city.vancouver.bc.ca/parks/parks/stanley/.

19. Thomas (2003) and Vancouver city website, http://www.city.vancouver.bc.ca/parks/info/stats/index.htm.

20. Stanley Park in Vancouver and Central Park in neighboring Burnaby were also military reserves, prior to becoming parks.

21. See the Seattle city website, http://www.cityofseattle.net/parks/Environment/.

22. See http://www.city.vancouver.bc.ca/parks/info/stats/index.htm. See the following websites for more information about the parks and recreation services described in Vancouver: http://www.city.vancouver.bc.ca/parks/rec/pools/index.htm; http://www.vancouverplus.ca/portal/profile.do?profileID=397184; http://www.city.vancouver.bc.ca/community_profiles/RecGuideInfo.cfm; http://www.city.vancouver.bc.ca/parkfinder_wa/index.cfm?

23. Seattle city website, http://www.cityofseattle.net/parks/aquatics/poolmap.htm, http://www.cityofseattle.net/parks/Centers/find-a-center.htm.

24. Mixed-use zoning integrates apartment and townhouse-style housing, as well as shops, schools, and community centers. Many Vancouver neighborhoods feature design elements—including lanes or alleys—consistent with "New Urbanism" as described by Duany, Plater-Zyberk, and Speck (2000). For more on the architectural and planning development of Vancouver's neighborhoods, see Berlowitz (2005).

25. MacDonald (1987, 202).

26. MacDonald (1987).

27. In contrast, in many U.S. cities services such as planning and transit are most often made at the county or state level, which can result in fragmented systems over a metropolitan region.

28. Vancouver city website, http://www.city.vancouver.bc.ca/commsvcs/Census2001/Kensington03.pdf. Statistics Canada measures poverty differently than the U.S. Census Bureau. Fewer households would be considered poor if the U.S. measures were used.

29. All statistics presented about Kensington-Cedar Cottage can be accessed at the Vancouver city website, http://www.city.vancouver.bc.ca/commsvcs/Census2001/Kensington03.pdf.

30. Vancouver city website, http://www.city.vancouver.bc.ca/commsvcs/Census2001/Kensington03.pdf.

31. Kozol (1992).

32. For more information about NIST programs and the United Nations Award, see the Vancouver city websites, http://www.city.vancouver.bc.ca/NIST/nist_teamarea.cfm?searchTeamID=7, http://www.city.vancouver.bc.ca/ctyclerk/NewsReleases2003/NRunaway.htm.

33. See http://www.city.vancouver.bc.ca/parks/cc/kensington/index.htm. More informa-

tion about Trout Lake Community Centre can be found at: http://www.city.vancouver.bc.ca/parks/cc/troutlake/index.htm

34. Kensington-Cedar Cottage website, http://vancouver.ca/community_profiles/kensington-cedar/services.htm.

35. Not surprisingly, respondents living in the wealthier west-side Vancouver neighborhoods were also very positive about their neighborhoods. For example, Jessica Roberts, a server at the Hotel Deluxe Vancouver, described her Kitsilano neighborhood: "I love Kits, I love the fact that I was three blocks away from the Beach. I love the fact that I was two blocks away from the grocery store, where I could walk to all the stores right there. And the neighborhood feel to it."

36. Several hotel employees in both Seattle and Vancouver live in low-quality housing and experience hardships in their material standard of living. More workers in Vancouver than Seattle reported problems with rats, mice, roaches, or other insects; with a poorly functioning heating system; with a fridge or stove not working properly; and with inadequate garbage pickup. At the same time, more workers in Seattle than Vancouver reported problems with toilets, inadequate hot water, and plumbing; with heating; and with wind drafts. Policy differences did *not* have much impact on the housing quality, although neighborhood differences did matter.

37. Kay Chiang was interviewed with the help of a language translator.

38. Glassner (1999).

39. Mercer Resources Consulting, 2004 Quality of Life report. Available at: http://www.mercerhr.com/. For more on recent "best city" awards won by Vancouver from *Condè Nast Traveler* and the "Economist Intelligence Unit," see Vancouver city website: http://vancouver.ca/aboutvan.htm.

40. See Rosentraub (1999).

41. For more information, see http://www.elevated.org/project/. Unfortunately, a recent referendum on projected cost overruns for the project resulted in its permanent cancellation.

CHAPTER 8. SUBJECTIVE PERCEPTIONS AND FUTURE OUTLOOK

1. We might hypothesize that this difference is an artifact of Canadian respondents' tendency to answer less extremely (less positively or negatively) than Americans to this survey question. Although the same percentage of employees ranked themselves and their families well above the middle rung in each city, the ladder data show that Seattle hotel employees perceived themselves and their families as far below the middle class more often than Vancouver employees did.

2. Jennifer Shih was interviewed with the assistance of a language translator.

3. Other employees expressed more fatalistic views—understandable given their tumultuous experiences before arriving in Seattle. Sumar Bonadu, a recently arrived refugee working as a banquet houseman at the Globe Hotel Seattle said of his future: "God Knows. I don't know. I don't know what will happen. I leave in hands of God."

4. Sennett and Cobb (1973).

5. Immediately after the new provincial government came into power, the tuition freeze was lifted and tuition rates increased approximately 30 percent in 2002–2003 and were slated to be increased again 30–40 percent in 2003–2004 (http://www.fact-index.com/u/un/university_of_british_columbia.html).

6. Association of American Universities (AAU) Public Universities Report, available at: http://www.ir.ufl.edu/nat_rankings/students/tuitinOld.pdf. In addition, although tuition scholarships are tax-exempt in both countries, Canada also allows students to exempt their first

$3,000 in nontuition scholarships from their annual income and provides a federal tax deduction of $400 per month of full-time enrollment (or $200 per month for part-time enrollment). Added to the standard deduction (over $8,000), this full-time student deduction and scholarship exemption combine to allow most typical undergraduate and graduate students on scholarships to earn up to $14,000 tax-free (these numbers are for the 2004 tax year). These credits can also be transferred to spouses or parents and can be carried to future years.

7. Kane (1999).

8. Jennifer Shih, Lan Zhang, Hue Chung, and Tung Sing Chan were interviewed with the assistance of a language translator.

CHAPTER 9. IMPROVING THE LIVES OF THE WORKING POOR

1. Wilson (1996, 209). These kinds of policy reforms can also be viewed as going beyond reducing hardship to extending citizenship rights to all people in a democratic society (see Marshall 1950).

2. Wilson (1996, 208).

3. Terkel (2003, xviii).

4. Newman (1999, 298).

5. Warren and Tyagi (2003, 6). For more on the importance of progressive policy makers focusing on working families, see Skocpol (2000).

6. Warren and Tyagi (2003, 80).

7. Edin and Lein (1997, 132). Other research on the negative consequences of poverty in the U.S. include Brooks-Gunn and Duncan (1997) and Furstenberg et al. (1999).

8. Wilson (1996, xxi–xxii). He expounds on this idea in Wilson (1999). See also Rose (2000); Clawson (2003); Schorr (1997); Borosage and Hickey (2001).

9. Bakan (2004, 107). See also Derber (1998).

10. Levy (1998, 189).

11. Derber (2002, 275). For more about social movements and activism in U.S. history, see Zinn (2003).

12. Lipset (1990).

13. The policy recommendations presented in this chapter are based on an ecological model: "In Brofenbrenner's model, the individual is at the center of a social system with different layers. He describes it as a set of nested structures, like a set of Russian dolls" (Johnson 2002, 162). Brofenbrenner was an original architect of the U.S. Head Start programs and his ecological model is a powerful one for thinking about how macro-level policies and institutions interact with the family level to influence individuals. Policy reform at one level can also improve outcomes at other levels.

14. Jencks (1992). For more U.S. policy recommendations, see Danziger, Sandefer, Weinberg (1994) and McFate, Lawson, and Wilson (1995).

15. Newman (1999, 276).

16. After considering many options, the state of Maine has recently adopted a health insurance reform scheme with the explicit goal of creating universal coverage in the next few years. Their example could prove to be a model for other states.

17. The Unemployment Insurance infrastructure could also be used to administer a new paid maternity leave system for new mothers, similar to the Canadian system described in chapter 6.

18. Youngblood and Jensen (2003).

19. Youngblood and Jensen (2003). For more research on revitalizing U.S. unions, see Milkman and Voss (2004).

20. Katz and Krueger, in Brofenbrenner (2000, 20).

21. According to Jennifer Johnson in *Getting By on the Minimum,* "the United States lags behind most similar countries in reducing poverty by means of taxation and income transfers. In fact, the United States has the dubious honor of being the only country where income transfers are redistributed from lower to higher income earners in the forms of benefits such as mortgage deductions" (2002, 225). See Sweeney and Kusnet (1996) for more on the declining financial position of low-wage workers in the United States.

22. One example of a tax that functions regressively is the social security tax, which is levied at a flat percentage on all workers, but only up to approximately the first $60,000 in income. Additional income is not taxed, so wealthy earners pay a much lower percentage of their income in social security taxes than the average income earner in the United States.

23. Taxes on high-income earners generate important revenue to fund government programs. The economic benefits from reducing the tax burden on the wealthiest are the smallest, and they also reduce government revenue most dramatically. Across-the-board and other tax cuts disproportionately benefit high-income earners, at a cost to average and low-income earners.

24. Newman (1999, 271).

25. Dryfoos (1994). For more on the negative consequences of social exclusion on child development, see Hertzman (2002).

26. Newman (1999, 275). See Chaudry (2004) for an excellent examination of the challenges facing low-wage mothers managing work and child care based on qualitative research in New York City.

27. For a discussion of this research, see Alexander, Entwisle, and Dauber (2002).

28. Warren and Tyagi (2003, 39).

29. Schweinhart (2005).

30. Head Start is a federal early childhood education program for low-income children.

31. Wilson (1996, 215). He draws on the cross-national child and family policy research of Kamerman and Kahn (1995).

32. Lareau (2003, 248).

33. See Weissbourd (1997).

34. Johnson (2002, 221).

35. In addition, tax loopholes allowing wealthy Canadians to reduce their income tax burden should be reduced. Restrictions on moving assets offshore should be closed to increase the resources available to end poverty.

36. The legislated goal was to eliminate child poverty in Canada by the year 2000. It is critical that this goal not be achieved through a redefinition of poverty or lowering of the poverty line, as advocated for by some conservative think tanks.

37. Zuberi (2004b).

38. All workers in Canada contribute to the Employment Insurance funds, which covers the costs of benefits. Since the Employment Insurance reforms, the federal government now collects more in Employment Insurance taxes than it provides in benefits to unemployed workers. As of March 2003, there was over a $44 billion surplus in the Employment Insurance Account (Source: http://www.oag-bvg.gc.ca/domino/other.nsf/html/04hr01_e.html, Date Accessed: September 21, 2005). See also: http://www.fin.gc.ca/consultresp/eiratesResp_2e.html.

39. See Reich (1991); Gordon (1996).

1. Wilson (1996).

2. Although their concepts of urban ecology are useful, the descendents of the Chicago School have been criticized for exclusively focusing on "lifeless" quantitative empiricism. My study uses an empirical methodology, but it also adds Erving Goffman's (1959) insights about the value of studying how people interact—their symbolic interactions—in their workplaces, neighborhoods, and homes.

3. There are some parallels between African-American and immigrant group experiences. As Nicholas Lehman (1992) describes, a large number of African Americans migrated from the rural South to the urban centers of the North and Midwest from the early 1940s to the 1970s.

4. Whyte (1993); Lewis (1966); For the document that is known popularly as the *Moynihan Report,* see Office of Policy Planning and Research United States Department of Labor (1965).

5. Newman (1999, 297).

6. Pierson (1994). See also Myles and Pierson (1997).

7. Wilson (1987, 142).

8. Massey and Denton (1993).

9. Sassen (2001); Reich (1991). Also meriting discussion is the role of the "creative class," as discussed in Florida (2004), which has also reshaped urban life in both Seattle and Vancouver.

10. Wilson (1996).

11. See Jahoda (1982); Johoda, Lazarsfeld, and Zeisel (1933 [1977]).

12. Edin and Lein (1997).

13. Anderson (1990, 1999); Venkatesh (2000). Even much of the working-poor literature focuses heavily on studying the cultural outlook and values of the working class, such as Kefalas (2003); Lamont (2000); Duneier (1999); Rubin (1976); Halle (1984); Lareau (2003).

14. I am certainly *not* arguing that Canada is better than the United States in all dimensions. Rather, my argument focuses on the impact of relatively recent (within the past four or five decades) policy divergences between the two countries on urban working-poor families. The wealthy pay lower taxes in the United States, and those with high levels of education and relative earnings may be materially better off than similar Canadians. I am also not arguing that *all* policy differences between the two countries are responsible for *all* outcome differences between the two countries. For example, the combination of a strict gun-control policy and long-standing cultural differences together explains lower levels of handgun ownership and violence in Canada compared to the United States.

15. Oliver and Shapiro (1997).

16. See Portes and Rumbaut (1996, 2001); Rumbaut and Portes (2001); Gans (1997); Fernandez-Kelly and Schauffler (1994,1995). Because European cities are also becoming the recipients of migration, rather than continuing in their traditional role of source, these issues are also now gripping the social science communities in Europe.

17. Mills (1967 [1976]).

18. Ragin (1987).

19. Johnson (2002).

REFERENCES

Adams, Michael. 2003. *Fire and Ice: The United States, Canada, and the Myth of Converging Values.* Toronto: Penguin Canada.

Adler, Patricia A., and Peter Adler. 2004. *Paradise Laborers: Hotel Work in the Global Economy.* Ithaca: Cornell University Press.

Alba, Richard, and Victor Nee. 1997. "Rethinking Assimilation Theory for a New Era of Immigration." *International Migration Review* 31(4): 826–74.

Alexander, Karl, Doris R. Entwisle, and Susan L. Dauber. 2002. *On the Success of Failure: A Reassessment of the Effects of Retention in the Primary School Grades.* 2nd ed. Cambridge, UK: Cambridge University Press.

Anderson, Elijah. 1990. *Streetwise: Race, Class and Change in an Urban Community.* Chicago: University of Chicago Press.

———. 1999. *The Code of the Street: Decency, Violence, and the Moral Life of the Inner-City.* New York: W. W. Norton.

Appelbaum, Eileen, Annette Bernhardt, and Richard J. Murnane. 2003. *Low-Wage America: How Employers Are Reshaping Opportunity in the Workplace.* New York: Russell Sage Foundation.

Armitage, Andrew. 1996. *Social Welfare in Canada Revisited: Facing Up to the Future.* 3rd ed. Don Mills, Canada: Oxford University Press Canada.

———. 2003. *Social Welfare in Canada.* 4th ed. Don Mills, Canada: Oxford University Press Canada.

Atkinson, Anthony B., Lee Rainwater, and Timothy M. Smeeding. 1995. *Income Distribution in OECD Countries: Evidence from the Luxembourg Income Study.* Paris: Organization for Economic Cooperation and Development.

Bakan, Joel. 2004. *The Corporation: The Pathological Pursuit of Profit and Power.* Toronto: Viking Canada.

Bane, Mary Jo, and David Ellwood. 1994. *Welfare Realities: From Rhetoric to Reform.* Cambridge, Mass.: Harvard University Press.

Banting, Keith, George Hoberg, and Richard Simeon, eds. 1997. *Degrees of Freedom: Canada and the United States in a Changing World.* Montreal: McGill-Queens University Press.

Baron, James N., and Andrew E. Newman. 1990. "For What's Its Worth: Organizations, Occupations, and the Value of Work Done by Women and Nonwhites." *American Sociological Review* 55(April): 155–75.

Beck, Ulrich. 1992. *Risk Society: Towards a New Modernity.* London: Sage Publications.

Beiser, Morton. 1999. *Strangers at the Gate: The 'Boat People's' First Ten Years in Canada.* Toronto: University of Toronto Press.

Bellah, Robert, Richard Madsen, William M. Sullivan, Ann Swidler, and Steven M. Tippleton. 1985. *Habits of the Heart: Individualism and Commitment in American Life.* Berkeley: University of California Press.

Bennett, Arnold, and Orvill Adams, eds. 1993. *Looking North for Health: What We Can Learn from Canada's Health Care System.* San Francisco: Jossey-Bass.

Berlowitz, Lance. 2005. *Dream City: Vancouver and the Global Imagination.* Vancouver, Toronto, and Berkeley: Douglas & McIntyre.

Bernhardt, Annette, Laura Dresser, and Erin Hatton. 2003. "The Coffee Pot Wars: Unions and Firm Restructuring in the Hotel Industry." In *Low-Wage America: How Employers Are Reshaping Opportunity in the Workplace,* edited by Eileen Appelbaum, Annette Bernhardt, and Richard J. Murnane, 33–76. New York: Russell Sage Foundation.

Bernhardt, Annette, Martina Morris, Mark S. Handcock, and Marc A. Scott. 2001. *Divergent Paths: Economic Mobility in the New American Labor Market.* New York: Russell Sage Foundation.

Berns McGowan, Rima. 1999. *Muslims in the Diaspora: The Somali Communities of London and Toronto.* Toronto: University of Toronto Press.

Blank, Rebecca. 1997. *It Takes a Nation: An Agenda for Fighting Poverty.* New York: Russell Sage Foundation.

Blank, Rebecca M., and Maria J. Hanratty. 1993. "Responding to Need: A Comparison of Social Safety Nets in Canada and the United States." In *Small Differences That Matter: Labor Markets and Income Maintenance in Canada and the United States,* edited by David Card and Richard B. Freeman, 191–231. Chicago: University of Chicago Press.

Blankenau, Joe. 2001. "The Fate of National Health Insurance in Canada and the United States: A Multiple Streams Explanation." *Policy Studies* 29(1): 38–55.

Blau, Joel. 1999. *Illusions of Prosperity: America's Working Families in an Age of Economic Insecurity.* New York: Oxford University Press.

Blau, Peter, and Otis D. Duncan. 1967. *The American Occupational Structure.* New York: Howe and Wiley.

Bloemraad, Irene. 2002. "The North American Naturalization Gap: An Institutional Approach to Citizenship Acquisition in the United States and Canada." *International Migration Review.* 36(1): 194–229.

Bluestone, Barry, and Bennett Harrison. 1982. *The Deindustrialization of America: Plant Closings, Community Abandonment, and the Dismantling of Basic Industry.* New York: Basic Books.

Bolaria, B. Singh, and Harley D. Dickenson. 2002. *Health, Illness, and Health Care in Canada.* 3rd ed. Scarborough, Canada: Nelson Thomson Learning.

Borosage, Robert L., and Roger Hickey, eds. 2001. *The Next Agenda: Blueprint for a New Progressive Movement.* Boulder: Westview Press.

Borjas, George J. 1993. "Immigration Policy, National Origin, and Immigrant Skills: A Comparison of Canada and the United States." In *Small Differences That Matter: Labor Markets and Income Maintenance in Canada and the United States,* edited by David Card and Richard B. Freeman, 21–43. Chicago: University of Chicago Press.

———. 2001. *Heaven's Door: Immigration Policy and the American Economy.* Princeton: Princeton University Press.

Boychuk, Terry. 1999. *The Making and Meaning of Hospital Policy in the United States and Canada.* Ann Arbor: University of Michigan Press.

Brofenbrenner, Kate. 2000. "Uneasy Terrain: The Impact of Capital Mobility on Workers, Wages, and Union Organizing." U.S. Trade Deficit Review Commission. Available at:

http://www.ilr.cornell.edu/extension/download.html?pub_id=1096. Date accessed: October 20, 2002.

Brooks-Gunn, Jeanne, and Greg J. Duncan. 1997. *Consequences of Growing Up Poor.* New York: Russell Sage Foundation.

Buchanan, Ruth. 2001. "Lives on the Line: Low-Wage Work in the TeleService Economy." In *Laboring below the Line: The New Ethnography of Poverty, Low-Wage Work, and Survival in the Global Economy,* edited by Frank Munger, 45–72. New York: Russell Sage Foundation.

Burbank, John R., and Michael Sullivan. 2001. *Expanding the Basic Health Plan through Increasing Cigarette Taxes: A Public Policy Partnership for Good Health.* Seattle: Washington Economic Opportunity Institute. Available at: http://www.eoionline.org/Health CarePolicyBrief2000.htm. Date accessed: May 13, 2003.

Card, David, and Rebecca M. Blank, eds. 2000. *Finding Jobs: Work and Welfare Reform.* New York: Russell Sage Foundation.

Card, David, and Richard B. Freeman, eds. 1993. *Small Differences That Matter: Labor Markets and Income Maintenance in Canada and the United States.* Chicago: University of Chicago Press.

Card, David, and Alan Kreuger. 1995. *Myth and Measurement: The New Economics of the Minimum Wage.* Princeton: Princeton University Press.

Card, David, and W. Craig Riddell. 1993. "A Comparative Analysis of Unemployment in Canada and the U.S." In *Small Differences That Matter: Labor Markets and Income Maintenance in Canada and the United States,* edited by David Card and Richard B. Freeman, 149–89. Chicago: University of Chicago Press.

Chaudry, Ajay. 2004. *Putting Children First: How Low-Wage Working Mothers Manage Child Care.* New York: Russell Sage Foundation.

Chin, Margaret. 2005. *Sewing Women: Immigrants and the New York City Garment Industry.* New York: Columbia University Press.

Ciulla, Joanne B. 2000. *The Working Life: The Promise and Betrayal of Modern Work.* New York and Toronto: Times Books/Random House.

Clawson, Dan. 2003. *The Next Upsurge: Labor and New Social Movements.* Ithaca: Cornell University Press.

Collins, Jane L. 2003. *Threads: Gender, Labor, and Power in the Global Apparel Industry.* Chicago: University of Chicago Press.

Coontz, Stephanie. 1992. *The Way We Never Were: American Families and the Nostalgia Trap.* New York: Basic Books.

Creese, Gillian, and Edith Ngene Kambere. 2003. "What Colour Is Your English?" *Canadian Review of Sociology and Anthropology* 40(5): 565–73.

Curtis, James, Edward Grabb, and Neil Guppy, eds. 2003. *Social Inequality in Canada: Patterns, Problems and Policies.* 4th ed. Scarborough, Canada: Pearson Education Canada.

Danziger, Sheldon H., and Peter Gottschalk. 1995. *America Unequal.* Cambridge, Mass.: Harvard University Press.

———. 1997. *Uneven Tides: Rising Inequality in America.* New York: Russell Sage Foundation.

Danziger, Sheldon H., Gary D. Sandefur, and Daniel Weinberg, eds. 1994. *Confronting Poverty: Prescriptions for Change.* Cambridge, Mass.: Harvard University Press.

Davis, Mike. [1990] 1992. *City of Quartz: Excavating the Future in Los Angeles.* New York: Vintage Books.

Deber, Raisa Berlin. 2003. "Health Care Reform: Lessons from Canada." *American Journal of Public Health* 93(1): 20–24.

DeParle, Jason. 2004. *American Dream: Three Women, Ten Kids, and a Nation's Drive to End Welfare.* New York: Viking Books.

Derber, Charles. [1979] 2000. *The Pursuit of Attention: Power and Ego in Everyday Life.* Oxford: Oxford University Press.

———. 1998. *Corporation Nation: How Corporations Are Taking Over Our Lives—and What We Can Do about It.* New York: St. Martins Press.

———. 2002. *People before Profit: The New Globalization in an Age of Terror, Big Money, and Economic Crisis.* New York: St. Martin's Press.

Devine, Fiona, and Mary C. Waters. 2004. *Social Inequalities in Comparative Perspective.* Malden, Mass.: Blackwell Publishing.

Dore, Ronald. [1973] 1990. *British Factory—Japanese Factory: The Origin of National Diversity in Industrial Relations.* Berkeley: University of California Press.

Duany, Andres, Elizabeth Plater-Zyberk, and Jeff Speck. 2000. *Suburban Nation: The Rise of Sprawl and the Decline of the American Dream.* New York: North Point Press.

Dryfoos, Joy G. 1994. *Full-Service Schools: A Revolution in Health and Social Services for Children, Youth and Families.* Boston: Jossey-Bass.

DuBois, William E. B. 1899. *The Philadelphia Negro: A Social Study.* Philadelphia: University of Pennsylvania Press.

Duneier, Mitchell 1999. *Sidewalk.* New York: Farrar, Straus, and Gitroux.

Dunn, James R. 2002. *Are Health Inequalities Making Canada Less Healthy?* Ottawa: The Health Determinants Partnership Making Connections Project, March.

Edin, Kathryn, and Laura Lein. 1997. *Making Ends Meet: How Single Mothers Survive Welfare and Low-Wage Work.* New York: Russell Sage Foundation.

Edin, Kathryn, and Maria Kefalas. 2005. *Promises I Can Keep: Why Poor Women Put Motherhood before Marriage.* Berkeley: University of California Press.

Ehrenreich, Barbara. 2001. *Nickel and Dimed: On (Not) Getting By in America.* New York: Henry Holt and Company.

Ehrenreich, Barbara, and Arlie Russell Hochschild, eds. 2002. *Global Woman: Nannies, Maids, and Sex Workers in the New Economy.* New York: Henry Holt and Company.

Elliott, Kimberly Ann, and Richard B. Freeman. 2003. *Can Labor Standards Improve under Globalization?* Washington, D.C.: Institute for International Economics.

Ellwood, David T. 1988. *Poor Support: Poverty in the American Family.* New York: Basic Books.

Esping-Andersen, Gøsta. 1990. *The Three Worlds of Welfare Capitalism.* Princeton: Princeton University Press.

Esping-Andersen, Gøsta, with Duncan Gallie, Anton Hemerijck, and John Myles. 2002. *Why We Need a New Welfare State.* Oxford: Oxford University Press.

Federal, Provincial, and Territorial Advisory Committee on Population Health. 1999. *Toward a Healthy Future: Second Report on the Health of Canadians.* Ottawa: Her Majesty the Queen in right of Canada, represented by the Minister of Public Works and Government Services Canada.

Fernández-Kelly, Patricia, and Richard Schauffler. 1994. "Divided Fates: Immigrant Children in a Restructured Economy." *International Migration Review* 28(4): 662–89.

———. 1995. "Social and Cultural Capital in the Urban Ghetto." in *The Economic Sociology of Immigration*, edited by Alejandro Portes, 213–47. New York: Russell Sage Foundation.

Findlay, John M. 1998. *History of Washington State and the Pacific NorthWest, Lesson 25: The Impact of the Cold War on Seattle: The 1962's World Fair*. Available at: http://www.washington.edu/uwired/outreach/cspn/hstaa432/lesson_25/hstaa432_25.html#uw13107. Date accessed: September 24, 2003.

Florida, Richard. 2004. *The Rise of the Creative Class: And How It's Transforming Work, Leisure, Community and Everyday Life*. Reprint ed. New York: Basic Books.

Foucault, Michel. 1995. *Discipline and Punish: The Birth of the Modern Prison*. 2nd ed. Translated by Alan Sheridan, 1977. New York: Vintage Books.

Frankel, B. Gail, Mark Speechley, and Terrance J. Wade. 1996. *The Sociology of Health Care: A Canadian Perspective*. Toronto: Copp Clark.

Freeman, Richard, ed. 1994. *Working under Different Rules*. New York: Russell Sage Foundation.

Friedman, Pamela. 2000. "The Earned Income Tax Credit." *Welfare Information Network Issue Notes* 4(4). Available at: http://www.welfareinfo.org/friedmanapril.htm. Date accessed: July 16, 2003.

Fuchs-Epstein, Cynthia, and Arne L. Kalleberg, eds. 2004. *Fighting for Time: Shifting Boundaries of Work and Family Life*. New York: Russell Sage Foundation.

Furstenberg, Frank F., Jr., Thomas D. Cook, Jaquelynne Eccles, Glen Elder, Jr., and Arnold Sameroff. 1999. *Managing to Make It: Urban Families and Adolescent Success*. Chicago: University of Chicago Press.

Gans, Herbert. 1995. *The War against the Poor: The Underclass and Anti-Poverty Policy*. New York: Basic Books.

———. 1997. "Toward a Reconciliation of Assimilation and Pluralism: The Interplay of Acculturation and Ethnic Retention." *International Migration Review* 31(4): 875–92.

Gardyn, Rebecca. 2002. "The Mating Game." *American Demographics* (July/August) 7: 33–37.

Glassner, Barry. 1999. *The Culture of Fear: Why Americans Are Afraid of the Wrong Things*. New York: Basic Books.

Goffman, Erving. 1959. *The Presentation of Self in Everyday Life*. New York: Anchor.

Gopnik, Adam and Malcolm Gladwell. 2000. "Health Care Forum: Canada vs. U.S." *Washington Monthly*. March. 3:25–36. Available at http://www.washingtonmonthly.com/features/2000/0003.gladwellgopnik.html. Date accessed: September 20, 2005.

Gordon, Milton M. 1964. *Assimilation in American Life: The Role of Race, Religion and Natural Origin*. New York: Oxford University Press.

Gordon, David. 1996. *Fat and Mean: The Corporate Squeeze of Working Americans and the Myth of Managerial "Downsizing."* New York: The Free Press.

Gore, Al, and Tipper Gore. 2002. *Joined at the Heart: The Transformation of the American Family*. New York: Henry Holt and Co.

Graham, John R., Karen J. Swift, and Roger Delaney. 2000. *Canadian Social Policy: An Introduction*. Scarborough, Canada: Prentice-Hall Canada.

Graig, Laurene A. 1993. *Health of Nations: An International Perspective on Health Care Reform*. 2nd ed. Washington, D.C.: Congressional Quarterly Inc.

Granovetter, Mark. 1995. *Getting a Job: A Study of Contacts and Careers.* 2nd ed. Chicago: University of Chicago Press.

"The Grass Really Is Greener to the North." 1999. *Health Letter.* 15(12): 8.

Halle, David. 1984. *America's Working Man: Work, Home, and Politics among Blue-Collar Property Owners.* Chicago: University of Chicago Press.

Hancock, Lynnell. 2002. *Hands to Work: The Stories of Three Families Racing the Welfare Clock.* New York: HarperCollins.

Harrison, Bennett, and Barry Bluestone. 1988. *The Great U-Turn: Corporate Restructuring and the Polarizing of America.* New York: Basic Books.

Hays, Sharon. 2003. *Flat Broke with Children: Women in the Age of Welfare Reform.* Oxford: Oxford University Press.

"Heavy Price Paid for Lack of Coverage." 2003. *USA Today* 131(2693): 1–2.

Hertzman, Clyde. 2002. *Leave No Child Behind!: Social Exclusion and Child Development.* Toronto: Laidlaw Foundation.

Heymann, Jody, ed. 2003. *Global Inequalities at Work: Work's Impact on Individuals, Families, and Societies.* New York: Oxford University Press.

Heymann, Jody, Alison Earle, Stephanie Simmons, Stephanie M. Breslow, and April Kuehnhoff. 2004. *The Work, Family and Equity Index: Where Does the United States Stand Globally?* Boston: Project on Global Working Families.

Hochschild, Arlie Russell. 1997. *The Time Bind: When Work Becomes Home and Home Becomes Work.* New York: Metropolitan Books.

Holzer, Harry. 1995. *What Employers Want: Job Prospects for Less-Educated Workers.* New York: Russell Sage Foundation.

"Homeless in Toronto Live Longer than U.S. Counterparts." 2000. *The Nation's Health* 30(5): 36.

Hondagneu-Sotelo, Pierrette. 2001. *Doméstica: Immigrant Workers Cleaning and Caring in the Shadows of Affluence.* Berkeley: University of California Press.

Hornberger, John C., Donald A. Redelmeyer, and Jeffrey Petersen. 1992. "Variability among Methods to Assess Patients' Well-Being and Consequent Effect on Cost-Benefit Analysis." *Journal of Clinical Epidemiology* 45(5): 505–12.

Hurtig, Mel. 1999. *Pay the Rent or Feed the Kids: The Tragedy and Disgrace of Poverty in Canada.* Toronto: McClelland & Steward.

Hutton, Thomas A. 1998. *The Transformation of Canada's Pacific Metropolis: A Study of Vancouver.* Montreal: Institute for Research on Public Policy.

Iceland, John. 2003. *Poverty in America: A Handbook.* Berkeley: University of California Press.

Imershein, Allen W. 2001. "Review of the Making and Meaning of Hospital Policy in the United States and Canada." *Contemporary Sociology* 21(30): 194–96.

Jahoda, Marie. 1982. *Employment and Unemployment: A Social-Psychological Analysis.* Cambridge, UK: Cambridge University Press.

Jahoda, Marie, Paul Lazarsfeld, and Hans Zeisel. 1933 [1977] *Marianthal: A Sociography of an Unemployed Community.* London: Tavistock.

Janigan, Mary. 2003. "What's a Wait Worth." *Maclean's* 116(2): 39.

Japsen, Bruce. 2003. "Uninsured Are Charged Twice as Much for Medical Services, Study Finds." *Chicago Tribune,* January 26, p. 1.

Jargowsky, Paul. 1997. *Poverty and Place: Ghettos, Barrios, and Slums.* New York: Russell Sage Foundation.

Jencks, Christopher. 1992. *Rethinking Social Policy: Race, Poverty, and the Underclass.* New York: HarperPerennial.

Johnson, Jennifer. 2002. *Getting By on the Minimum: The Lives of Working-Class Women.* New York: Routledge.

Kamerman, Sheila B., and Alfred J. Kahn. 1995. *Starting Right: How America Neglects Its Youngest Children and What We Can Do about It.* New York: Oxford University Press.

Kane, Thomas J. 1999. *The Price of Admission: Rethinking How Americans Pay for College.* Washington D.C.: Brookings Institution.

Kanter, Rosabeth Moss. 1977. *Men and Women of the Corporation.* New York: Basic Books.

Katz, Michael B. 1986. *In the Shadow of the Poorhouse: A Social History of Welfare in America.* New York: Basic Books.

Kawachi, Ichiro, and Bruce P. Kennedy. 2002. *The Health of Nations: Why Inequality Is Harmful to Your Health.* New York: The New Press.

Kefalas, Maria. 2003. *Working Class Heroes: Protecting Home, Community, and Nation in a Chicago Neighborhood.* Berkeley: University of California Press.

Kozol, Jonathan. 1992. *Savage Inequalities: Children in America's Schools.* New York: HarperPerennial.

Lamont, Michèle 2000. *The Dignity of Working Men: Morality and the Boundaries of Race, Class, and Immigration.* New York: Russell Sage Foundation.

Lareau, Annette. 2003. *Unequal Childhoods: Class, Race, and Family Life.* Berkeley: University of California Press.

Lee, Mark, and Andrea Long. 2001. Behind the Headlines 2001: A Review of Public Policy in BC. October. Canadian Centre for Policy Alternatives—British Columbia Office, Vancouver, Canada.

Lehman, Nicholas. 1992. *The Promised Land: The Great Black Migration and How It Changed America.* New York: Vintage.

Leidner, Robin. 1993. *Fast Food, Fast Talk: Service Work and the Routinization of Everyday Life.* Berkeley: University of California Press.

Lemieux, Thomas. 1993. "Unions and Wage Inequality in Canada and the United States." In *Small Differences That Matter: Labor Markets and Income Maintenance in Canada and the United States,* edited by David Card and Richard B. Freeman, 69–107. Chicago: University of Chicago Press.

Levitan, Sar A., and Isaac Shapiro. 1987. *Working but Poor: America's Contradiction.* Baltimore: Johns Hopkins University Press.

Levy, Frank. 1998. *The New Dollars and Dreams: American Incomes and Economic Change.* New York: Russell Sage Foundation.

Lewis, Oscar. 1966. *La Vida: A Puerto Rican Family in the Culture of Poverty—San Juan and New York.* New York: Random House.

Liebow, Elliot. 1967. *Tally's Corner: A Study of Negro Streetcorner Men.* Boston: Little, Brown.

Lightman, Ernie. 2003. *Social Policy in Canada: Who Benefits, Who Pays?* Don Mills, Canada: Oxford University Press.

Lipset, Seymour Martin. 1990. *Continental Divide: The Values and Institutions of the United States and Canada.* New York: Routledge.

Lipset, Seymour Martin, and Noah M. Meltz. 2004. *The Paradox of American Unionism: Why Americans Like Unions More Than Canadians Do, but Join Much Less.* Ithaca: Cornell University Press.

MacLeod, Jay. 1995. *Ain't No Makin' It: Aspirations and Attainment in a Low-Income Neighborhood.* Revised ed. Boulder: Westview Press.

MacDonald, Norbert. 1987. *Distant Neighbors: A Comparative History of Seattle and Vancouver.* Lincoln: University of Nebraska Press.

Manuel, Douglas G., and Yang Mao. 2002. "Avoidable Mortality in the United States and Canada 1980–1996." *American Journal of Public Health* 92(9): 1481–84.

Marmor, Theodore, and Kip Sullivan. 2000. "Canada's Burning!" *Washington Monthly* 32(7/8): 15–20.

Marshall, Thomas H. 1950. *Class, Citizenship, and Social Development: Essays by T.H. Marshall.* Chicago: University of Chicago Press.

Massey, Douglas, and Nancy Denton. 1993. *American Apartheid: Segregation and the Making of the Underclass.* Cambridge, Mass.: Harvard University Press.

McDonald, Robert A. J. 1996. *Making Vancouver: Class, Status and Social Boundaries, 1863–1913.* Vancouver, Canada: UBC Press.

McFarlane, Lawrie, and Carlos Prado. 2002. *The Best Laid Plans: Health Care's Problems and Prospects.* Montreal & Kingston: McGill-Queen's University Press.

McFate, Katherine, Roger Lawson, and William Julius Wilson, eds. 1995. *Poverty, Inequality, and the Future of Social Policy: Western States and the New World Order.* New York: Russell Sage Foundation.

McLellan, Faith. 2003. "Uninsured People in the USA Put A Strain on the Health System." *The Lancet* 361(9361): 938.

McMullin, Julie. 2004. *Understanding Social Inequality: Intersections of Class, Age, Gender, Ethnicity, and Race in Canada.* Don Mills, Canada: Oxford University Press.

Mead, Lawrence. 1986. *Beyond Entitlement: The Social Obligations of Citizenship.* New York: The Free Press.

———. 1992. *The New Politics of Poverty: The Non-Working Poor in America.* New York: Basic Books.

Millman, Michael, ed. 1993. *Access to Health Care in America/Committee on Monitoring Access to Personal Care Services, Institute of Medicine.* Washington, D.C.: National Academy Press.

Mills, C. Wright. 1967 [1976]. *The Sociological Imagination.* New York: Oxford University Press.

Milkman, Ruth, and Kim Voss, eds. 2004. *Rebuilding Labor: Organizing and Organizers in the New Union Movement.* Ithaca: Cornell University Press.

Morgan, Murray. 1982. *Skid Road: An Informal Portrait of Seattle.* Seattle: University of Washington Press.

Moss, Philip, and Chris Tilly. 2001. *Stories Employers Tell: Race, Skill, and Hiring in America.* New York: Russell Sage Foundation.

Munger, Frank, ed. 2001. *Laboring Below the Line: The New Ethnography of Poverty, Low-Wage Work, and Survival in the Global Economy.* New York: Russell Sage Foundation.

Murphy, Barbara. 1999. *The Ugly Canadian: The Rise and Fall of a Caring Society.* Winnipeg, Canada: J. Gordon Shillingford Publishing.

Murray, Charles 1984. *Losing Ground: American Social Policy 1950–1980.* New York: Basic Books.

Myles, John, and Paul Pierson. 1997. "Friedman's Revenge: The Reform of Liberal Welfare States in Canada and the United States." *Politics and Society* (Stoneham) 25(4): 443–72.

Newman, Katherine S. 1989. *Falling from Grace: The Experience of Downward Mobility in the American Middle Class.* New York: The Free Press.

———. 1993. *Declining Fortunes: The Withering of the American Dream.* New York: Basic Books.

———. 1999. *No Shame in My Game: The Working Poor in the Inner City.* New York: Alfred A. Knopf/Russell Sage Foundation.

———. 2003. *A Different Shade of Gray: Mid-Life and Beyond in the Inner City.* New York: The New Press.

Oberlander, John, and Theodore R. Marmor. 2001. "The Path to Universal Health Care." In *The Next Agenda: Blueprint for a New Progressive Movement,* edited by Robert L. Borosage and Roger Hickey, 93–125. Boulder: Westview Press.

Office of Policy Planning and Research United States Department of Labor. 1965. *The Negro Family: A Case for National Action.* March. Available at: http://www.dol.gov/asp/programs/history/webid-meynihan.htm

Oliver, Melvin L., and Thomas M. Shapiro. 1997. *Black Wealth/ White Wealth: A New Perspective on Racial Inequality.* New York: Routledge.

Osberg, Lars. 2000. Poverty in Canada and the USA: Measurement, Trends, and Implications. Presidential Address to the Canadian Economics Association, Vancouver, June 3.

Ozyegin, Gul. 2001. *Untidy Gender: Domestic Service in Turkey.* Philadelphia: Temple University Press.

Park, Robert E. 1996. "Human Migration and the Marginal Man." in *Theories of Ethnicity: A Classical Reader, edited by* Werner Sollers, 156–67. New York: New York University Press.

Parrenas, Rhacel Salazar. 2001. *Servants of Globalization: Women, Migration, and Domestic Work.* Palo Alto: Stanford University Press.

Parvaz, D. 2000. "Experience, but at What Cost?" *Seattle Post-Intelligencer,* 24 June, p. A9.

Pear, Robert. 2004. "Academy of Sciences Calls for Universal Health Care by 2010." *New York Times,* 14 January, p. A21.

Pierson, Paul. 1994. *Dismantling the Welfare State?: Reagan, Thatcher, and the Politics of Retrenchment.* Cambridge, UK: Cambridge University Press.

Portes, Alejandro, and Rubén G. Rumbaut. 1996. *Immigrant America: A Portrait.* Berkeley: University of California Press.

———. 2001. *Legacies: The Stories of the Immigrant Second Generation.* Berkeley: University of California Press/New York: Russell Sage Foundation.

Pratt, Geraldine. 2004. *Working Feminism.* Philadelphia: Temple University Press.

Presser, Harriet. 2003. *Working in a 24/7 Economy: Challenges for American Families.* New York: Russell Sage Foundation.

Pulkingham, Jane, and Gordon Ternowetsky, eds. 1996. *Remaking Canadian Social Policy: Social Security in the Late 1990s.* Halifax, Canada: Fernwood Publishing.

Quadagno, Jill. 1994. *The Color of Welfare: How Racism Undermined the War on Poverty.* New York: Oxford University Press.

Ragin, Charles C. 1987. *The Comparative Method: Moving Beyond Quantitative and Qualitative Strategies.* Berkeley: University of California Press.

Rainwater, Lee. 1970. *Beyond Ghetto Walls: Black Family Life in a Federal Slum.* Chicago: Aldine Publishing.

———. 1993. "The Social Wage in the Income Packaging of Working Parents." Luxembourg Income Survey Working Paper Series no. 89. Available at: http://www.lisproject.org/ publications/. Date accessed: February 6, 2004.

Rank, Mark Robert. 2004. *One Nation Underprivileged: Why American Poverty Affects Us All.* Oxford: Oxford University Press.

Reich, Robert B. 1991. *The Work of Nations: Preparing Ourselves for 21st Century Capitalism.* New York: Alfred A. Knopf.

Reisman, David. 1969. *The Lonely Crowd: A Study of the Changing American Character.* New Haven: Yale University Press.

Reitz, Jeffrey G. 1998. *Warmth of Welcome: The Social Causes of Economic Success for Immigrants in Different Nations and Cities.* Boulder: Westview Press.

Reitz, Jeffrey G., ed. 2003. *Host Societies and the Reception of Immigrants.* San Diego: Center for Comparative Immigration Research.

Reitz, Jeffrey G., and Raymond Breton. 1994. *The Illusion of Difference: Realities of Ethnicity in Canada and the United States.* Toronto: C. D. Howe Institute.

Riddell, W. Craig. 1993. "Unionization in Canada and the United States: A Tale of Two Countries." In *Small Differences That Matter: Labor Markets and Income Maintenance in Canada and the United States,* edited by David Card and Richard B. Freeman, 109–48. Chicago: University of Chicago Press.

Rieder, Jonathan. 1985. *Canarsie: The Jews and Italians of Brooklyn against Liberalism.* Cambridge, Mass.: Harvard University Press.

Romanow, Roy J. 2002. *Building Our Values: The Future of Health Care in Canada.* Ottawa: Commission on the Future of Health Care in Canada. Available at: http://www.hc-sc .gc.ca/english/care/romanow/hcc0086.html. Date accessed: April 22, 2003.

Rose, Joseph B., and Gary N. Chaison. 2001. "Unionism in Canada and the United States in the 21st century: The Prospects for Revival." *Relations Industrielles/Industrial Relations* 56(1): 34–65.

Rose, Fred. 2000. *Coalitions across the Class Divide: Lessons from the Labor, Peace, and Environmental Movements.* Ithaca: Cornell University Press.

Rosen, Ellen Israel. 2002. *Making Sweatshops: The Globalization of the U.S. Apparel Industry.* Berkeley: University of California Press.

Rosentraub, Mark S. 1999. *Major League Losers: The Real Cost of Sports and Who's Paying for It.* Revised ed. New York: Basic Books.

Rubin, Lillian B. 1976. *Worlds of Pain: Life in the Working-Class Family.* New York: Basic Books.

———. 1994. *Families on the Fault Line: America's Working Class Speaks about the Family, Economy, Race, and Ethnicity.* New York: Harper Collins.

Rumbaut, Rubén G., and Alejandro Portes, eds. 2001. *Ethnicities: Children of Immigrants in America.* Berkeley: University of California Press/New York: Russell Sage Foundation.

Rutstein, David D., William Berenberg, Thomas C. Chalmers, Charles G. Child III, Alfred P. Fishman, and Edward B. Perrin. 1976. "Measuring the Quality of Medical Care: A Clinical Method." *New England Journal of Medicine* 294: 582–88.

Sassen, Saskia. 2001. *The Global City: New York, London, and Tokyo.* 2nd ed. Princeton: Princeton University Press.

Schlosser, Eric. 2002. *Fast Food Nation: The Dark Side of the All-American Meal.* New York: HarperPerennial.

——. 2003. *Reefer Madness: Sex, Drugs, and Cheap Labor in the American Black Market.* Boston and New York: Houghton Mifflin.

Schorr, Lisbeth B. 1997. *Common Purpose: Strengthening Families and Neighborhoods to Rebuild America.* New York: Anchor Books.

Schulman, Beth. 2003. *The Betrayal of Work: How Low Wage Jobs Fail 30 Million Americans and Their Families.* New York: The New Press.

Schwartz, Thomas, and Kathleen Maas Weigert, eds. 1995. *America's Working Poor.* Notre Dame and London: University of Notre Dame.

Schweinhart, Lawrence J. 2005. *The High/Scope Perry Preschool Study through Age 40: Summary, Conclusions, and Frequently Asked Questions.* Ypsilanti, Mich.: High/Scope Foundation Press. Available at: http://www.highscope.org/Research/PerryProject/PerryAge40SumWeb.pdf. Date accessed: May 14, 2005.

Sennett, Richard, and Jonathan Cobb. 1973. *The Hidden Injuries of Class.* New York: Vintage Books.

Sered, Susan Starr, and Rushika Fernandopulle. 2005. *Uninsured in America: Life and Death in the Land of Opportunity.* Berkeley: University of California Press.

Sherman, Rachel Ellen. 2003. Class Acts: Producing and Consuming Luxury Service in Hotels. Ph.D. diss., University of California, Berkeley.

Shipler, David K. 2004. *The Working Poor: Invisible in America.* New York: Alfred A. Knopf.

Simmel, Georg. 1972. *On Individuality and Social Forms.* Chicago: University of Chicago Press.

Skocpol, Theda. 1992. *Protecting Soldiers and Mothers: The Political Origins of Social Policy in the United States.* Cambridge, Mass.: Belknap Press/Harvard University Press.

——. 1997. *Boomerang: Health Care Reform and the Turn Against Government.* New York: W. W. Norton (new ed.).

——. 2000. *The Missing Middle: Working Families and the Future of American Social Policy.* New York: W. W. Norton.

Small, Mario Luis. 2004. *Villa Victoria: The Transformation of Social Capital in a Boston Barrio.* Chicago: University of Chicago Press.

Smeeding, Timothy, and Katherine Ross. 1999. "Social Protection for the Poor in the Developed World: Evidence from the LIS." Luxembourg Income Survey Working Paper no. 204. Available at: www.lisproject.org/publications. Date accessed: June 16, 2003.

Sollers, Werner. 1986. *Beyond Ethnicity: Consent and Descent in American Culture.* New York: Oxford University Press.

Stack, Carol. 1974. *All Our Kin: Strategies for Survival in a Black Community.* New York: Harper and Row.

Statistics Canada. 1991. Statistics Canada Data Books. Available at: http://www.statcan.ca. Date accessed: June 14, 2000.

——. 1996. Statistics Canada Highlights. Available at: http://www.statcan.ca. Date accessed: June 14, 2000.

Stern, Linda. 2003. "Grown-Up and Uninsured." *Newsweek* 141(3): 78–79.

Stier, Haya, and Marta Tienda. 2000. *The Color of Opportunity: Pathways to Family, Welfare, and Work.* Chicago: University of Chicago Press.

Sweeney, John J., and David Kusnet. 1996. *America Needs a Raise: Fighting for Economic Security and Social Justice.* Boston: Houghton-Mifflin.

Tannock, Stuart. 2001. *Youth at Work: The Unionized Fast Food and Grocery Workplace.* Philadelphia: Temple University Press.

Taras, Daphne G. "Why Nonunion Representation is Lawful in Canada." *Relations Industrialles/Industrial Relations.* 52(4):736–86.

Taylor, Fredrick Winslow. 1919. *Principles of Scientific Management.* New York: Harper & Brothers Publishers.

Terkel, Studs. 2003. *Hope Dies Last: Keeping Faith in Difficult Times.* New York: The New Press.

Thomas, Sandra. 2003. "Kit's Beachhead." *Vancouver Courier,* 6 April. Available at: http://www.vancourier.com/issues03/042103/news/042103nn1.html. Date accessed: November 6, 2003.

Troy, Leo. 2000. *Beyond Unions and Collective Bargaining.* Armonk, N.Y.: M. E. Sharpe.

Tuohy, Carolyn H. 1999. *Accidental Logics: The Dynamics of Change in the Health Care Arena in the United States, Britain, and Canada.* New York: Oxford University Press.

U.S. Census Bureau. 1990. U.S. Census CD-ROM. Washington, D.C.

——. TIGER 2000 Line Files. Available at: http://ftp2.census.gov. Date accessed: April 23, 2005.

U.S. Geological Survey. National Atlas of the United States. Online data archive. Available at: http://www.nationalatlas.gov. Date accessed April, 23, 2005.

Venkatesh, Sudhir Alladi. 2000. *American Project: The Rise and Fall of a Modern Ghetto.* Cambridge, Mass.: Harvard University Press.

Vogel, Donna. 2001. In Search of the Good Life: "Competitiveness" and Well-Being in British Columbia and Washington State. June. Canadian Centre for Policy Alternatives—British Columbia Office, Vancouver, Canada.

Waldinger, Roger, and Michael I. Lichter. 2003. *How the Other Half Works: Immigration and the Social Organization of Labor.* Berkeley: University of California Press.

Warren, Elizabeth, and Amelia Warren Tyagi. 2003. *The Two-Income Trap: Why Middle-Class Mothers & Fathers Are Going Broke.* New York: Basic Books.

Warren, James R. 1997. *King County and Its Emerald City: Seattle.* Sun Valley, Calif.: American Historical Press.

Waters, Mary C. 1999. *Black Identities: West Indian Immigrant Dreams and American Realities.* Cambridge, Mass.: Harvard University Press.

Weale Albert. 1998. "Rationing Health Care." *BMJ.* 316: 410.

Weiss, Lawrence D. 1992. *No Benefit: Crisis in America's Health Insurance Industry.* Boulder: Westview Press.

Weissbourd, Richard. 1997. *The Vulnerable Child: What Really Hurts America's Children and What Can We Do about It.* Boston: Addison-Wesley Publishing.

Westhues, Anne, ed. 2003. *Canadian Social Policy: Issues and Perspectives.* 3rd ed. Waterloo, Canada: Wilfred Laurier University Press.

Whyte, William Foote. 1993. *Street Corner Society: The Social Structure of an Italian Slum.* 4th ed. Chicago: University of Chicago Press.

Willis, Paul E. 1977. *Learning to Labor: How Working Class Kids Get Working Class Jobs.* New York: Columbia University Press.

Wilson, William J. 1980. *The Declining Significance of Race: Blacks and Changing American Institutions.* Chicago: University of Chicago Press.

——. 1987. *The Truly Disadvantaged: The Inner City, the Underclass and Public Policy.* Chicago: University of Chicago Press.

——. 1996. *When Work Disappears: The World of the New Urban Poor.* New York: Alfred A. Knopf.

——. 1999. *The Bridge over the Racial Divide: Rising Inequality and Coalition Politics.* Berkeley: University of California Press.

Winston, Pamela, Ronald J. Angel, Linda M. Burton, P. Lindsay Chase-Lansdale, Andrew J. Cherlin, Robert A. Moffitt, and William Julius Wilson. 1999. *Welfare, Children, and Families: A Three City Study.* Baltimore: Johns Hopkins University Press.

Youngblood, Pat, and Robert Jensen. 2003. "U.S. Workers Deserve Choice on Union Issues." *Austin American-Statesman,* 10 December. Available at: http://www.statesman.com/opinion/content/editorial/othertakes/1203/1210jensen.html, Date accessed: September 22, 2005.

Zinn, Howard. 2003. *A People's History of the United States: 1492–Present.* New ed. New York: HarperCollins.

Zuberi, Daniyal. 2004a. Differences Matter: The Impact of Social Policy on the Working Poor in Canada and the U.S. Ph.D. diss., Harvard University.

——. 2004b. "Transfers Matter Most: How Changes in Transfer Systems in Canada and the United States Explain the Divergence of Household Poverty Levels from 1974–1994." *International Journal of Comparative Sociology* 45(1–2): 87–110.

Zucchino, David. 1997. *Myth of the Welfare Queen.* New York: Scribner.

INDEX